The
Outer
Beach

The
Outer
Beach

A THOUSAND-MILE WALK

ON CAPE COD'S ATLANTIC SHORE

ROBERT FINCH

W. W. NORTON & COMPANY

Independent Publishers Since 1923

NEW YORK | LONDON

Copyright © 2017 by Robert Finch

For information about permission to reproduce selections from this book, write to
Permissions, W. W. Norton & Company, Inc., 500 Fifth Avenue, New York, NY 10110

For information about special discounts for bulk purchases, please contact
W. W. Norton Special Sales at specialsales@wwnorton.com or 800-233-4830

Manufacturing by Berryville Graphics
Book design by Chris Welch Design
Production manager: Julia Druskin

ISBN: 978-0-393-08130-5

W. W. Norton & Company, Inc., 500 Fifth Avenue, New York, N.Y. 10110
www.wwnorton.com

W. W. Norton & Company Ltd., 15 Carlisle Street, London W1D 3BS

2   3   4   5   6   7   8   9   0

In memory of Jim Mairs (1939–2016),
dear friend and steadfast editor for four decades

And landscape, that vast still life, invites description, not narrative.
It is lyric. It has no story: it is the beloved, and asks only to be
contemplated. For contemplation is, in poetic form, love.
This lyric response to the world tends toward rhapsody.

—PATRICIA HAMPL, *SPILLVILLE*

Description is always bad.

—JOHN KEATS, *LETTERS*

CONTENTS

Majestic and mutilated, the great glacial scarp of Cape Cod's Outer Beach rises from the open Atlantic, separating it from Cape Cod Bay. Its many-colored sands and clays flow grain by grain, or in sudden shelving slabs, to replenish the shore below. The beach itself, broad and gently sloping in summer, short and steep in winter, arcs northward for more than thirty miles, giving the walker a curved prospect two or three miles ahead at most. And always, coming onto the shore and reforming it, with measured cadences in calm weather, with life-destroying fury during northeast gales, is the sea. Here, as Henry Beston put it, "the ocean encounters the last defiant bulwark of two worlds." There is no other landscape like it anywhere.

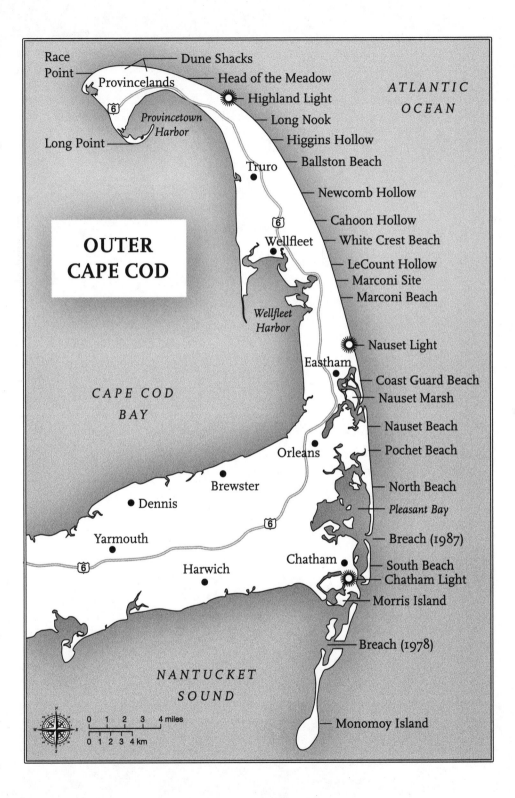

INTRODUCTION:
A VIEW FROM THE BEACH

The somewhat misleading subtitle of this book—"A Thousand-Mile Walk on Cape Cod's Atlantic Shore"—originated a few years ago when, in an idle mathematical mood, I calculated that I had spent some forty years walking the back side of Cape Cod, otherwise known as the Great Beach or the Outer Beach. In a rough estimate I calculated that I had averaged, conservatively, about a half mile of beachwalking every week, or a mile every two weeks. That, rounded off, equaled about twenty-five miles a year, or roughly a thousand miles of walks during my tenure here. I don't claim much for that figure, certainly not any physical achievement, which is pretty modest for that span of time. I can only claim a longtime acquaintance, irregular but constant.

The essays that follow trace nearly a half century of walking the shoreline of Cape Cod's Outer Beach—a forty-mile stretch of glacial bluffs, dunes, barrier beaches, and islands running north from the southern tip of Monomoy Island to Provincetown's Long Point. They document the interactions and the changes that have taken place between the beach and myself at different points over that span of time. The walks were not regular, and certainly not purposeful. It was the powerful but undefined character of the beach itself that drew me. It seemed a space and a place full of nonhuman meaning, and I was determined to walk it until it spoke to me. No attempt has been made at—nor should the reader look for—any comprehensive natural, human, scientific or cultural history of the beach. My intent has been simply to reflect the many moods, voices, and aspects of the beach, and to demonstrate the variety of encounters, reactions, and reflections one individual can experience in such a place over a long period of time. As such, it is a mosaic rather than a narrative.

Nonetheless, for structural purposes I have divided the book into fourteen chapters, moving geographically from south to north. Within each chapter the essays are arranged roughly chronologically, in part to emphasize how each portion of the beach has its distinct character, but also to give the reader a sense of what it has been like to return to the same section of the beach year after year. The awkward artificiality of this division will be apparent, more evidence that the beach resists the imposition of any human form upon it.

Finally it should be said that, given my approach, the following views of the beach are necessarily restricted. Perhaps the most glaring restriction is that they are the views of an essentially *shorebound* observer. For whatever reasons, there is no perspective from the sea itself, though that is probably the most familiar view of the beach that the old Cape Codders had, and one that no doubt provides the observer with views he or she cannot have from the beach. There are occasional views from the top of the glacial bluffs or from the estuaries behind barrier beaches that provide certain perspectives—for example, the shape of offshore bars, the patterns of tidal currents— unavailable from the beach, but these are few. I cannot claim a lack of opportunity for this. The truth is that, by temperament or by choice, right from the start, I have always instinctively preferred to be not off the beach or above it, but *on* it. It is there I have felt most in the midst of things, on the front lines of what has been described over and over, by poets and scientists, as the struggle for supremacy between land and sea. If this preference has resulted in a somewhat narrow, or even myopic point of view, perhaps it has at least provided a vivid one.

The
Outer
Beach

1

....

Beginnings

FIRST CONTACT

The first time I ever saw the Outer Beach was in the spring of 1962—April, I think—when I was nineteen. My freshman roommate at Harvard was John Hagenbuckle, whose father ran one of the dozen or so sailing camps that dotted the inner shores of Pleasant Bay in those days.

It was not the first time I had seen the ocean. Growing up in urban New Jersey, I went with my family on one or two excursions to Asbury Park, and I have a memory, when I was about five, of standing in the waves, which were as tall as I was then, and of being lifted by them, gently and with a sense of benignity. But we were mostly lake people in the summers, and after our family moved to West Virginia when I was twelve, I did not see the ocean again until that spring on Cape Cod, seven years later.

John and I left Cambridge sometime after eleven at night, driving in his old VW Bug. There was a full moon and no other traffic on Route 3 for most of the way down. Somewhere around Plymouth, having seen no other cars for a while, John turned off the headlights and we drove for several miles by the light of the moon. It was like entering another world.

We stayed that night in one of the camp cottages in South Orleans. The next day a late spring northeaster strafed the land, whipping up a wild surf that assaulted the beach. We drove out to Nauset Beach, buttoned up in the foul-weather gear that John had provided, and shouldered our way against the wind and rain out of the parking lot and through a gap in the dunes. When I first beheld that wild beach, it overwhelmed whatever anticipations or expectations I might have had. My reaction totally surprised me and was, at the time, inexplicable: I turned full front to the ocean, raised both my arms—and began to conduct. I waved my arms out and in, up and down, in rough time to the surf's irregular rhythm. Of course I was conducting nothing. Even then I felt that the ocean was something that took absolutely no cognizance of me. If anything, it was I who was being conducted by the sea, trying to catch its rhythms and tempi, trying, awkwardly, to become a part of its overwhelming majesty.

Now, at a distance of more than five decades, my reaction seems understandable, even predictable. The only thing in my life thus far that was at all commensurate to what I was experiencing on that beach was symphonic music, mostly the Romantics: Tchaikovsky, Rachmaninoff, Dvořák, and Sibelius—especially Sibelius. I had spent much of my adolescent years in West Virginia in our family's darkened pine-paneled basement rec room listening to 33⅓ LPs of those composers on my Motorola portable stereo with detachable speakers. It was my drug of choice in those predrug days, my substitute for sex in those presex days. I would often stand in front of the turntable, conducting the music in the dark as a way of becoming part of it. It called forth a depth of emotional and psychic response unlike any I had ever experienced, or would—until that day on the beach. Like the music, but of vastly larger proportions, the storm waves gave me the sense of illimitable power and irresistible force, of lavish, inexhaustible beauty, a mix of desire and fear, all held within laws, patterns, and a sense of order too vast and complex for my adolescent mind to recognize, let alone understand, but which I nevertheless felt deeply. I stood on the brink of something that could, if I overstepped my bounds, swallow me up instantly, annihilate me utterly, but which, if I showed the proper respect, caution, and patience, might tolerate me, not shut me out, and perhaps eventually might even allow me an audience with its august presence. My awkward attempts at conducting, I can see now, were unconscious and instinctive, an *homage*, a recognition of a power I had never encountered before—and a desire to somehow be a part of it.

April 1962

OUTER BEACH OVERNIGHTS

We always called it the Outer Beach. Later—not that much later—I would learn that it had many names: Nauset Beach, Cape Cod Beach, the Great Beach, the Backside. But during my first summer on Cape Cod, when I was nineteen and worked as a counselor at Camp Viking, a boys' sailing camp in South Orleans located on Namequoit Point in upper Pleasant Bay, I thought the "outer beach" was the local colloquial name for the Atlantic shore of Cape Cod.

Actually, the term was used at Camp Viking to refer specifically to the part of the outer shore that we could see across Pleasant Bay from the camp's beach. From that perspective, it was, literally, the *outer* beach. The camp's own shoreline was located on the *inner* beach of the bay—the original glacial coastline shaped some twenty thousand years earlier by the Wisconsin Stage Glacier. This beach was the site of the archery target range, swimming lessons, the wooden docks, and, above all, the large flotilla of sailboats—Winabouts, Whistlers, Mercurys, Beetlecats, Wood Pussys, Sharpies, Sunfish, Sailfish, Moths, plus two black twenty-six-foot whaleboats, the *Sea Hawk* (the camp director's inboard launch), and an assortment of skiffs, prams, and dinghies— that formed the core of the camp's activities.

The camp beach was a somewhat muddy shoreline, lined with beds of eelgrass. Innocent as we all were of marine ecology in those days, eelgrass was regarded as an itchy, slimy nuisance, and campers who committed infractions of camp rules were assigned to rake the encroaching eelgrass out of the swimming area.

The air that summer was always sweet and tangy with salt, the decaying piles of eelgrass, and the sun-warmed sap of pine resin. East of the camp the long, low islands of Pleasant Bay—Pochet, Little Pochet, Hog, Sampson, Money Head—lay like long, low dinosaurs in the shallow waters. Beyond the bay, through the gaps in the islands, we could see a thin, ivory line of sand—the "outer beach"—stretching from north to south, interrupted here and there by the tiny, square, almost abstract silhouettes of the outer beach cottages, like mirages on the horizon. Some of these were old hunting cabins, some were used as summer getaway places by local residents of Orleans or Chatham. But one of the cabins belonged to the camp and was referred to as the Overnight Cabin.

On occasion a couple of counselors would take their cabin's campers in a whaleboat across the bay to the Outer Beach for one or two nights in the Overnight Cabin. These trips were always sparked by a spirit of adventure and even mild lawlessness that would hardly be tolerated now. Distinctions between counselors and campers tended to break down out on the beach, and sometimes we encouraged, and even aided, the boys in the prohibited, but universally-indulged-in, nighttime activity of digging "beach-buggy traps."

A beach-buggy trap consisted of a deep hole dug on the beach in one of the existing vehicle tracks that recreational fishermen followed when driving their ORVs down the beach for nighttime fishing. At dusk we would dig the hole two or three feet deep, then hide behind a dune, waiting for the next pair of headlights to come bouncing down the beach from the north. We watched in anticipation until one of the headlights suddenly dropped at an angle, signifying that we had "caught" a beach buggy in our trap. Then we stifled our conspiratorial laughter as a stream of profanity issued from the invisible driver.

Sometimes the whaleboat left the counselors and campers at the cabin and returned to camp. In such a case, after a night or two in the cabin, counselors and campers, carrying their backpacks, trekked along the outer beach to be picked up by the camp bus at the Nauset Beach parking lot, some three miles north of the cabin. It was not an easy hike, and to keep the young campers going, especially on a hot July day, we would hold out the prospect of an ice-cream cone at Philbrick's Clam Shack at the end of the walk.

It was on such a slog from the cabin to the parking lot that I learned two of my earliest lessons about the Outer Beach. The first was that a mile of walking on the beach was roughly equivalent to walking two miles on firm land. (As an adjunct to this lesson, I was instructed by the more experienced counselors that the most efficient technique of walking on the beach was to walk as flat-footed as possible on the sand, instead of the usual hiking method of stepping on the balls of your feet.) The other lesson was the usefulness of the subtle but continuous convex curve of the Outer Beach along its entire length. Such a curve limits one's view of the beach to about a mile, even on a clear day. Thus, when (as inevitably happened) some of the campers began to complain about the arduousness and length of the trek and demanded to know how far it was to Philbrick's, we could honestly, if somewhat misleadingly, tell them that it was "just beyond the next curve."

But my peak experience with the Overnight Cabin, and one that secured me a small place—or notoriety—in the legends of the camp, came during that first summer. One day my co-counselor, Pete Ferreira, and I took our cabin of boys, aged eight and nine, to the Outer Beach for an overnight. That evening, totally against all camp rules, Pete and I rigged a makeshift sail on the whaleboat from bedsheets and sailed back across the bay into Chatham Village, some five miles to the south. There we took all the boys to see Sean Connery and the sensuously bikinied and suggestively named Ursula Andress in the first-ever James Bond movie, *Dr. No*. After the movie we took them all for ice-cream cones and then sailed back to the Overnight Cabin.

Of course in retrospect I should be appalled, not so much at what we did that night as at what *might* have happened—but at the time whatever risk we took seemed insignificant in the light of the wide-eyed and unbelieving faces of those young boys as we sailed back across the bay under starlight. And though Pete and I swore them to secrecy about our adventure, I'm sure it has been told many times in many places over the years, and that that moment still shines bright in many of their memories across the decades.

Summer 1962

CED

Since 1947 Camp Viking had been run by Ced Hagenbuckle, the father of my freshman college roommate, which was, of course, the only reason I got a job there, since I knew absolutely nothing about sailing or boats. I was hired as a general gofer and custodian, making trips into town in the camp jeep for supplies, driving the old school bus that was used to take campers on infrequent excursions to Nauset Beach, making camp signs in the shop, and helping out the mess crew.

Ced (pronounced with a hard C) was a World War II navy veteran, and as a camp director he looked as if he came from central casting. He had rugged good looks, a strong jaw, dark bristly eyebrows, steel-gray hair, penetrating blue eyes, a wiry tanned body, a swaggering walk, a deep resonant voice, and a commanding presence that belied his actual five-foot-eight-inch height. The nautical ethic permeated the fabric and the running of the camp. Not only was Viking primarily a sailing camp, but the structure, language, and protocol of its day-to-day routine were based on those of the U.S. Navy. The daily schedule was based on navy routine; there was Reveille, Morning Colors, Cleanup and Inspection, Assigned Activities, Mess, Evening Colors, Quarters, and Taps—all scheduled in military time (for example, "0710 Reveille Bell"). Each day there was appointed an OD, or officer of the day, whose job it was not only to see that the daily schedule was followed but to record the day's activities in the camp log. Campers were divided into seven crews: Able, Baker, Charlie, Dog, Easy, Fox, and George. Campers with minor scrapes and infections were treated in sick bay; candy, stationery, and other small luxuries were purchased by campers at small stores; and counselors and campers alike relieved themselves in the head. (One of my daily tasks was to clean and restock the camp toilets, as a result of which I was inevitably known to both campers and staff as the "head counselor.")

The tone of navy discipline and order was set by Ced, though once the camp got up and running he was seen only infrequently. Like any good leader, he realized that by limiting his appearances, they had more of an impact when he hove into sight. Ced seemed to have a sixth sense if there was dissension among the counselors, or a food fight in the mess hall, or a camper with a bad case of homesickness, or any other "disturbance in the force." He would suddenly show up, jumping out of his jeep, and with a few words or sometimes just a look, set matters to rights.

On the other hand, within the seemingly tight camp schedule there was plenty of individual freedom, and behind Ced's commanding manner and gruff voice there was a mischievous playfulness and an instinct for what boys aged eight to fifteen really needed and loved. Viking was framed in navy discipline and regulations, but these were enforced only enough to keep natural enthusiasm—which included practical jokes, comic skits, and open-ended adventures—within safe boundaries. Ced himself would often join in the fun, engaging in his patented ape imitation or finding ways to prank a prankster. Like an autocratic but humane sea captain, he commanded respect and loyalty, but more than that, he inspired affection. As one former counselor said, "We would have worked for free—hell, we would have paid *him*."

By my second summer at Viking, I became a shop counselor, which meant I helped, and in some cases more than helped, campers make the model sailboat that each boy could take home with him. That was the extent of my official seamanship, but during free periods

I was allowed to take out one of the smaller boats and eventually gained a modicum of sailing ability.

That summer I was also passionately engaged in my first full-blown love affair. During the preceding winter, when I was living in Provincetown, I would hitchhike to Orleans on weekends to see a woman who was ten years my senior and recently divorced with four young children—a typical Cape Cod romance. As it turned out, she and the kids were living that summer in an old windmill on a bluff on the east side of Little Pleasant Bay. It was several miles by bicycle, but less than a half mile by water from Camp Viking.

It did not take me long to realize that the easiest and quickest way of seeing her was by boat. After lights out, counselors were allowed to assemble in the mess hall until 11 p.m., when we would return to our cabins. About once a week, abetted by my cabin cocounselor, I would leave the mess hall at eleven, then make my way stealthily down to the beach, push one of the prams into the water, and row across the bay to the windmill on the bluff. It was a hopelessly romantic setting, rowing under the moon and stars and weaving through the black silhouettes of the sailboats and whaleboats that rocked gently at their moorings like tethered horses. Far to the east the white strip of the Outer Beach shone in the moonlight like an illuminated bar. All that was missing was a green light at the end of her dock.

I was not so smitten, however, that I wasn't diligent about rowing back well before dawn, beaching the pram, climbing my way back up to the cabin, and getting perhaps an hour of sleep before reveille. After one of those nights I usually dragged through the next day, but I congratulated myself on concealing these nocturnal excursions.

After the campers left at the end of August, most of the counselors stayed around for another week to help put the camp to bed for the winter—closing up the cabins, taking in the docks, storing the boats in the boathouse, the canoes in the shop, and the mattresses in the mess hall. At the end of that week there was a postseason counselors' party, held at an old boathouse belonging to one of Ced's neighbors, Buzz Wilcox, just on the other side of Viking Point. It was a laid-back affair, full of the bonhomie that comes from having completed another successful campaign or season. There was a thoroughly democratic air that evening, beer and wine lubricated the sense of camaraderie, and for once even Ced removed his mask of authority. About ten o'clock, as the party was winding down, he turned to me, slung his wiry, muscular arm around my shoulder, and said in a conspiratorial tone, "Bob, wouldn't you like to take one of the prams out for a row tonight?"

Summer 1963

SEASON'S END

Late on a late September afternoon I got out of the car and started to walk slowly, as I had done so many times that year, across the long sandy stretch of Pochet Beach toward the unseen sea. I crossed the little wooden footbridge that spanned the shallow tidal river, its two-faced current now flowing gently southward, its depth ebbing with the tide. Here, on countless occasions, I had accompanied four blond-haired children as they ran their stick races, dropping twigs or bits of marsh grass over one side of the bridge, then dashing to the other side to see the winner emerge. Their imaginations made a great tunnel of the four-foot width of that bridge—a safe tunnel with a predictable exit, and yet one whose unseen currents could, as they crossed that width of planks, sort out and change in a matter of seconds the order and fate of the passive sticks.

The children and their mother were gone now, though the alternating currents of the stream continued in their lunar rhythms, and one could only guess whether the long-abandoned sticks lay stranded somewhere, bleaching on the upper limits of its course, or were unimaginably scattered and refunded into the anonymous depths of the sea itself.

Such tidal streams are in a sense ambiguous frauds, having no real living headwaters, no complete natural cycle as rivers do, only an end-less regurgitation and reswallowing of their own substance.

The sky was in that state of brilliant instability so characteristic of this land. At a very low altitude, thin-bodied sheets of cloud raced madly out to sea, while higher up, majestically aloof, a cumulus layer, like a fleet of flat-bottomed boats, floated in slow whiteness in the opposite direction. Amid all this the sun periodically broke through and splashed in broken patterns on the sand, pursuing the cloud shad-ows across the plain and the sculptured dunes of the beach. It was as though the heavens were engaged in a playful, or at least thoughtless, kind of end-of-the-season housecleaning.

The wind was clean, new, and sharp with the salt of distant spray. It scattered sand, light sticks, and dead straws of beach grass. It com-pelled the grass clumps to draw circles around themselves in the sand, as though marking off a new domain and a new episode in their end-less struggle for survival, while at the same time it subtly moved the dunes, which threaten always to bury whatever life they foster.

All this flurry of inanimate activity discomposed me. I felt like something left over from a bygone season that might be swept away capriciously, deposited in the sea or buried in the sand for a dark and mindless renewal. I wanted things quiet and still, solemn, even gray—something to feed my inarticulate need for a sense of finality, of closure, which, it seemed, could only be fed from without. There are, after all, no endings or beginnings to human things unless we make them in our imaginations, and the imagination can only feed on facts, can only create from and transform what *is* there.

I walked on, over the bridge, across the wide central plain of the beach, on which only traces of beach-buggy wheels were left in the moving sand. And then, about a hundred feet from the final rise of dunes, as though to startle expectation, the sea threw up an unbidden gesture. It leaped up through the narrow cleft in the dunes: a sudden surge of wave that reached out toward me, gaining for an instant the irresistible shape of a hand before its lengthening fingers sank, turned to foam and dribbles, and disappeared into the sand. It was a moment's apparition, an arm spawned, shaped, thrust, amputated, and buried in the space of a few seconds. And that was all. Nothing followed. But it was something, and it would have to be enough. I turned and headed back to the bridge, the capricious wind now at my face, now at my back, but in the end undirected and uncompelling.

Late Summer 1963

2

....

Monomoy

THE SANDS OF MONOMOY

I

I have been burned. I sit here in the cool morning shade of our oaks and I can feel my face burning, radiating the heat of yesterday's sun, sun that glinted off emerald swells, bone- and shell-strewn sands, silvered flats. Was it only yesterday I was there? It seems a thousand days away. Yet last night in my sleep I still felt the rocking of the waters beneath me, heard and saw the rush and rise of ten thousand wings before me, and drank in the clean tide of solitude that rolled over the flats, across the rippling expanses of marsh grass, the hidden, salty ponds, and the hollows and gentle rises of the dune battlements.

I feel a lump in the pocket of my jeans, reach down, and pull out a handful of sand. It is not ordinary Cape Cod sand, but an extremely fine variety, twice-sifted, water-milled, and wind-distilled. There are more than a thousand grains to the square centimeter. They roll and flow into the veins of my palm almost like water, like diamond dust. They are the sands of Monomoy.

Monomoy Island drops off the chin of Chatham like the beard of the Cape, the barbel of its codfish. Like beards and barbels it is an outgrowth of the main body, though at the moment a disconnected one. A product of wind and sea, it is composed of glacial material worn from the cliffs of the Outer Beach to the north, carried southward by strong longshore currents, and deposited below Pleasant Bay, first as an underwater bar, then as exposed shoals, and finally as an eight-mile barrier island of low sand dunes, sculptured by the wind and held tenuously stable by beach grass.

If Cape Cod is a metaphor for time, a constantly changing landform registering the geological hours, then Monomoy Island is its sweep second hand, caught in the grip of the same forces of change, but recording them much more quickly and visibly. It is the cartographer's despair and the coastal geologist's delight.

Seen from the air, the long, thin island appears as some giant seabird, soaring seaward out of Nantucket Sound, its great wings feathered out into the marshes and flats to the west. Seen in time-lapse photography, it would appear to form the southern end of a twenty-mile whip of barrier beaches and barrier islands lashing the inner coast of Chatham, dissolving and re-forming over and over again through the centuries.

There is something about the nature of Monomoy that invites metaphor, as though with enough images we might somehow shackle its shifting, protean shape. It seems, in its constant mutations, an image itself, illusory, ephemeral; yet it is as rooted in reality as the Rockies, and its changes merely attest to the intensity of its existence.

I had for several years wanted to visit Monomoy. From the mainland portion of the Monomoy National Wildlife Refuge the island looms across the channel, teasingly close, like a floating mirage, like Oz, white and green. There are Audubon trips and other groups that go regularly to the island by charter boat, but it seemed to me to be one of those natural presences that asks, initially at least, to be encountered alone, unguided, to see what it has to offer.

And so yesterday I borrowed a canoe and set off from the Morris Island Dike, paddling down through the narrow outlet of Pleasant Bay toward Monomoy's northern tip. It was a beautiful August day of premature fall weather, cool, with a light breeze out of the northeast and white sprays of high cirrus clouds spouting up to the south over the island.

I rode rapidly down its ocean-facing shore, riding with the tide on clear, heaving swells. I was surprised at how gentle these sea swells remained, but the long curving tip of North Beach to the east still extended itself like a shield, and beyond that, farther south, the rush and clash of whitecaps indicated the presence of the Monomoy shoals. These bars and shoals have threatened and claimed hundreds of ships ever since the early French explorers named it Cape Malabarre— "Cape of the Evil Bar"—but today they offered protection to me and to Monomoy itself.

I first made a landing about a half-mile down the outside shore, and was almost immediately assaulted by hordes of biting greenhead flies, which breed abundantly in the nearby marshes. Wildlife on Monomoy is not "managed," not even the flies. The wooden greenhead-fly trap boxes so common on the mainland are missing in these marshes, and the visitor without long clothes and insect repellent comes here in August at his peril.

Just inside the dunes at this point is the Monomoy tern colony, the largest in the state, posted and patrolled by the Massachusetts Audubon Society. During the past breeding season some two thousand common, several hundred roseate, a few dozen least, and a handful of arctic terns nested here. Largely protected from human disturbance, the terns of Monomoy are, according to the Audubon tern warden, Peter Trull, "barely holding their own" against beach erosion, encroaching herring gulls, and natural predators such as owls and night herons. Their numbers, in fact, have been slipping gradually but steadily in recent years.

When I arrived, in mid-August, breeding had been over for several weeks and the posted signs had been removed. The arctic terns had long departed, having the farthest to travel, and while many birds could still be seen on the island, they no longer hovered and screamed over their nests.

Now, in late summer, the colony had a strange, deserted look. I walked down through the hollows between the dunes, out onto a kind of flattened alley, a pathway of some former flood tide. Its floor was laced with lovely lavender mats of seaside spurge. Here and there among the spurge I came upon the remains of nests and, occasionally, pairs of mottled greenish-beige eggs encircled, as though by the tide, with bits of marsh grass and blackened seaweed. Most were abandoned, but some were still warm, a second clutch probably, still being incubated by a few of the adults, but standing almost no chance at this late date of hatching and fledging before the parents deserted them. Under one of these egg-filled nests I saw, protruding from the sand, the skull of a night heron, blown white and clean by the abrading wind.

To the west of the colony spread the broad green expanse of salt marsh and the beginning of the tidal mudflats. Here many of the terns were resting, the young fledged common terns easily distinguished at close range by their darker plumage, white foreheads, black bills, and prominent black wing bars. There were also several peep—small sandpipers, sanderlings, and plovers—running and poking about in the mud and the undrained tidal creeks. But here, on the island's back side, the tide was still a half mile or more out, and most of the thousands of migrating shorebirds that congregate on Monomoy in late summer and early fall would not be visible for several hours yet.

I returned to the canoe on the ocean side and set off again, paddling toward Hammond's Bend, the narrowest point of the island, about two miles farther south. There I planned to portage across, explore the area to the south on foot, and paddle back on the Sound side in the afternoon in time to catch the shorebirds.

Paddling south on the outside of Monomoy is a curious and tricky business. The farther one goes, the more one emerges from the protection of the shoals and bars to the east. Although the swells themselves were still relatively gentle, they began to break higher and higher as I continued down the beach. I started to wonder if I could make a landing at Hammond's Bend without capsizing.

But the landing proved easier than I had anticipated. Working my way carefully in, I was lifted by a swell and deposited as carefully as a plover's egg on the beach. Before I could pull the canoe out of the surf's reach, however, a second wave came in and swamped the stern. No farther by boat, it seemed to say. Foot it from here.

II

I dragged the canoe onto the upper beach. The isthmus at Hammond's Bend was barely a hundred yards wide, and drift lines from high tides on either side came within half that distance of each other.* Shouldering a small pack, I crossed the narrow waist and set off along the long inner curve of Hammond's Bend to explore the older, southern portion of the island. Except for a large splotch of tidal flats off Inward Point, the shallows and marshes south of this bight are much narrower than those of the northern end. It makes for fewer greenhead flies, but also for fewer shorebirds. This is more than made up for, however, by a much greater variety of terrain, including a number of small brackish ponds, higher dunes, shrub forests containing Monomoy's elusive but sizable deer herd, and patches of the largest, sweetest blackberries I've ever tasted.

At Inward Point there was the remnant of a colony of old beach shacks—small, indigenous, eccentric wooden structures with whimsical names like "Tinkerbell School" and "Whelk-um"—slipped between

---

* Six months after my visit here, on February 7, 1978, a massive ocean storm breached this isthmus, separating the upper third of the island from the rest. It remains today as a wide, open channel through which small boats may pass at high tide.

dune hollows or perched on slender sand pillars as though on stilts. I
investigated one that looked empty, a low-built shack with a junkyard
of mattresses and other debris scattered outside. Dozens of migrating
barn swallows perched and soared about it, celebrating the discovery
of a human-built oasis in this structural desert, and giving it at once
an air of domesticity and abandonment. At least it looked abandoned,
but when I peered through one of the loose windows I saw a wet wash-
cloth hung up to dry and a clock on a small table, ticking loudly away.

I counted only three cottages at Hammond's Bend, in an area
where my 1964 Geological Survey Map showed nine. These buildings
are part of a vanishing species, doomed by Congress in 1970 by the
designation of Monomoy as part of the National Wilderness Preservation system (the only official wilderness in Massachusetts and one
of the few on the entire East Coast). Except in this handful of preex-
isting buildings, no overnight camping is allowed on the island, and
even these cottages will gradually be eliminated as tenancy agree-
ments with the U.S. Fish and Wildlife Service expire—unless, as
seems more likely, the ocean swallows them first.

As such, these few remaining cottages represent the last act in
a long drama of human use and occupation of Monomoy. As early
as 1711 an intrepid settler came here and opened a tavern at Wreck
Cove, a former harbor just south of these cottages. In those days the
island, then attached to the mainland, served as common pasture for
the Chatham townspeople, and the "Common Flats" were harvested
for salt hay. In the 1820s Monomoy Light was built at the south end
near Monomoy Point, and during the mid-nineteenth century a good-
size fishing community, known as Whitewash Village, flourished west
of Monomoy Point around a deep harbor, complete with stores, a
tavern, and a school.

In its time the sands of Monomoy have also harbored four lifesaving
stations, a Coast Guard Station, hunting clubs, and summer cottages.
Of all the many human footholds on the island, only the abandoned
lighthouse tower, the Coast Guard boathouse, and a handful of summer camps remain. By law, nothing more may be built.

I took lunch in the shade of one of the shacks near the beach and then, rolling up my pants, forded Train's Creek, a wide tidal stream connected to a large stretch of ditched inland marsh and a shallow brackish impoundment known as Hospital Pond. This marsh system and the pond are all that is left of the old Wreck Cove. I do not know how Hospital Pond got its intriguing name, but a possible source is an incident that occurred during the winter of 1729 when the *George and Ann*, sailing from Dublin with a shipload of emigrants, took refuge there. Storms, disease, overcrowding, and a lack of provisions had already claimed more than one hundred lives and brought the survivors close to mutiny when they were spotted by a Captain Lothrop and led to harbor in Wreck Cove. The passengers and crew spent the winter boarding with the village families, receiving both hospital care and hospitality, and finally resumed their voyage in the spring.

South of Train's Creek I came upon a graveyard of shells—large sea scallops, knobbed and waved whelks, moon snails—a sea chest of delicate, sculptured, pastel forms. There were hundreds of them, lying in dense concentrations and windrows as though carried in by some previous flood tide and deposited in piles, crowning the low sand hills with fans and whorls of purple, yellow, and orange shells.

Beyond the shell piles was a stretch of small barren sand bowls where the island's numerous gulls apparently came to congregate, and to die. Their gray mummified bodies were stretched indecorously about, legs up, and here and there a whitened bone thrust up through the sand. I came upon one carcass that looked recently dead and experimentally pushed on its diaphragm; it uttered a series of soft, hoarse honks, like a rusty harmonium.

III

The felicities of political language, which flowered in the early days of the Republic in the noble phrases of declarations, constitutions, and judicial decisions, seem in our time to survive, when they do so at all, largely in legislation relating to the preservation of natural areas. Public Law 88-577, better known as the Wilderness Act of 1964, provides one of the few contemporary examples. It contains the terms under which Monomoy Island was established as a Wilderness Area: "an area where the earth and its community of life are untrammeled by man, where man himself is a visitor who does not remain."

As I walked down and across the rims and bowls of the sand hollows south of Train's Creek, the fittingness of these words seemed to spread all about me. Here was life and death in untrammeled freedom; here were the skulls of herons supporting tern eggs, mollusk shells building their own lovely monuments atop sand knolls, gull corpses singing their own dirges, and weathered shacks, wreathed with swallows, sinking gracefully toward oblivion.

"Untrammeled"—what a marvelous word! Commonly confused with "untrampled," it has a very different meaning, namely, "unrestricted in activity or free movement." It derives from "trammel," a shackle attached to a horse's leg to teach it the artificial gait of ambling. Here on Monomoy, at least, nothing was forced to march at an unnatural pace.

I crossed east from the Sound shore over some low dune ridges to Hospital Pond. On the far side of the pond were half a dozen large white egrets, four snowies and two common, standing still as cardboard cutouts on stalked legs in the shallow water. As I squatted down to watch them, something rustled in the marsh grass nearby. I rose up slightly and saw a movement of mottled gray and white among the dark-green blades: a juvenile herring gull, probably unfledged and hiding.

I did not want to disturb the egrets by flushing it, but all at once the bird flapped jerkily out of the grass and onto the pond into view. Something was horribly wrong with it. Its neck was twisted, bent backward and down to one side nearly into the water. It seemed to have no control over its movements and began to drift away from me in the slight breeze toward the far side of the pond.

I shed my pack, stripped off my clothes, and plunged with a loud splash into the shallow lukewarm water. The egrets, startled, rose with hoarse croaks and broad, slow wingbeats, while hordes of marsh minnows spread out in waves before me. In a few strokes I caught up with the crippled gull and discovered its plight. It had become hooked by a fishing lure that had probably washed up with the tide. One of the lure's three hooks had pierced the bird's left knee joint and another was jammed into its left nostril, bending the bird nearly double.

I stood up in the shallow water and clasped its body to me with one arm while I removed the hook in its knee with my other hand. The gull, with a wild stoicism and weakened resistance, kept its beak clamped shut, but I managed to pry it open and free the second hook. When I looked in its mouth I thought at first that its tongue had been ripped, but on closer inspection I realized that a gull's tongue is curiously detached and serrated at its rear end.

I released the bird and watched it float across the pond to the far bank, where it limped ashore, fluttered in the air a few yards, and came to a wobbly landing on its injured leg.

I waded back to the near shore, shivering for several minutes as the sun dried me off, and put my clothes back on. However Hospital Pond had gotten its name, I had no illusions about its efficacy in this case. There was a good chance the gull would die of gangrene from the rusted hooks, but surely it would have died a painful and hobbled death by starvation if I had not come upon it, a fate no creature deserves.

Shouldering my pack, I headed south once more. Why had the bird's plight affected me so much? Surely nature is capable of equally pitiless means of starvation—wolves with snouts full of porcupine quills, beavers with mouths hopelessly propped open by ingrown incisors, Canada geese wandering futilely across marshes locked in ice.

Moreover, gulls are among the more expendable of Monomoy's birds, a menace to the dwindling tern colonies. Their numbers here are unnaturally large—some fifty thousand pairs—nurtured by the prevalence of open garbage dumps on the nearby mainland. Their scavenging nature leaves them open to fates like the one I had just prevented. Often I have seen them on public beaches and at town landfills with necks or legs encumbered by plastic beer rings. Would I have been so quick to come to this gull's aid if I had found it ensnared so on the mainland? Perhaps I would have done Monomoy's beleaguered terns a favor by leaving the bird to its fate? But there is nothing like the proximity of pain to bend our stiffest ecological prejudices.

Besides, something in the mangled nature of the bird's predicament made it seem especially wrong for such a thing to happen here. The grotesque angularity of its posture had been painful and unseemly. I have seen too many natural contours and shapes—tidal creeks and marshes, gentle pine-studded hills, pond bluffs, rolling heaths, all flowing things on the Cape's mainland—mangled and wrenched by human greed, blindness, and indifference. My sudden, intense passion to help the hobbled gull had sprung in part from the chronic helplessness I usually feel to correct such deformity, to restore the proportion of grace and shape and line, to put things aright again.

It was time to be getting back to the canoe. The tide, and with it the shorebirds, would soon be coming to the marshes at the north end. I struck off east across Monomoy's thin shank toward the ocean beach, crossing several old vehicle tracks shown on my map. These had nearly disappeared, and I had to look closely to see where a slight difference in the vegetation still marked their former passage.

On the beach the surf broke gently and evenly along the shore, where sanderlings ran nonchalantly at the edge of the waves. I stripped again, placed the clothes in my pack, and for nearly a mile walked the August solitude of Monomoy's sands unencumbered, while only the gulls looked on.

IV

It was nearly four o'clock when I reached the canoe again. The tide was coming in rapidly now. I would have to travel fast to reach the marshes before the shorebirds. I dressed and portaged the canoe across the narrow isthmus to the Sound side. Paddling hard up the west shore, I skirted the marshes around Shooter's Island—an island in name only now, but which during the late 1800s was the site of the famous Monomoy Brant Club, a collection of shanties where gentleman sportsmen from New York congregated for the spring shooting of Monomoy's once-abundant flocks of brant (a smaller cousin of the Canada goose). Here I flushed several more snowy egrets, a few willets with their bold black-and-white wing patterns, and some small flocks of Hudsonian godwits, one of Monomoy's "specialties."

Then, toward the north end of the island, I began to see them: an armada of dark silhouettes, still more than a hundred yards out, working their way in with the snaking of the tide. A canoe will work pretty well as a blind if you sit low and quietly in it. I found a tidal creek and worked my way into the edge of the marsh, pulled the canoe up onto a peat bank, and sat down in the bottom to watch.

First to come in were the small, short-legged peep—least and semi-palmated sandpipers, sanderlings, ring-necked plovers, the chunkier knots and ruddy turnstones—running and probing just ahead of the tide. Behind them were the larger, long-legged wading birds: short-billed dowitchers, flocks of a hundred or more godwits, tall whimbrels with striped heads and graceful downcurved bills, and neat sets of greater and lesser yellowlegs wading in as if for comparison.

They continued to weave in closer with the advancing shallows, probing in the mud with an energetic stitching motion, embroidering the hem of the tide with their own lovely barred-and-streaked patterns of beige, buff, cinnamon, and light gray. No doubt in all their numbers were some of the serious birder's "catches"—a golden plover, a marbled godwit, perhaps even a ruff or a wandering tattler—but I was a novice, content to feast on spectacle, where dimension matched the primal nature of their movement.

Now they approached very close, coming within a few yards of the canoe before parting and flowing around me up into the marsh. As they came near, their separate personalities became more clearly defined. The dowitchers, greatest in number, with their long, slightly hooked bills and white triangular rump patches, seemed curiously single-minded, probing deeply and rhythmically into the mud, using sensitive, prehensile bill tips to extract small crustaceans and interstitial organisms from the sand grains.

The Hudsonian godwits, by contrast, were taller, with slightly upcurved bills and striking black-and-white tail patterns. They appeared more wary and dignified than the dowitchers, did not probe in so far with their bills, and frequently lifted their graceful heads to look about. Gideon would have chosen godwits for his army.

As the shorebirds advanced and parted around me, I could see, farther out, terns swinging and gliding over the water and, far beyond them, some small dark birds flitting out over the waves, petrels perhaps. From the cordgrass behind me came the high, bright *chips* of sharp-tailed sparrows as they flushed, fluttered up weakly, and dropped back down again. And far inland, across the broad rippling expanse of marsh grass, I heard the muted cacophony of the vast gull colony, one hundred thousand strong. Occasionally large rafts of shorebirds lifted in a rush of wings and silvery crying, making dark clouds against the lighter real ones gathering from the south. I sat, it seemed, in an element of birds, surrounded as though by rain, wind, and fog, a living fullness that tantalized the mind with visions of an abundance that once rendered waste and decimation so innocent to the minds of men. They formed an electric band of life, so intense, so intent on their probing, running, stalking, dipping, diving, and flitting that I was only minimally regarded, as a wreck or some rock might have been.

The shorebirds passed, the waters encircled the canoe and lifted it off the bottom, and I began to drift with the breeze, turning lightly like a leaf, out into the Sound. The terns now filled the air with their harsh cries, dipping and skimming over the shallows. Most of these were black-billed juveniles that seemed to be drinking and practice-diving rather than fishing in earnest. With the terns I spotted three or four larger birds, striking in appearance: black on top, white underneath, with long red tapered bills tipped with black. These were black skimmers, larger relatives of the terns that can usually be seen in small groups on Monomoy in summer and early fall. Skimmers were nesting on the Cape when Samuel de Champlain sailed into Nauset Harbor in 1605, but were rapidly extirpated along the New England coast in colonial times by egg hunters. During the past twenty years, after an absence of more than two centuries, they have begun nesting on Monomoy again.

A skimmer's bill is an improbable structure at first glance; its lower mandible is fully one-half again as long as its upper. The skimmer feeds by flying low over the water with its lower bill plowing the surface. When it strikes a small fish, the upper part clamps down. Often the skimmer will work the same "row" of water several times, back and forth, attracting the fish to the surface with its first passage and gathering them up on the next.

In flight the skimmers are handsome, dark-winged birds with flat, slightly arched wingbeats adapted to their unique fishing method. I watched them sail close above the shallows, bright-billed heads dipped low, wings raised high and arched, uttering low *aawrks*. They looked like flying wheelbarrows, or plows, furrowing the contours of the bottom, lowering the bill deep in a channel and raising it to avoid bars. Feeding with the adult skimmers was one immature bird, speckled brown and white above, with a bill still pale in color. It apparently had not yet mastered the skills of its elders, for several times it appeared to misjudge the depth of the water and strike bottom, tripping on its bill, so to speak.

How many uses a single tide could be put to! How many times the same ground could be gone over, harvested and gleaned by a seem-

ingly endless array of bills and beaks, and still yield up fresh suste-
nance. It seemed a stately procession, a dance of new prey rising up
to meet new predators, all riding together on the major rhythms of
the tide.

I wanted to stay and see them all go out again, but dusk was coming on and the tide would be against me going back. I took up my
paddle and headed back toward the mainland. Since I was already
on the west side of the island, I decided to take the cut-through at
Harding's Light into Chatham's Stage Harbor. By the time I reached
the entrance to the harbor, the color was draining from the sky in
the west and the breeze had freshened from the north. I bucked both
wind and tide through the channel, making snail progress, my limbs
aching with exhaustion.

It was nearly nine o'clock when I finally entered the inner harbor.
In the blackness I could make out the shapes of more than a hundred moored boats, from small dinghies to large, expensive yachts. I
weaved among their silent, rocking forms, feeling alien and unallied
to these vessels and their inhabitants. The smell of steaks barbecuing
assailed my nostrils, and I was suddenly ravenous. I saw a charcoal
grill standing on the stern deck of one of the larger yachts. From
inside its cabin the sounds of talk, laughter, and ice-filled glasses fil-
tered out through lighted windows. I could have scaled the ladder
that hung down the stern and made off with a steak without com-
punction. I felt *outside* this human order and its restraints—an unexpected legacy of my day on Monomoy.

But I paddled on through the harbor, leaving the steaks unmo-
lested, back to the dike where my van was parked. As I rounded the
mainland shore, the unaccustomed sound of whippoorwills exploded
from its full, dark hills.

August 1977

A DANGEROUS EDGE

Yesterday I spent four hours on North Monomoy Island with Peter Trull, the Massachusetts Audubon tern warden, collecting the signs he had posted in the spring around the tern nesting areas. It was a perfect day for it, sunny and windy with a strong breeze out of the south-southwest. We put in at Horne's Marina in Chatham and went down the outside channel, the metal launch banging, dancing, and slamming like a bronco against the concrete-hard swells. I held onto the gunnel for dear life, but Peter looked as if he was enjoying himself immensely. He is a lanky, outgoing, loquacious, and enthusiastic naturalist in his early thirties with a perpetually boyish face and an indefatigable curiosity, who treats the natural world as if it were an unexpected, endlessly fascinating toy.

We landed about a quarter mile down the outside shore, near the tern colony. Peter says about 1,900 common terns are here this year, 290 leasts, and a scattering of arctics. Nauset Beach's least tern colony, by contrast, had no production this year, having been completely wiped out by the Pochet foxes. He believes that, even under "natural" conditions, that colony would have been wiped out, but now they have nowhere to go. We have removed the margin, he says, the "free play" of the prey-predator relationship, the freedom to fluctuate, to relocate, and for many species have reduced the tolerance for survival to a narrow dangerous edge: Stay where you are, or be wiped out.

Peter's words brought to mind a harrowing National Geographic documentary, *Death in Eden*, on the elephants of Kenya, which I had recently watched on PBS. Recognizing the economic if not the environmental value of these animals, the Kenyan government had established what they thought were sufficient elephant "refuges" in the highlands. What they had not sufficiently recognized were the elephants' traditional seasonal migratory routes, which took them through recent human settlements and farmland, creating widespread destruction for the inhabitants of those areas. After several failed attempts to contain or reroute the elephants, the government had resorted to "culling" or killing dozens of them in the more "troubled" areas. The final, horrific scene showed dozens of elephant trunks against the sky, moving in increasingly panicked circles as they dropped one by one to the bullets of the government-approved hunters—one of the most dramatic images of environmental failure I have ever seen. The plight of these tern colonies is nowhere near as horrific, of course, but the principle is the same: We have failed to "make room" enough for them, and we are loath to remove ourselves.

Peter and I walked through the colony to the marsh on the western shore and made our way south across "marsh flats," those curious expanses of muddy sand, barren of grass, covered with a slippery black mat of algae about one-eighth-inch thick, which in turn are covered with pale, hopping flies. The biting greenhead flies were abundant, both on the beach and the flats, but the wind kept them down.

On Monomoy this year's crop of young terns were all fledged, though most still hung over the colony, tearing the air with their screams. We saw a number of common tern "fledgies" with white foreheads, dark-brownish plumage, and noticeable black wing stripes when at rest. Several were practicing ineffectual dives, as if to say, Look, Ma—I'm a tern! Peter said he has seen terns mobbing toads on Monomoy, for no apparent purpose.

There were still several late nests with eggs in them, some still warm, being futilely incubated, others abandoned. Breeding schedules are mercilessly tight here, in addition to heavy predation from owls and black-backed gulls.

There were no arctic terns to be seen now. Peter said they leave earlier than the rest, on a trek that will take them to the southern tip of South America. Monomoy is a kind of international avian airport, with constant arrivals and departures, all with built-in tower controls. Fledglings continue to be fed by adults, probably through migration.

We walked back to the boat along the perimeter of the tern colony, gathering up the tern nesting signs as Peter urged the birds: "The season's over, guys, get going." We had lunch on the beach, a stiff wind blowing sand into my sandwich as I held it, and filling my pockets with a fine shower of sand. Like snow, Peter said.

After lunch we walked around the north tip of the island, where we came upon the nine-foot skeleton of a tuna that Peter had found stranded there a few weeks ago. The head was still covered with a net of flies. Then around to the flats again, where the hordes of shorebirds were working their way in at the edge of the tide.

We sat down on the sand flats at one point and waited for the tide and the shorebirds to approach us. The peep—small sandpipers and plovers—stayed pretty much on course, passing within twenty feet or so of us, but the larger birds—dowitchers, whimbrels, godwits, yellowlegs—gave us a wide berth. I felt the birds must quickly eat their fill in such fertile diggings, but Peter said that, unlike ground-feeding land birds, there is likely much probing before a strike is made. Earlier this summer he had found a dead plover and examined its stomach. It was all sand grains.

We examined fistfuls of marsh sand, finding a few threadlike red worms and a single large mealworm-like larva in one batch. I did not see how the birds could extract such tiny animals, but Peter said their bills are extremely sensitive and that the dowitchers' tips are prehensile, like those of woodcocks. As we walked from the shallows toward the tide's edge at one point, myriads of sand shrimp and killifish, millions of unseen motions in the water, teemed on the surface, filling it with tiny, rippling, popping explosions, giving it a live, electric edge before dispersing invisibly, like the wind, as we gained the disappearing shore.

In places the concentrations of shorebirds were impressively dense. On the sands they crowded together, like sow bugs on a wet foundation. Flushed, they made dark clouds of flashing wings against the sky, which, with the cacophony of the nearby gull colony, and the sweeping rippling green of summer's fullness across the marshes and dunes, tantalized the mind with visions of original abundance that rendered decimation innocent.

As the tide reached the edge of the marsh grass, it began to sprinkle, a cold, hard refreshing patter. We came back through the marsh across the herring gull colonies. Among the nests and the live birds there were also dozens of dead gulls, their bodies seemingly unmarked. When I asked Peter about them, he said, "It happens." He told me he once found a dead gull with an automobile air filter in its throat.

We loaded the signs in the boat and then tried to go down to the new cut-through that the February blizzard had made at the island's waist, but the swells got too rough. So we skimmed back up into Pleasant Bay with the swells, swerving between buoys, sun showers, and emerald shallows. It did not begin to rain in earnest until we put in at Arey's Boatyard in South Orleans, where Jonnie Fisk, an old friend of ours and an amateur ornithologist whose pioneering studies of migratory songbirds earned her the sobriquet of the "Bird Lady of Orleans," invited us in for tea and homemade English muffins.

August 1978

LIFE AND DEATH IN THE OPEN

My friend Ralph MacKenzie and I have landed on Monomoy Island in his 4 hp skiff. We put in about 8:30 a.m. with some trepidation (Ralph's boat is unlicensed) at the Mitchell Bridge Landing in Chatham, right across from the Coast Guard patrol boat with its flashing blue light. The Coast Guard was testing its lights, horns, sirens, and the like for the Memorial Day patrol. We putted around in the Mill Pond for a while, trying to look inconspicuous, then made a run for it under the bridge. They didn't even look at us.

It is a beautiful day, calm, sunny, already near seventy. It took us about an hour to run down to the new Inlet (now permanent enough to be capitalized), where we have landed on its south shore—a surreal landscape of mudflats, trunk roots, and shrubs half buried in the sand where three years before I had picked blackberries.

We are pleased to find that Dana Eldridge's family cottage—

"Tinkerbell School"—is still here. I first saw it on my first trip to Monomoy in 1977. Then it had been a quarter mile inland; now it is only about two hundred feet from the Atlantic beach and badly storm damaged. Just under the window is a penciled line labeled "Great Storm of '78 water line—zowie!" Still, the cottage preserves a touching sense of domesticity even in the face of imminent destruction. There is a swallow nest under the window and an adult pair perched on the roof peak. There are fresh deer tracks, occasional dead gulls, and feathers everywhere in the tidal wrack.

Since the tide is running out, we decide to motor down the inside channel to the south end of South Monomoy Island without delay, a run of about four miles. We squeak our way west out of the shallows and around the outside of the tidal flats. The wind picks up as we head south, forcing us to run close in toward the shore, with terns and laughing gulls diving everywhere all around us.

We beach the boat in a narrow tidal creek just south of Powder Hole, near the site of Whitewash Village, a nineteenth-century fishing village that presumably got its name from the ubiquitous paint on its structures. From there we explore a chain of small ponds to the south—human-made ponds built back in the 1940s when Monomoy became a state wildlife refuge. In the largest one, Big Station Pond, there are four perfectly round, regularly spaced nesting islands populated by a dozen or so pintails and baldpates. Though there are deer tracks everywhere, we have not yet seen one, since they tend to bed down for the day in the low stands of bayberry and beach plum that dot Monomoy's landscape. On the sandbar between our tidal creek and Powder Hole we find the decayed carcasses of ten harbor seals, their white skulls picked clean, the hides maggot-infested and full of holes—all facing the lagoon as they must have been when they died. What brought them to this spot? What caused this mass die-off? Despite their decomposed state, they make an oddly formal group, as if they were arranged in their positions for a painting or a sculpture. (I thought again of that uncharacteristically naive comment by the essayist Lewis Thomas: "You do not expect to see dead animals in the open. It is the nature of animals to die alone, off somewhere, hidden. It is wrong to see them lying out on the highway; it is wrong to see them anywhere." Thomas is a wonderful writer, but he clearly never spent much time on the beach.)

We flush what I think is a whippoorwill, which quickly lands and lets us get within twenty feet of it before flushing again. Now I can see it is a nighthawk, with long pointed wings and white patches, an even rarer bird than a whippoorwill on Monomoy, seen only once every two to five years.

We return to the skiff and investigate a tar-paper shack on the east side of Powder Hole, the only one remaining of seven buildings shown in that location on the 1964 topo map. Inside is a gas stove, gas refrigerator, sink, a small side bedroom with two bunk beds, a functional outhouse with swallow nests inside—and a note on the table that reads "Thank you for treating this cottage as if it were your own.— THE OWNERS." There are considerable penciled graffiti on the whitewashed walls—effusive thank-yous, sketches of birds, facetious requests for air-conditioning and mail delivery—but not one obscenity.

It would seem that there are now only two cottages remaining on the island—this one and the Eldridges'—where not that long ago there were dozens. In all probability there will soon be none, fulfilling the vision for Monomoy in the enabling legislation establishing it as a National Wilderness Area in 1964: "an area where the earth and its community of life are untrammeled by man, where man himself is a visitor who does not remain." Despite the fact that Ralph and I both fight to preserve as much land in our town as we can from rampant development, we feel sad at the imminent disappearance of all human structures in this place. The proportion, the mix, is all; or, as Ralph put it, "A few houses improve a landscape."

We haul our gear up to the shack and sack out for a couple of hours. Ralph gets up first and heads toward the abandoned lighthouse, built in 1828, about three-quarters of a mile to the northeast. I join him later on the poverty-grass prairie between the shack and the light, where he tells me he jumped four deer in the swales. There are lots of prints going up into the sand dunes that look like small diamondback turtle tracks, but turn out to be muskrats, several of which we saw in the marsh ponds. We find the half-buried and decayed remains of an old Model A Ford in the sand, a relic of the early decades of the twentieth century when Monomoy was attached to the Chatham mainland and joyriding down the sands of Monomoy in old jalopies was a favorite pastime for local teenagers. The chassis has a "double-glass tail-light" still intact, which Ralph says is "quite rare." He will try to remove it tomorrow for his brother John, who owns a Model A.

Ralph heads back to the lighthouse, while I go back to the shack to take notes and prepare dinner. Later, at dusk, as I go to get water in the pond behind the shack, there is a deer across the water, looking at me calmly. Later I surprise another one a hundred feet from the house. It bounds away, passing very close to the seal carcasses and through the bayberry bushes into the dusk, looking like a giant rabbit, its large white tail flag waving back and forth.

In the evening gulls settle like eyelids on surface of Powder Hole. Ralph says there were lots of sunspots prominent at sunset tonight. Attached pairs of horseshoe crabs promenade along the edges of the lagoon as the tide rises. We fall asleep to the toneless screams of Fowler's toads in the dunes, grateful we are too early for greenhead flies.

The next morning begins calm and muggy and full of Monomoy mosquitoes, which seem to get high on DEET. I walk south to the herring gull colonies, and then on to the Salt Pond, where the variety of ducks is astonishing. I stand there with my *Peterson Bird Guide* open to ducks, flipping the pages and checking off virtually every species: Gadwall, Green-Winged Teal, American Black Duck, Mallard, Northern Pintail, Blue-Winged Teal, American Widgeon, Oldsquaw, Black Scoter, White-Winged Scoter, Common Goldeneye, Bufflehead, Hooded Merganser, Red-Breasted Merganser, Ruddy Duck.

On the south side of Salt Pond is perhaps the most puzzling find of the trip: a large bulldozer, probably used to build these nesting ponds back in the 1940s. It still sits upright, its gears, tracks, and sides full of decades of rust, reminding me, for some reason, of the collection of seal corpses we came on the day before. I have the odd sense that if I climb up into the cab I might find the mummified body of its last operator. But the big mystery isn't *why* it is here or why it was abandoned, but the fact that the machine's carcass is covered three to four feet up its rusting yellow sides with barnacles. The bulldozer is now several hundred yards from salt water, but even if it had been in water when it was abandoned and had subsequently been coated with barnacles, how did the entire machine come to rest at least several feet above the current sea level? That would have required the sea level to have dropped several feet in the past several decades, which is the opposite of what is actually happening here.

But after a while on Monomoy, nothing seems improbable, and as the wind picks up and the fog rolls in, the line between animate and inanimate begins to blur. A two-foot-long green and yellow snake wiggles out from between the dozer tracks. A deer skeleton lies, like a fossil, on the east side of the last nesting pond, fragments of attached, parchment-like skin waving in the wind like prayer flags. It is hard to focus on anything on Monomoy—new things keep crossing the field of view and the eye is distracted.

I wander through the gull colony, whose birds now begin diving at me. I wonder if this might have been the site of the old Whitewash Village. Hard to tell, even looking at maps, for there are so few stable reference points in such a place. In any case, this site is certainly whitewashed now, with the constant bombardment of the diving gulls.

Doubts grow. The gulls seemed a negative force, their screams urging me to Go, go, go. I trek north along the spine of the dunes toward the abandoned lighthouse, one of the few clear landmarks on the island, to find Ralph. The weather begins to clear, and a cloud of black ducks rises in the west.

As I approach the lighthouse Ralph is standing on the empty ramparts, looking at me through his binoculars. I climb the circular iron staircase and join him. This is the best vantage point on the island. In fact from here one can see the entire length of the island, which resembles a giant thighbone, thick at both ends and now fractured in the middle. From here we can see several deer, hunkered down in the brush. A redheaded woodpecker, very rare even on the mainland, dips and flaps across the dunes, looking for a tree. A hawk skeleton lies next to one of the light's outbuildings. Everywhere life and death are blatantly commingled.

We trek back across the sand bowls to the shack. Surprisingly, two or three of the deer stand up, in broad daylight, staring at us. Perhaps they know their cover has been blown and there is no use continuing to hide. It is curious how deer will stand broadside when looking at you, almost as if to present a better target. We follow an old jeep road, which now seems to be primarily a deer trail, full of their split-pear tracks—a process reversing the usual order of succession. Loons call from somewhere on the fog-shrouded ponds.

We set out for home in the skiff about six thirty, going up the outside with the wind and tide. The long, long eastern shore of Monomoy presents a profile of cuts and truncated dunes. The clear deep-green water, shingled with shells, slides beneath us. A cloud of terns rises up from North Beach to the east, half a thousand at least, like sticks thrown up from a fire. Ralph calls them the "most aesthetically appealing of birds." They blend into a battery of RV campers at the southern end of the beach. Then, to the left, an impossibly large swarm of gulls rise like bees over the island and settle on the beach. They seem an unstoppable number, like sand grains, like ticks.

As we approach the bluffs of Morris Island the very trees sift human words to us on the breeze, and with great surprise, we rediscover our wonder.

It is now about nine o'clock, less than an hour after Ralph and I got back to the Mitchell River Bridge. I am sitting in my neighbor Judy's living room, drinking a glass of wine, shivering under a tartan she has spread over me, trying to flush the chill of the hour and a half ride in an open boat back from Monomoy that is still in my bones. Outside, a spring thunderstorm of unusual violence has begun. When the first lightning flashes hit the mantel and the walls, I take them, from habituation and tiredness, for the flashes from Chatham Light. The strokes flash brilliantly and silently from all points of the horizon, like heat lightning, though the night is cool.

By the time I return to my own house, the thunder is starting to creak and crackle in from the edges, and a few minutes later the rain begins: thick, hard, icy drops, like a garden hose trained on my roof. It soon becomes a stagestruck tempest, drumming on the roof, shredding the sky from one end to the other, and lighting up the yard with brilliant scattered blue-white flashes, like some mad shutterbug running about outside snapping strobe-light pictures.

The storm surges, retreats, and surges again for several hours. I lie in bed, waiting for sleep. In my mind I have simultaneous flashes, like some frantic slideshow, of that whitened island landscape under the storm: of clumps of deer bedded down in bayberry thickets, looking up with each crash and flash with black, staring eyes; of the ducks, milling and turning on the surface of the nesting ponds, black silhouettes on a roof of old quicksilver; of the gulls, like thousands of white stones padding the scalloped dunes; of the lightless black-and-red tower, shedding illumination no more but illuminated itself, an arbitrary and powerful symbol of the absence of human presence in that long, low landscape.

All through the storm the little phoebe who has been nesting on my front door light sits on her nest, white tail feathers pushed up against the clapboards, rocking, with steady breathing, back and forth.

May 1980

FOR ANNIE

I remember now, Annie, that foggy, sunny, late-summer day when we all met—you and Gary, Beth and I, our young daughter, Katy, and her friend Mahri, our friends Georgene and Ralph—on that shrouded causeway to Morris Island. We brought three canoes, one on a trailer, one mounted upside down on a car top, and one stuffed in the back of a station wagon that looked like a whale calf being born. We stood around talking, wondering if we should wait for the fog to lift—Gary congenial and knowledgeable as always, your motormouth going with a kind of determined sociability—until finally we decided to set out and paddle to the south end of Morris Island. We portaged the three canoes across the sand flats to the little cove on the east side of the island, set Katy in the middle of our canoe, Mahri in the middle of yours, and then paired up like the middle-class couples we were.

The tide was going out as we rounded an old weir where cormorants sat, then hugged the eroding coast and the expensive, sandbagged battlements of Morris Island and its newly built window-walled castles. We had to go nearly out of sight of land to avoid the bars where dozens of gulls stood in a line on the riffling water, past pungent fishing boats and graceful sailboats swinging at anchor, testing the waters and one another in our newly formed friendship, you waving to small groups of people on the shore, shouting, "Is this Massachusetts?" beaching at last at the lower end of Morris Island in a wall of fog.

We walked about and watched hermit crabs and ate lunch on the beach and made forays inland into the fog to pee, and Gary and Ralph talked boats—killing time for a couple of hours, waiting for the fog to lift, until, just as we were about to accept a thwarted day (you kept saying it wasn't, kept encouraging us, kept appreciating everything), the fog lifted like a silver cover off a main-dish platter, and there lay North Monomoy, low and revealed, shining like Shangri-La in the southern early afternoon sun. We quickly got into our canoes and set off, reaching the flats at the northern tip in minutes, but then going at least twice as far on the outside before we beached the canoes next to a large sailboat in front of the North Island's eroding dunes. As soon as we landed the fog dropped like a curtain, thicker than before, like a joke we had all assented to.

We circled the northern tip of the island, finding a partially disintegrated Nerf football and tossing it around, then walked down the outside beach, endlessly, it seemed, as the swift green current kept pace with us. Katy found one large sandal in the sand. A hundred feet farther we came on the other, and you said, "I've been waiting for the other one to drop"—[beat]—"They call him 'Stretch.'"

We saw only a few shorebirds, but you, as usual making the best of things, said, "I don't care much for shorebirds. I prefer passerines."

You told us of a song you had dreamed the night before. It went something like this:

Who makes the birds to fly?
Who makes the fish to swim?
McNature does—[strumming an air ukulele] chordy-chordy-chordy
McNature does.

We found a stranded Christmas tree on the beach, already tinseled with eelgrass, which we planted in the sand and decorated with crab shells and gull feathers. You took a horseshoe crab shell and held it up to your face by the tail and it became a Greek or Japanese mask; then you put it on your head and wore it all afternoon as a helmet, like Johnny Appleseed's pot. It seemed to hold on to your braided golden hair like an ardent male. Your invention inspired us all, and we transformed everything we found that afternoon, turning dead life into decoration or sound or movement. At one point Georgene came upon an intact duck leg. You picked it up and entertained the children by pulling the exposed dangling tendon so that the leg jerked, the foot moved, and the toes splayed as in life. We all exclaimed and giggled at the outrageous humor of it. We were ready to pull migrating warblers out of the air to use as darts, or stranded bass for baseball bats.

We walked, it seemed, endlessly over the flat moonscape toward the Inlet. Somewhere along the way you said that nearsighted peo-ple were more introspective and bookish than others, and I almost believed you. At last, though, about three thirty, we realized that we had to try to get back. The tide had turned, though the fog had not lifted at all. None of us had brought compasses, though you, Ralph, and I had all thought of it but had decided not to, thinking that if it was bad enough to need one, we wouldn't have gone.

But, necessity being the mother of conviction, we reasoned that we had both wind and tide with us, and at worst would end up in Little Pleasant Bay. So we set off, going by dead reckoning, keeping the southeast wind behind our right ears, running with the current over the sinking bars. What I remember most is how quickly all signs of land disappeared and there we were, three disembodied canoes, running on wind and tide, in a soft, muffled silence of light and fog, wanting above all to stay in sight of one another, yet letting our different senses of direction (all baseless, merely willful) nearly carry us apart again and again, so that most of the time only one of the other two canoes was in sight, the other existing only by voice. There was a shared sense of fragile connection, that we might easily be lost to one another.

But soon we hit an unfamiliar stretch of shore and spent some time arguing whether it was Morris Island, the Outer Beach, or the moon—but in the end it was just where we had aimed, a short unfamiliar bar on Morris Island that made the current go the wrong way. And so we made our way back, as fishing boats chugged and boomed in and out of view at less than a hundred yards. We got Mahri back to her parents just after they had called out the Coast Guard. The rest of us went back to our house for showers and clam chowder and wine and lots of good talk. When the conversation drifted dangerously toward the threat of nuclear war, you began to fiddle with an empty Land O'Lakes butter carton, folding it so that the Indian maiden's rosy knees were transformed into boobs beneath her deerskin jacket, delighting and turning us all into children once again.

September 1982

3

....

North Beach /
Pleasant Bay / Pochet

HIGH SURF AND A BREAKTHROUGH

We Americans live so much within ourselves, we think we must physically move in order to experience change. Perhaps that is why we travel so much and have so little to show for it.

On New Year's Day, on the morning following a furious ocean storm, I walked several miles down the beach from the Pochet parking lot. The storm itself had blown rapidly out to sea during the night, and the wind had careened around to the west, giving rise to that strange sight: a clear and sunlit beach on which a mighty surf, still in the throes of the offshore storm and now approaching its flood, dashed itself in magnificent chaos.

Such surf, swept back by the wind and etched in light, had passed through all stages of watery fury. No longer a series of breakers, it had become a shattering wall of green and white, crest breaking upon crest, wave receding crashing into wave oncoming. The sound it made was not a roar but more like a wind—a low, hollow, invidious whine that slowly grew in pitch and intensity, like the sound of an approaching tornado, before it broke and dissolved into the next oncoming whine.

The air itself was full of the mist of its destruction, intersecting rainbows and flashes of light, and the air smelled sweet, newmade, and wonderfully exhilarating. In no other place can you get so close to ultimate force with so little risk as on the shore.

Yet there was more than spectacle to see that day. The ocean was stretching its borders and trying out new shapes. The access to the beach at Pochet is a long one. From a small, private parking lot a wooden pedestrian bridge leads across a shallow but broad tidal stream, representing the uppermost reaches of the waters of Pleasant Bay to the south. Beyond this is a stretch of dunes and swales nearly a thousand feet wide, bisected by a north-south beach-buggy trail that provides access to fishermen and the owners of beach cottages on North Beach. The beach itself is finally gained through a cut, or gut, in the front line of dunes that was formerly used by vehicles but is now closed off.

During the storm and again that morning the ocean had broken through this gut and was now flowing shallowly west and downhill to meet the already swollen tidal stream coming up from Pleasant Bay. This had in effect made a temporary island out of all North Beach to the south. Halfway across the sand it flowed into the beach-buggy tracks and was spreading out north and south, filling up this premade bed and some of the side trails as well.

Despite this, a stream of holiday trucks and jeeps trickled buoyantly and doggedly south from the Nauset Beach parking lot. Some, when they encountered the salt water creeping up the track, attempted to circumvent it by going into the bordering vegetation, but most churned right through. One driver stopped his pickup, got out, and waded into the middle of the stream in his boots, held a stick in the water to gauge its depth, and then, judging that his horsepower still outweighed seapower, got in and plowed safely access.

How confidently he and the others trusted in this beach! I thought. And how I, who often played games with the violent surf, trusted the ocean. How we all trust natural processes, knowingly or not, even in our abuse of them, like the wife beater whose violence is founded in large part on the conviction that his victim will not, or cannot, leave. These motorized pilgrims were implicitly affirming that this was, after all, only a temporary break, that the waves would subside, the tide recede, the beach would hold, and they would be able to get back.*

I had to agree with them, watching the edge of the breakthrough on the ocean side where the waves still crested over the top of the berm, rolling stones and shells and bits of seaweed before them. The flow through the break was only about ten to fifteen feet wide and a few inches deep; I could easily have crossed it myself on foot. Yet it was not the actual magnitude of the breakthrough but the power of suggestion behind it that made me stop and ponder: What if a massive, permanent cut-through occurred on this beach, putting an end to all foot and vehicular traffic?

This is not, after all, too far-fetched a fancy. Geologically speaking, all of the Outer Beach from Coast Guard Beach in Eastham to the southern tip of Monomoy Island nearly twenty miles to the south is a barrier-beach system created by material chewed from the Eastham-Wellfleet sea cliffs and carried south by the prevailing littoral drift. As such the barrier beach has served to protect the headlands behind it, those of Pleasant Bay, Pochet, and Nauset Harbor.

Yet the beach itself has been far from stable. It has a long and cyclical history of shifting inlets, new breakthroughs, lengthening sand spits followed by sudden amputations—a series of connections, discon-

---

* I do not want to get drawn into the controversy over beach buggies here, except to note that one of the worst reasons recently offered in their defense is the assertion that nature, after all, destroys the beach far more wantonly and extensively than vehicles. This is not only illogical, it is also a manifestation of that dangerous tendency to identify ourselves with nature when it suits our purposes by the lowest common denominator—namely our ability to imitate nature's destruction.

nections, and reconnections, like honey dripping from a spoon. Nauset
Inlet, for instance, has shifted north and south continually ever since
Champlain entered it in 1605 and drew the first map of Nauset Harbor. Many older residents of Orleans still remember the sizable cottage
colony known as "Nauset City" on Nauset Beach during the 1920s
that was washed away by a single storm. North Beach itself has had an
even more erratic history. An 1883 U.S. Geological Survey map shows
entrances to Chatham Harbor at a point opposite North Chatham, at
the former site of the Old Harbor Coast Guard Station. At one point
this old breach became so large that the unprotected town lost both
of the old Chatham Lights and portions of two streets before the spit
began to lengthen and the break closed up. And Monomoy Island is, of
course, a mere breath of land, the flicking end of a marine whip of tide
and sand. In other words, as Galileo might have said, *Si muove*.

Granted, so far as I know, no permanent breakthrough has ever
occurred on this particular stretch of beach, but this day's work had
at least opened the possibility. And what a sudden dividend such a
breach would produce: six or seven miles of North Beach separated
from the mainland and added to the Monomoy Wilderness Area in
one fell swoop!*

Wilderness! The ocean itself is the final repository, the holder of its
secret, and, it seems, the only source that can create more. We need
more wilderness, if only because humans need to look outward and
behold something other than their own faces peering back at them
and their machines circumscribing the landscape.

I looked longingly across the brief and intermittent island created
by the breach. Then, pocketing a piece of kelp that had been flung

---

* A bit of unintentional prognostication, for which I take no credit except that
of wishful thinking. This, in fact, took place in 1991 when the southern part of
North Beach, already separated from North Beach by a storm in January 1987
and thence known as South Beach,, connected its northern end to Chatham
Light Beach and then, several years later, connected its southern end to South
Monomoy Island, providing, at least temporarily, a land bridge between the
mainland and the Monomoy Wilderness.

in over the dunes, I turned my back on the still-howling beach and picked my way back across the beach-buggy ruts, thickening like veins with the blood of the ocean.

January 1975

NORTH BEACH JOURNAL

I

I have been living alone for three days now in a cottage on the west shore of North Beach, a long and narrow barrier spit of low sand dunes and salt marsh lying a mile or so east of Chatham at the elbow of Cape Cod. Chatham is one of the fog capitals of New England, especially in spring. Since I arrived on Sunday evening the fog has poured nearly continuously over this naked beach like some great silent river; but late this afternoon the wind shifted to the west and the gray shroud at last began to lift.

I do not live alone easily. In solitude I find myself inordinately affected by the weather. It is as though meteorology takes the place of intimate company, and the distinction between outer weather and inner mood is gradually obliterated. In such situations it is not so much a question of trying to give myself over to nature as trying to hold something back, some bit of perspective and self-evaluation. This is just what fog loves to steal from you.

There was already a dense fog at the water's edge and a light north-west wind blowing when I set off about five last Sunday afternoon in a small red rowboat from Scatteree Town Landing on the Chatham mainland. My wife, Beth, and daughter, Katy, were there assisting and forming a farewell committee. Within a few minutes their shapes dissolved and melted into the ghostly background of low bluffs and houses, and soon that, too, disappeared.

According to the map I had, the cottage lay across Pleasant Bay about a mile to the southeast, at the northern end of a group of twenty or so beach cottages known as the South Colony. I steered by compass, due east, to compensate for the southerly push of wind. A small squadron of terns flew close by heading north, gray on gray over gray.

Rowing is a strange method of traveling, even within the contained waters of a pond. One is always pulling oneself backward, into the unknown, steering by what one has already experienced or left behind. Here, in an open-ended estuary, with no visible landmarks, I had the curious feeling that I was rowing into the center of my own mind where figures vanished and loomed like memory.

I passed a pair of channel markers and heard the deep thrum of a motor approaching from the south. It turned out to be Buzz Hutchins, a bulldozer operator who had dug my house foundation a few years ago.

"Hello, Robert, where you going?" he called out cordially. Cape Codders are rarely surprised by anything they find at sea.

"Cabin," I yelled back, jerking my head toward the Outer Beach as I kept rowing, and he disappeared with a wave back into my past.

Fifteen minutes later I stopped to check my compass bearings. Though the bay at this point is relatively shallow and not very wide, it is notoriously deceptive in fog with back currents and sudden shifts in wind. The water around me appeared calm, quiet, and completely empty. I had wanted to cut ties for the duration, but not this quickly.

Suddenly the water was filled with the pulsing bodies of moon jellies, domed and translucent, drifting north with the incoming tide over beds of dark, streaming eelgrass. I reached out and stroked a long, slick frond of grass. A biological oddity, eelgrass is a true marine flowering plant descended from some terrestrial angiosperm that, like the land ancestors of whales and walruses, has returned for some reason to the sea. What are you doing out here, grass, among jellyfish and seabirds? Where are we all heading?

After a half hour or so of rowing and neck twisting, I finally saw a beach materializing behind me, still vague and undefined in the fog.

The large, dark silhouette of a cottage loomed straight ahead. I could not believe my blind luck in hitting it on the mark. But when I came ashore, the building did not fit the description at all.

I wandered around the ghostly dunes for some time before stumbling upon a family at another cottage, packing up their Blazer and about to leave after a weekend's vacation. They told me I had landed not at the South Colony but at the North Colony, a second cottage group nearly a half mile north of where I wanted to be.

I had erred twice, it seems: first, in not taking into account the push of the incoming tide, and second, in not correcting my compass readings for magnetic declination—some sixteen degrees at this longitude—a stupid, amateur's mistake.

By the time I returned to the boat, the light had begun to fail and it was raining lightly. I set off again, rowing south against the tide just a few yards offshore. The fog now alternately closed in and lifted, revealing at brief intervals the dim outline of the mainland across the bay, ridiculously close. Black-bellied plovers and small sandpipers lined the water's edge, probing the tideline with short, dark bills. Fog and dusk were thickening to darkness when I finally came to the cottage, pulled into a little cove just south of it, and hauled the boat ashore.

The beach cottage belongs to a neighbor of mine, Tia Tonis, who had offered me the use of it for a week. She had taken my heavier gear down by jeep on Saturday and had returned to the mainland that afternoon. When I entered the cottage I found my trunk full of food and books set against one wall, and on the table a nice welcoming note from Tia with a pair of sharpened pencils.

It was too late to begin lighting the gas lamps or cooking a meal, so I made myself a sandwich by candlelight and threw a sleeping bag on one of the cots and myself after it. All around me was the dull roar of wind and surf, and the occasional compacted thud of a breaker on the ocean side of the beach a quarter mile away. The tide was still rising. The fog had lifted again, and now, to the southwest, across the dark waters of Pleasant Bay, the great double beams of Chatham Light raced out into the night, chasing each other like demons up the dark strip of the Outer Beach until they broke against the south wall of the house, exploding in star-shaped flashes through the screens.

This place is now home, I thought, my neighborhood for a week. It has the feeling of being wholly contained in nature, of existing within its terms. What a strange crossing it has been! Never could I have gotten so swiftly detached from the mainland, emotionally and psychologically, under clear skies. Lying here now at night on this open strand, listening to the dull roar of the surf and the unobstructed wind, it seems years since this morning when I was down in the bog below our house, only a few miles from here, gathering the eggs of wood frogs and salamanders beneath a thick forest canopy, finding woodland lady's slippers and trailing arbutus, listening to the calls of ovenbirds and other woodland warblers, and the strange whistles of wood ducks in the bog.

There are other cottages near this one, but they are all dark. There are no other lights as far as I can see up or down the length of the beach. Now the fog has closed in again, this time for good, it seems, and not even the drumming demon beam of Chatham Light can pierce it.

II

I like this house, its bright, spare, unfinished look. It is a shell: twenty-four by twenty-eight feet, shingled and roofed on the outside, with studded walls pierced everywhere by the exposed tips of shingle nails, a trussed and strapped ceiling, open doorless partitions where the bedrooms will be, and a bare plywood floor.

The house sits about sixty yards from the gentle waters of the bay. Like many beach cottages, this one seems largely an excuse for windows. There are five on the west side, facing the bay, two on the south, three on the east, two on the north, plus three windowed steel doors. One large white table sits in the center of the unpartitioned area— for the typewriter and "heavy work"—with a smaller pine table next to the west windows, complete with two ice-cream-parlor twisted-wire chairs, for meals, reading, journalizing, and bay watching. A few white curtains hang on rods above the windows, more to wave inward in the breeze than to veil anything. There is a gas stove, three gas-lights, a gas refrigerator, a hand pump and sink, and a flush toilet in the outhouse. The refrigerator has been acting up a little. It won't shut off, so I disconnect it now and then. I wish I had brought an onion.

In exchange for the use of the house I have agreed to paint the wood trim, window sashes, and screens. Four gallons of white paint were left stacked in one of the partitioned rooms. I planned to begin Monday morning, but when I woke at dawn the fog and mist still clung tenaciously around the house. After breakfast I decided to take a walk across to the ocean shore, hoping they would burn off by afternoon.

North Beach is about a thousand feet wide here, a terrain of low dunes and wet swales, with a higher broken ridge of primary dune just before the Outer Beach. At no point does the land rise twenty feet above sea level.

This barrier beach has undergone more changes than most: length-ening, contracting, breaking up into archipelagoes of sandy islets, dis-solving and re-forming again every couple of hundred years. Though the spit is at present some ten miles long and extends more than four miles south of the Tonis cottage, the section of dune I was now walk-ing was a harbor entrance into Pleasant Bay a hundred years ago. Until recently a large, turreted wooden building stood just behind the first ridge of dunes—the Old Harbor Life-Saving Station, built in 1897. The former harbor entrance had long since silted in, and the station had been abandoned for decades, but gradual erosion of the Outer Beach had brought the old building dangerously close to the surf. Last fall the Cape Cod National Seashore, in an exception to its official policy of letting nature take its course and whatever lies in it, had the station sawed in two and floated on barges twenty miles north to Provincetown's Race Point Beach, where it has been reas-sembled and turned into a museum.

It was a timely move, as it turned out, for only a few weeks later one of the most powerful ocean storms ever to hit the Cape submerged 90 percent of this beach, washing over the former site of the lifesaving station, and in the process smashing the original Tonis cottage, which had stood near it.

When I reached the beach I found the half-buried rubble of the station's foundation, and just north of it the charred remains of Tia's old family cottage, which had to be burned before they were allowed to build the new one earlier this spring. Tia blames the government for its loss, claiming that they destroyed the dune in front of the original cottage when they moved the station. "They did pile some sand back in the cut when they were through," she told me, "but no more than that. For heaven's sakes, even a child would have patted it down."

Several other cottages in the vicinity survived the storm, though the prevalence of new walls, new shingles, scattered pilings, bedsteads, and other debris in the overwash area testified that they had not escaped unscathed. A few stunted cedars, burnt orange and dead, looked planted around the houses.

The buildings all wear the aspect of a Western ghost town, one that suffered some wild, violent raid, was partially rebuilt, and was then abandoned as not worth it. I am its sole inhabitant these days, but it is only the lull before the first human inundation of the season, the week before the Memorial Day weekend, when all these beach shacks will spring back to life and hundreds of beach buggies will form a nearly continuous line of vehicles on the Outer Beach.

I walked back from the ocean to the bay in the sandy ruts of a vehicle trail. In the sand overwashes immediately behind the beach I found fox scat, the strong smell of skunk, and the tiny tracks of a piping plover, a small sand-colored shorebird that nests at the base of these dunes. The trail wound by some juncus bogs, bright and green and level, and passed a small brackish pond surrounded by reeds, where toads call at night.

The dune cover here is almost pure beach grass, interspersed with dusty miller and new leaves of beach goldenrod. The new green blades of Ammophila are just about to overtop the dead, dry stalks of last year. There is little beach plum growing, and what there is seems about two weeks behind that on the mainland, which has already blossomed. Along the crest of the road banks are dark blue-gray tufts of poverty grass, little rag-mop plants just beginning to green again. I stopped to stoop down and look at them, anticipating the tiny, delicate yellow flowers they would cradle in June.

I felt like a farmer walking his fields, in that mixture of remembrance and anticipation between seasons. Nature is everywhere familiar in macrocosm and microcosm, in the dip and resurgence of the night-sky constellations and in the shower of green leaves welling up around old dead seed stalks. Only in the middle distance is it alien, are landscapes foreign.

III

That second night I slept a troubled sleep, a sleep of too much caffeine and germinating doubts. It rained through the night, slattering on the new asphalt roof, and through the rain and wind I heard the distant, mournful calling of a piping plover on the night beach.

As usual, following an initial, buoyant surge of self-reliance and selfish delight at having such a place all to myself, I now began to feel insufficient. Already, by Tuesday morning, I found myself thinking of my daughter's irrepressible, continual engagement with life, my father's quiet, strong, indirect love. Life is always deeper on the other side of the water, it seems, though that morning the other side remained hidden in mist and swirling fog.

The house slipped into insubstantiality as I walked down to the bay shore. I followed the dry, twisting bed of what was formerly a salt marsh creek. Now there is only a thin fringe of marsh along the western shore here. The barrier beach, gradually retreating westward in the face of the ocean's assaults, buries these tidal creeks and marshes even as it forms new ones farther west. Eventually they emerge again on the ocean side in the form of exposed peat ledges, some of which still carry the prints of old cart wheels and foraging cattle made generations ago.

The old creek bed here now fills only at high tides, the water winding cautiously, like some semi-tame animal, up to the cottage deck each morning. At ebb tide it contains a few pools, warm soupy bowls full of marsh minnows that flip about as they slowly cook.

Because of the fog I could see no birds, though I heard the *chips* and clicks of terns feeding in the currents offshore, and the purring, clattering hum of lobster boats laying down pots somewhere out in the bay.

I worked through the morning, writing at the large white table. Outside, the wind shifted back and forth from southeast to southwest; the fog flowed, pausing, lifting, and dropping again over the bay and the bluffs on the mainland.

I ate lunch on the deck, where tree swallows buzzed me and a trio of crows, wearing new glistening black coats, paused briefly on the roof ridge to consider, then flew on. A horned lark landed in a bush and breasted forth a buzzy, tinkling, rising trill, one not described in the bird books. I have begun to notice that birdsong, like the flowering schedule of plants, seems to be affected by the exposed environment here. The song sparrows, for instance, all have thin, scratchy, attenuated voices here, as though all the sap had been dried out of their notes by the salt air.

After lunch I took a short nap. When I awoke a thin cloud cover had sucked the fog up into itself, and the wind had shifted to the southwest. I painted rake trim for a few hours and then, at about four thirty, walked out to the beach.

The smell of the surf, just coming in, hit me with a rich fish and salt odor, carried along on the crashing mist of its edge by a southerly breeze. I stood and inhaled it deeply, rhythmically, timing my breaths with the rush and surge of the combers.

I walked south along the undulating, ivory, grist-laced slope of

the beach as the white crests caught some of the red from the sinking sun. A green glass bottle, thrown up on the sand, glinted in the
reflected light. It was corked and had a message inside, written in
German, which I cannot read, accompanied by several pornographic
sketches—probably thrown overboard by some bored crewman not
far offshore. I recorked it and threw it back into the surf, where it
floated north at about two knots.

I stopped and sat on a low dune crest pitted with ant holes and
wolf-spider traps and watched the day wheel slowly down, the tide
climb slowly and ponderously in. I wished I were staying for a year. I
would not write for a week at a time, except to record weather, perhaps, and certain telling and vulnerable details: how the light slanted
in the evening, or the taste of seaweed picked up on the beach. I
would let the personal dry up or seep slowly out, regarding all inner
turmoil as external, the tortuous and self-conscious processes of
thought as trivial and of no account. I would let my mind be picked
clean by the crows and ants and bleached by the sun, ride this thin
spar of sand as it slides back and forth between the tides. I would let
all feelings and their objects drift out with the daily currents and wait
to see what came back ashore at the end of each week.

Walking back, I found an unfamiliar beach sparrow perched on
the gable of the little outhouse. I had a sudden, fierce desire for positive identification, but I had not brought field glasses with me. "Sing,
damn you, sing," I muttered. But it only shit and flew off.

Late Tuesday afternoon the wind shifted to straight west, and
now, after forty-eight hours of fog, the evening is blessedly still and
clear. Only a few high, thin clouds trail among the simple stars in a
rich dark-blue sky. For the first time since arriving here I can see the
mainland clear and sharp across the bay: a darkening pleat of low glacial bluffs surmounted by a line of peak-roofed houses against a red
afterglow. I feel at once reattached to the world and shot with a sense
of how far I have come from it. The bay waters are silky smooth and
gently undulating, but the gaily colored lobster buoys in the offshore
channel reveal a strong incoming current; they strain hard at their

submerged lines and lean steeply northward, sending small wakes ahead of them.

Small flocks of plovers fly by overhead—silent, heavy-bodied forms. A pair of black-crowned night herons utter deep, guttural *quawks* and head south with strong, steady wingbeats to feed on the flats at the far end of the spit. Behind me, from the wet marshy hollows between the dunes, breeding Fowler's toads scream their dry, toneless screams.

The night seems to be calling me with its clarity, so in the last of the light I slip my skiff from its mooring in the creek bed, set the oars, and pull out into the current toward the straining lobster buoys. Anchoring about fifty yards out, I thrust my rubberized lantern beneath the surface and flick it on. The water is very clear and not deep, and my beam reveals its running night life. Moon jellies, with bright orange cloverleaf patterns on their domes, pulse up and down in the currents like ghostly hearts. Beneath the jellyfish are large female horseshoe crabs, ancient arthropods that resemble dark spiked shields trailing long spearpoints, plowing along the floor of the bay as they have for four hundred million years. Most have one smaller male, and in some cases two or three, clinging piggyback fashion to their shells.

Drifting everywhere through the cold green waters is a fine white rain of dustlike particles. This is the phytoplankton bloom, a seasonal explosion of minute waterborne single-celled marine plants, the source of it all, the base of the estuary's rich food chain, the year's investment, bone of its body, the tiny universal foundations on which all our lives rest. Among this fine, passive dust of phytoplankton swim larger motes of zooplankton: adult copepods and arrowworms, the larval stages of crabs, barnacles, mussels, and oysters. Many of these respond positively to light; they turn and swim, jerking and twisting up toward my beam.

My light sweeps across the dark, domed forms of the submerged, lead-weighted lobster pots resting on the bottom. Inside one I sense a blurred movement and, yielding to a sudden lawless impulse, I grab its buoy line, haul it up out of some two fathoms of water, and heave it, tipping and dripping, over the gunwale of the skiff and onto the ribbed floor between my legs. Shining my light between its wooden slats and inner netting, I behold the white, ghoulish head of a large codfish spiked to the bottom of the cage for bait. The head stares up at me out of empty eye sockets, and around it dances an antic, dark collection of spider crabs, rock crabs, starfish, and one undersized lobster. The exposed creatures click, scuttle, and twist around the white fish head as though protecting their grisly treasure. I feel as though I have unearthed some undigested bit of night business.

I reach in and remove the small lobster (the owners would have to throw it back anyhow, I rationalize), then quickly heft the pot back over the side, where it sinks back down to the bottom. I row back to shore and moor my boat in the creek at the head of the tide, which tonight has almost reached the cottage. As I bolt up the steps, a splash of light from Chatham Light, two miles to the south, catches me and throws my guilty shadow up against the raw shingles like a prison searchlight. Inside, I can barely wait for the water to boil. The shell is thin. I rip the arms from the body and crunch the claws open with my teeth. To the east, beyond the dunes, beyond the mindless screaming of the toads, the night surf crawls toward its flood.

IV

I sleep a deep, dreamless sleep and awake Wednesday morning to a dawn clear but still gray. The sun, though an hour above the horizon, is in a race to overcome a rising cloudbank out over the ocean. By eight o'clock the sun wins, the bank recedes, and the morning becomes brilliant, sparkling, breezy. The bay is plied by small lobster boats, the crews checking and resetting pots. As I eat breakfast a large marsh hawk with down-swung head and upheld wings comes tilting and veering into the wind within a few yards of the west windows; it takes no more thought of this house than of a dune.

I spend the morning painting the west windows under prairie skies and rolling prairie grass, flanked by Mississippis and Missouris on all sides. The hidden surf beyond the dunes sounds like a herd of buffalo or antelope thundering down the beach, about to break through the dune hollows at any moment. The dunes themselves seem like the slick and shiny coat of some great healthy beast, muscles rippling, galloping under my feet as I paint.

And the clouds! What a gallery of vapors there is! Tumbled cumuli pile over the mainland to the west, backed and overarched by cirrus streamers, spiderlike bursts, and paint smears. Mottled salmon clouds spread high overhead, crossed by spreading jet trails—an electron microscopy of nerve ganglions. And below these, thin, light patches of fleece race up the Outer Cape from the south.

Despite the variety of clouds, the morning remains bright. The fog, it seems, has not left for good, but has retreated north and lies, just offshore there, like some low, snarling, purplish-brown, snakelike presence—treading air, indecisive, advancing hesitantly and retreating again like some cowardly dragon, kept at bay by the offshore wind.

Painting in the lee of the house, bathing in the first good sun in three days, I lapse into the simple, expanding motions of the day. Normally I hate to paint, and might resent the time it takes away from me here. But I am doing it to help a friend who has helped me, a favor for a favor; it is only a bonus that I get to do it in such a magnificent arena. I remember, when I earned my living in a classroom, how often we all complained about the "damned mechanics" of teaching, the drudgery of it. A colleague once remarked that the touted boredom of assembly lines is only a liberal cliché, no worse than that of most jobs. But it is not drudgery or boredom per se that is unbearable, only labor or life without purpose, and no amount of bonuses, rest breaks, sabbaticals, or public recognition can make up for that. On the other hand, give us a good-enough reason and we will go to hell and not resent it.

At one o'clock the fog still crouches offshore. I decide to take an after-lunch circuit walk of the south colony of cottages. The 1974 Geological Survey map shows twenty-four cottages in this group, spread out over a half mile or so of beach. That afternoon I count twenty-two, indicating that two besides the original Tonis cottage were lost in last winter's great storm.

Beach-cottage colonies tend to acquire very individual characters in different locations. Those on North Beach seem modest, middle class, and largely conventional, like the cottage owners themselves. These Chatham cottages lack the idiosyncratic elaboration of Provincetown's dune shacks, or the clustered communality of the "Village" at the tip of Barnstable's Sandy Neck. They are, instead, simple, restrained, and solid (or as solid as beach shacks can be), placed two to three hundred feet apart, as though seeking neither solitude nor true society, but comfortable association, seeking to be with but not of their own kind—not unlike certain nesting seabirds. They represent a kind of pared-down, unlandscaped counterpart to the settled, bourgeois character of the mainland community, an escape from some of the latter's specific restraints, the sharp edges and binding fabrics of communal living, without losing its basic forms. So our outriders are still characteristic of the main mountain ranges.

The owners these days tend to be from neighboring Cape towns like Dennis and Brewster, but some name signs I encounter are pure Chatham still: "Nickerson" and "Lumpkin" on my nearest neighbors' cottages, "Crowell" on a beached boat.

Inside, most of these cottages are plain, even negligently spartan. Some have imported trappings of suburban rec rooms: Masonite paneling, captain's chairs, coasters, "Old Philosopher" wall paintings, et cetera. But outside, all retain an enforced simplicity, a perpetually nomadic look, like dice thrown and rethrown again on the gaming table of the beach. There is little of that external, self-conscious, quaint cuteness that infects so much of the mainland's dwellings, from lobster pots on the lawns to hawser-and-pier fencing to "Cod's Little Acre" and "Our Hide-Aweigh" carved quarter boards over the garages. What there is of this is relegated mostly to the outhouses, perennial source of amusement among refugees from indoor plumbing. One has a "Lobster Potty II" sign above its door, with a genuine wooden pot mounted on the roof. The few signs attached to the cottages themselves tend to be self-deprecating—"Nauset Hilton" on a boathouse—or bristly—"Warning: Trap Gun Set" on a boarded-up window.

There is a kind of landscape humor to them as well. Their owners seem to enjoy bringing in useless artifacts of civilization and planting them around their houses: fire hydrants, newspaper boxes, "Keep Off the Grass" signs. It is a kind of inverse boasting, a reveling in their temporary freedom from the tyranny of what these objects symbolize. One owner has nailed an electric meter to the side of a wall.

I wonder about the origins of these colonies. Why did they cluster just where they did, a couple of dozen here, another twenty a half mile to the north, and nothing in between? Most of the buildings appear to have been built after World War II. I have an older map, surveyed in 1940, which shows only seven structures on the entire beach. The cottages in each colony are connected to one another by a complex series of trails threading through a maze of wet swales full of bayberry, beach rose, poison ivy, and wild cranberry.

It would be fun, given the time and opportunity, to study the social organization of such informal multigenerational beach communities, to chronicle the connections, civilities, folklore, and customs that have grown up in them. There must, I think, be conflicting tendencies toward privacy and intercourse in a setting so open and impressionable. Already I can discern a light but definite path running along the top of the dune ridge between the new Tonis cottage and the one immediately south. But I am just as glad to have the neighborhood to myself this time, not to have to get to know people as well as their dwellings: One set of neighbors at a time.

V

Sometime during the night the fog returned, blanketing the house again. I awake and feel islanded in its midst, like some cloudy, dilating eye unable to focus. I open the door and listen to the thin, high, attenuated calls of the birds of this outer land: the twinkling, metallic cries of the least terns, scratchy notes of song sparrows, *chips* of savannah sparrows, rising tinkles of larks, old-man coughs of black-beaked gulls, strident cackles of laughing gulls.

By midmorning a light, spitting rain begins; it lifts the fog some but drives all boats on the bay to shelter. The gulls, unperturbed, promenade like burgomasters on the bars in front of the cottage. The rain hits the asphalt roof with a pliant softness, gurgles down off the eaves.

I try to write, but it is no go. It is hard writing about the life one is actually living. I came out here in part to put some distance between it and me, but I find I carry it around with me, unfinished. Thoreau wrote about Walden mostly after leaving it. The best accounts are always separate finished episodes—Melville at sea, Whitman in the first flush of self-discovery, Hemingway at war—rather than the impossibly disparate grist of one's current daily existence. In such situations short, quick raids seem to be best: a day on the beach, a week in the garden, an hour on the road. Beyond that there is too much life to order, to give shape and meaning to. One never seems to get to the end of it.

It rains all afternoon, heavily at times. The air has turned soft and thick. I paint screen doors inside, and for the first time I miss having a radio. What I miss most is music. Thoreau took his flute to the pond. Henry Beston brought his concertina to his Eastham beach cottage in 1926 when he wrote his classic book, *The Outermost House*. I play piano.

By evening my schedule has crumbled away completely. No painting. A cold dinner. I prowl the empty neighborhood for novelty and find, in one of the open outhouses, two old copies of *Playboy* from 1966, its heyday. So innocent and positive they seem now, so *therapeutic* about sex. Having largely succeeded in what it set out to do, the magazine now seems forced to do more than it wants to, to appease the endless craving for novelty and the forbidden that it helped to legitimize.

Oh, we are all such horrible mixtures! It is amazing that anything clean and simple ever comes out of any of us. Any writer's honest journal is at once a revelation and an enigma.

VI

Friday. The holiday weekend begins with yet another morning of general fog, southeasterly wind, and spattering rain. Gulls perch like hungry senators at the edge of visibility. Terns call invisibly out of the gray. The southeast corner of the house soughs with surf, and the marsh hawk tilts over the bending, wind-stirred grass like some great brown and white butterfly.

South-southeast! It is as though someone opened a quadrant of the globe and forgot to close it, letting loose the unending, rearing tides of wind and fog. There is no birdsong anywhere this morning. Even the terns seem quieted by the monolithic persistence of this weather. The fog is a great gray god, a silent river like the flowing plankton borne ceaselessly along by the channel currents, impregnating the bay.

South-southeast! Flow on, moon jellies, flow on, plankton! The lobster buoys strain at their lines, leaning desirously northward, throwing their wakes ahead of them, held by the weighted, slatted traps on the sea bottom, where claws, horny shells, and disked feet dance, click, and scuttle around eyeless, spiked fish heads. The circus-colored buoys bend like the dune grass in the wind, flying ceaselessly but going nowhere. I would fly away too, now, but am held down here by lead weights and dead lures of resolution and commitment. I feel like a barnacle or a spirobus worm anchored to this house, throwing out feathered legs and tentacles of myself, then withdrawing to digest my finds.

Late in the morning the first campers of the weekend begin to lumber down the beach, fog or no fog. The rain stops by noon, and I spend most of the afternoon painting trim and windows on the north side. The fog lifts enough so that through my field glasses I can see a small-craft-warning flag flying from the Coast Guard Station next to

Chatham Light. I think about rowing across tonight to see a movie, maybe calling home. . . . But the wind picks up till there are white-caps on the bay, and by dusk the fog has closed in again, shutting out the shore lights, keeping me honest.

It is after eleven at night now. Beyond the dunes the surf is rising, its imperative thumping penetrating the thin walls of this uninsulated house. It has been a makework, make-play day, and I feel both enervated and restless. Placing a Coleman lantern in the east window as a beacon, I set out across the dunes to the ocean. I walk southeast, oblique to the shore, following the sound of the surf. Sights and sounds are both muffled in the darkness and fog. Chatham Light is only an obscure, intermittent glow off to my right. Offshore the deep bleating of two ship horns far apart carries like the baying of two great sea beasts in the night. Toads breed, screaming at one another in the wet hollows.

I seem to be traveling in a dim world of homogenized senses, where distance and dimension cease to exist. For an indeterminate time I walk without seeming to get any nearer the sound of the surf, then all at once I smell it, a wall of sea odors immediately ahead—rich, salt spiced, redolent of fecundity and decay.

The tide is approaching its high. The seethe of incoming foam laps and sloshes just below the wrack line on the upper beach, sliding back toward the dark breakers in a bubbly, sucking withdrawal. The breaking crests of the waves and the foamy swash edge appear to be outlined with a faint phosphorescence, but it is hard to tell in the obscurity of the fog. The wrack line itself—a knotted tangle of rockweed, dulse, mermaid's tresses, broken claws and shells—is speckled with thousands of tiny, pale, yellow-green coals of light. This is bioluminescent plankton, hordes of diatoms, dinoflagellates and copepods that in summer fill vast stretches of the ocean with their cold, chemical glow—a sort of *Aurora maritima*—so that ships plowing through these living shoals of light leave wide wakes of flickering fire behind them.

Some of the larger glowing particles in the wrack line are hopping about, like sparks from resinous kindling. Shining my flashlight on them, I see the bouncing forms of sandhoppers, or beach fleas—miniature, shrimplike crustaceans about a third of an inch long, with huge eyes and pearly white bodies. By day they live in burrows on the upper beach, coming out at night to feed on the tide's leavings. They ingest the tiny phosphorescent plankton, and their semitransparent bodies begin to glow like miniature jars full of fireflies.

The ocean shows no inordinate ambition tonight, staying contained for the most part, in orderly restlessness, within the high, steep berm of its own making, content to spit up these luminous bits of life. Yet now a larger wave than usual breaks, invisibly, far out; its grating roar seems to spread and encircle me, the dark beach loses definition and place, and though its seethe only curls up and licks my boots like a puppy, I feel a rush of vertigo beneath me, shiver deeply, and involuntarily step back. Vulnerable of spirit, I seem no more than one of those pale, glowing specks of moribund animal life in the wrack line before me, invisible except for the cold, weak light I give off, lasting a few moments, then going out forever.

Now there are other lights moving on the beach. A trio of beach buggies looms out of the fog from the north, their headlight beams lurching drunkenly over the inner sand trail behind the dunes. As they pass the cut where I stand, I can make out fishing poles erect in quivers mounted to their front bumpers. One tries to cut out to the beach over a dune, fails, and roars back onto the track. A man in another jeep curses loudly in the darkness as he passes. For a moment I think he is shouting at me, but then a woman's crackly voice, unangry, bantering, answers him unintelligibly on his CB radio.

They pass swiftly, their lights disappearing into the fog before them, and where they have been I hear the lovely, mournful, solitary note of the piping plover.

For once I do not resent the intrusions of these machines on our beaches, their meaningless lights and harsh sounds. I understand what draws them out here and feel a strong urge to follow them down the dark strand, down past the last of the cottages to the far tip of the spit where the sands perpetually shift and the night herons feed, where men cast their hooks into the curved breakers and pull living, flapping, cold fish flesh out of the side of the sea.

We all have a desire to seek out such primal encounters, however clumsily or blindly. And the relentless complexity and growing numbers of our society seem to force us to seek them at ever-odder hours and in ever-stranger places, as on this exposed and shrouded beach, flooded and freshened by the night.

VII

Saturday. Last night I dreamed that I was riding down North Beach in the company of clowns on unicycles. We kept avoiding holes that had been dug in the sand, laughing and singing as we went. Eventually we came to what seemed to be a small tourist or information center, somewhere south of this cottage. It had a makeshift telephone system, and I tried to call home but was frustrated by operators too friendly and chatty to bother placing my call, phones with complicated and obscure dialing instructions, intermittent connections with the mainland that seemed to be dependent on the tides. There was one strange phone that had been jury-rigged from old washing-machine parts and that kept agitating on me as I tried to use it. It is time to go home.

But there will be no going over this morning. I awoke at five thirty to heavy rain, fog, and strong southwest winds. After breakfast it cleared somewhat, but has closed down again and the fog has been dense ever since. Nonetheless the holiday clammers and beachcombers continue to arrive, replacing the shorebirds and terns on the bars and flats in front of the cottage. I have cleaned up and packed, will paint some more inside, and will try to go over after lunch.

At noon the fog finally lifts. Leaving the heavy gear again for Tia, who will arrive this afternoon, I row across, touching the mainland at

about two o'clock. I walk the boat upcurrent along the shore of Tern
Island to the Chatham Fish Pier. Rows of patterned plover heads follow me above the tall, bright-green juncus grass of the inner marshes,
and a large flock of mixed gulls sits along the southern dunes, unfazed
as always.

I haul the boat out beside the pier, with the strange sense of landing on a foreign shore, realizing that I have spoken to no human being
for nearly a week, wondering if I still know the language. I call Beth
at work—my voice works, she seems to recognize me—but she can't
pick me up for another two hours. So I decide to walk into Chatham
center, to reacquaint myself with civilization.

I set off along Seaview Street, carrying my backpack and drinking
a Coke. I am grungy, and my clothes are dirty and wrinkled, but I feel
strangely elated and unself-conscious. As I walk I become gradually
aware of and infused by sounds and sights I seem to remember as if
from childhood: the smooth hum of lawnmowers, the song of a full-
throated song sparrow, hedges, robins. A woman in white golf clothes
swings at a ball on the public course, misses, swings again, and hits it
about eight feet—some strange native ritual, no doubt. And there are
unexpected patterns of wires overhead, and pavement under my feet,
and children playing and fighting on front porches, and tourists walking along Main Street, arms around each other, and the smell of cut
flowers from florist shops, and the sight of women with done hair and
clean blouses sitting on high stools inside ice-cream shops—I want to
go in and buy them something.

There are cars, of course—but it is not the sight of cars that touches
me, not car noises and car smells, not the fast food and motel strips,
not any of the harsh contrasts of civilization that my mind has unconsciously set up defenses against, but rather these easy motions and
simple signs of our occupation of the earth.

Chatham, with its long-settled, well-cared-for look, its easy access
to wider horizons—where the Atlantic lies literally at the end of Main
Street—is probably one of the best ports of reentry into the human
world. The afternoon is a kind of decompression chamber for me,

leaving the marvelous and dreadful vacuum of the Outer Beach, moving away from that intense, consuming pressure of self-consciousness, expanding in the sunlit crowds.

I walk along, soaking up the sights, giving myself over to the human currents that are just beginning to fill the sidewalks and the shops. I walk into a florist shop and buy blue cornflowers for Beth, some small toys for the kids in the five-and-ten, and carry the packages around proudly like badges of readmittance. Everyone seems so helpful and pleasant. I have forgotten the simple but deep pleasure of being waited on courteously by a store clerk or a waitress. I play willingly the role of tourist and consumer, talking with people I would not normally speak to, just to hear the sound of their voices, the varieties of timbre and accent. It seems amazing that I can get people to speak to me just by speaking to them. It is as though I had at last mastered birdcalls.

I had expected to feel a certain letdown upon returning, but the effect is just the opposite. Somehow the fact of human existence strikes me as miraculous, as though never seen clearly before. I feel a little like Emily in *Our Town*, returning to earth for one day after her death, as a child. I want to cry out to those I pass and who pass me the simple wonder of us all being here together in this lovely place under sky and shade and sun-dappled yards and the song of birds. I know that inevitably I will sink back into the dulling effects of routine, into possessiveness, into trivial irritation, into the shortsighted pursuits that hobble and frustrate so much of our brief lives. But for a few hours I am granted a fresh look at what I have left, which—if not, as T. S. Eliot claimed, the sole point of all our exploring—is reward enough.

It is a little after four now, and I am back at the fish pier, standing on the loading platform, waiting for my family. Less than a mile across Pleasant Bay, the cottage where I lived alone for a week sits clear and gray now under the first sun in three days. It seems so close, and yet years away, across the gleaming boat-plied waters. Below me crews in yellow rubber aprons fork the gutted flapping carcasses of codfish from their boat decks into a large metal hopper. When the hopper is full it is raised by hydraulic winch and dumps its load, letting go a cascade of bloody disemboweled fish that goes sliding down a white ramp into the icy-breathed hold of the packing plant. Though most of the fish will be shipped off to New York or Boston in huge refrigerated trucks, and though whole striped bass now sell for more than prime rib in the public fish market next door, we can still see the elemental processes of our survival in such places as this.

A young man on the dock calls to a friend who is just getting into a new green Toyota with a Connecticut license plate: "Those Canadian girls, they going to be back this summer?" The friend smiles, raises his thumb, and drives off. I smile, too, content to be where I am, standing in this place of migrations and appetites, listening to the endless talk of fish, weather, and the chances of love.

May 1979

AGROUND

On March 29, 1984, I went out to Coast Guard Beach with a Boston television crew from Channel 5 to videotape a program about barrier beaches and how they cope with storms and erosion—part of their series, *Survival.* It was a cool, dry day, and the crew had set up on the parking lot overlooking the Eastham barrier beach, still recovering after it was smashed flat six years earlier by the "Great Storm of '78." I was interviewed by a friendly man with a boyish face. He told me that the previous *Survival* segment had recounted the story of one of Boston's homeless alcoholics who, after ten years on the streets, reformed, remarried his wife, and is, presumably, no longer homeless. He seemed to be hoping that I might come up with some equally inspiring story about beaches. ("Hello. My name is Coast Guard, and I'm a barrier beach.")

The crew pinned lapel mikes on us and then led us around on electronic leashes, looking for a spot where the wind wouldn't cause audio
problems. The actual interview was very informal. After each question
the reporter would comment on my answer ("Great!" "Super!"), then
turn to the producer, a young woman with a shock of dark red hair, to
get the next question. I thought it was only a warm-up, but then they
said, "How about some reversals and listening shots?" The reporter
and I switched places, and they shot some footage of him asking the
same questions, and then nodding at my nonexistent answers—which
would later be cut into the previous footage. So I learned that day, if I
didn't already know, that even news interviews are staged.

The questions bordered on the inane and the inaccurate: "Will this
beach always be here?" "Is it true that nude bathers endanger a beach
because other people trample the vegetation to get a look at them?"
"Would Henry Beston, author of *The Outermost House*, an account of
a year he spent living on this beach in 1973 [it was actually 1926–27],
recognize this beach today?"

At one point he asked me about the history of wrecks along this
shore, which he referred to portentously as "the Graveyard of the
Atlantic," and whether they still occurred. I bristled inwardly at his
cheap drama and said no, we didn't get wrecks along here very much
anymore, big ones, anyway; that the Cape Cod Canal and electronic
and satellite navigation equipment had changed all that.

After the wrap we headed back to the National Seashore Visitors
Center, where Warren Perry, a park ranger and an old Provincetown
native, pointed out a cloud of gulls circling high above the Salt Pond,
whose waters were so calm you could follow the birds' shadows on
its surface. "When they wheel like that," he said, "it's a sure sign of a
blow to come."

That was Wednesday. By late Thursday morning the winds had
increased to fifty knots, with higher gusts. At 4:53 p.m., on March
30, 1984, the *Eldia*, a 451-foot Maltese-registered freighter, empty of

cargo and carrying no ballast, was blown ashore on Nauset Beach in
Orleans. It beached about a mile south of the Nauset Beach parking
lot and some five miles south of where, in my interview just the day
before, I had assured the public that large wrecks no longer occurred
on the Outer Beach.

The following morning I drove down to the Nauset parking lot.
It was already crowded with vehicles. Even from a mile away, the
ship's great blue-and-red hull and massive trapezoidal loading rigs
rose impressively, incongruously, above the dunes like an apparition.
Hundreds of people were converging on this immense, unexpected
visitation. There were crowds of older retirees, young couples with
squalling infants, high school students whose parents thought they
were in class, workingmen and women—all borne along by the wind
and our curiosity. We brought our wonder, our unaging appetite for
spectacle, to this fantastic apparition, this visible manifestation of the
massive traffic of the sea come ashore—this, the largest vessel ever to
strand on the Outer Beach.

The great ship sat sideways against the beach, with its starboard
side landward, about two hundred feet above mean low water. It
seemed impossible that anything so huge could have been carried so
far up the beach, but its hull was empty and, drawing only five feet of
water, it had floated like a balloon on the surface of the sea. It seemed
completely deserted—a present and a presence beyond our expectations, at once resigned, enchained, majestically self-possessed, and
mysterious. Anyone or anything might be aboard.

The *Eldia* sat, if not quite high and dry, at least in soft, seemingly
safe sands. In a way it was no more of a spectacle than it would've
been if it had been docked at a pier. One visitor was quoted in the
local newspaper as saying, "It looked much bigger on TV."

Although its hull was empty of cargo, it carried considerable fuel
oil of its own, and there were rumors of a crack forming in the hull.
Yet there was no apparent damage to the vessel, and it seemed as if
it were simply the victim of some trivial mistake, waiting only for the
next tide take it back out onto the high seas. As it turned out, the

Eldia would remain aground on Nauset Beach for nearly two months, during which time it would become a major local tourist attraction, a boon to local businesses—and an environmental threat.

Over the first weekend after the *Eldia* grounded, some thirty thousand people congregated on Nauset Beach and made the mile-long trek to the stranded vessel. Vehicle traffic bottlenecked Beach Road halfway back to Orleans center, but gladdened the hearts of local businessmen with an unexpected off-season rush of tourists. Within a week *Eldia* T-shirts and postcards were being sold at Dave Bessom's Country Store in East Orleans. The following weekend Philbrick's summer clam shack reopened in the parking lot—the earliest ever. There were rumors that the selectmen were considering a proposal to let the ship remain on the beach indefinitely and turn it into a casino.

In fact the *Eldia* was becoming something of a municipal headache. In addition to the traffic problems, the dune line on the beach was showing considerable wear from the trampling of thousands of undirected feet, an effect that would shape up to be the greatest environmental damage resulting from the wreck.

The ship's captain and its Filipino crew had been lifted off by helicopter the night of the stranding. (Reportedly a standby rescue team had been dispatched with an antique breeches buoy, on loan from the Orleans Historical Society, in case the helicopter failed to reach the crew.) At this point the ship was officially abandoned, though it had not yet been claimed by the Coast Guard. The only banner visibly flying from the ship was an American flag, its front half ripped to shreds in the wind.

A week later, on the morning of April 6, I returned to the site of the stranding. Less than two hours before high tide, the great rusty bow was visibly shifting and moving above the dunes, like an immense dormant creature stirring to life.

When the ship first grounded, the twin bow anchors were set high up on the beach, their chains stretched tautly shoreward to keep the vessel from being swept off on the outgoing tide. But the ship had drifted some seventy yards down the beach, and both heavy chains were now wrapped beneath the forward hull. With each inward swing the chains grated heavily against the hull, producing a deep groaning sound, like some massive animal in labor.

The ship had moved landward half its original distance to the dry shore. Now the waves were breaking against the base of the dunes. Swells smashed majestically against the back side of the hull, swinging the bow in toward shore, while the prop and rudder remained grounded like a pivot, digging the stern deeper into the sand.

It was a different creature now, no longer a passive stranded vessel, but alive and responsive to its imprisonment. It moved against the beach as though it might come up into the dunes, across the marsh, along our streets, and into town. To keep it from drifting farther two three-inch-thick red nylon cables had been attached from its stern to two bulldozers in back of the dunes. The ship now seemed to have settled in even deeper. It sat there, like Gulliver, while Lilliputian men deliberated, scrambled, and worried over its fate.

Once, when a large swell hit its stern square on, the whole enormous bow tilted slowly, stately, steeply landward, until I could see its decks towering six stories above me. Those of us who were on the beach emitted a collective gasp and stepped several paces backward. But the ship righted itself, and seemed to settle in for good where it was. It was clear it was going nowhere by itself.

The *Eldia* was finally taken off Nauset Beach on May 17, 1984, fifty-one days after it came ashore. The strategy was simple but effective. First, excavators and bulldozers dug a deep bowl around the ship at low tide, which filled at high tide, allowing it to float. Next a floating dredge dug a short channel off its stern. Then a cable was attached to the stern and run out to an offshore derrick rig. Finally, on the night of May 14, on a flooding moon tide, the rig began to pull the *Eldia* out to sea. Nonetheless, there were some doubts as to whether the ship could be brought off intact, as there were several bars just offshore and it was more than a thousand feet to deep water.

I arrived at Nauset Beach that night about eleven thirty, a half hour past high tide. There were only a handful of people stretched along the dark beach from the Nauset parking lot down to the ship. It was a spectacular scene. The moon was hidden by clouds, but the entire vessel was lit up with deck lights, work lights, and searchlights—like some great party ship. Several hundred yards offshore the giant derrick rig sat on its barge, also lit with green and white lights, accompanied by a similarly lit tugboat. A launch with running lights raced back and forth between the derrick and the *Eldia*. As I got closer I could hear the deep thrumming of the ship's winch motors, and the derrick's, too, pulling on the great cables. I thought it would be appropriate if it left tonight, under the same cover of darkness and cloud in which it had arrived, but as it turned out, it would be another four days of pulling it slowly, five to ten feet at a time, dealing with snapped cables and other problems, before it finally came free and, on a windy, sunny afternoon, was tugged ignominiously out of sight.

Now that the ship was finally afloat and safely at sea, the entire operation, earnest and spectacular as it was, seemed curiously without significance. No lives had been lost or saved, no salvaging or looting had occurred, and, despite the trampled dune vegetation, no lasting environmental damage had been inflicted on the beach. The day the ship finally came off, hundreds of spectators were in attendance, cheering for no particular reason. Then Philbrick's clam shack closed up again until June, the sales of T-shirts and postcards diminished to a trickle, and local officials sighed with relief. It was already old news.

I visited the beach again a few days later. It felt strangely empty. In less than two months the stranded ship had already become oddly familiar, like a new moon in the sky. But it had been more like a comet than a moon, making a dramatic appearance, then vanishing from sight. The beach had been thoroughly cleaned, and the massive depression the *Eldia* had made in the sand had already filled in. Unlike other wrecks in the past, no crushed hull or broken spars remained on the beach to rot and blacken in the sun. No souvenirs were collected or pried or wheeled off the ship to adorn local lawns or mantels or sheds as memorabilia of a remarkable visitation. There were snapshots and Super 8 videos and newspaper photos, of course, but already the ship seemed less than palpable. Had it been real? Was it actually here? Did we imagine it? A few days later we read that the *Eldia* had been towed to a port in New Jersey and there sold for scrap.

March 1984

"YOU JUST NEVER KNOW WHAT'S GOING TO HAPPEN TO YOU WHEN YOU GET UP IN THE MORNING"

It was a springlike day in early February, and Ralph and I—along with his two Brittany spaniels, Hannah and Goober—were planning a trip to South Beach, a three-mile section of Chatham's barrier beach that separated from North Beach during a fierce winter storm two years ago. It was the day after an extreme high tide, and when I arrived at his house in Brewster, Ralph half-seriously blamed the full moon for a more than usual amount of the minidisasters that seem to be the normal milieu of his life. Yesterday, he told me, he had been trying to track down a leak in his water line but couldn't because a "blind and frothing skunk, possibly rabid," was standing directly over the line. Today he was fulminating over the perverse omissions of his WordStar manual: "They don't tell you that the printer has to have paper, oh no—*but there's a photograph of the plug being inserted into a wall socket*—give me a break!"

More than anyone I know, Ralph has retained, intact, at the age of forty-seven, a core of boyish enthusiasm, curiosity, and naïveté, overlain with a gentle, constant layer of adult cynicism, frustration, and irony. When I called him that morning to ask what time I should show up, Georgene answered first, and when he picked up the other phone, he said, "Hi—have you lined up the babes? . . . Uh-oh. . . ."

What I admire most in him, though, is his intense fascination with the anomalous particularities of the world. Once, when I mentioned an article I was writing about hummingbirds, he retrieved a jar from a bottom shelf in his shop and poured out the tiny, desiccated carcasses of four small iridescent green birds with tail feathers whose bases formed an orange-gold ring—female rufous hummingbirds, a West Coast species. They were all wrapped in cobwebs. Ralph had found them in an old barn on a trip to Oregon years before. He surmised that the birds had been gathering spider silk for their nests, and had perhaps been startled into the web by a cat. They were nearly weightless, with hard, dark, thorn-sharp bills about an inch long. Their wings were nearly colorless, diaphanous, like a dragonfly's wing. One was noticeably smaller than the others. Another's head was attached to the body only by an exposed, dark, rigid string of minuscule vertebrae. "Look!" said Ralph, pointing to a wing. "Look at that—there's an insect still attached!"

We hooked up the small trailer carrying his Boston Whaler to his van and headed toward Chatham. As we drove down 6A, Ralph thumbed his nose at the cars passing us, chortling. "Ha-ha, you're going to work and we're not!" Then he turned to me and said with a perfectly open smile, "Gee, this is the kind of day that makes me wish I'd gone into insurance. You know, so I could have spent the day in downtown Orleans in an office behind a desk!"

I nodded conspiratorially and refrained from pointing out that two of those poor working stiffs in offices were Georgene the travel agent and Beth the banker—thus helping to make it possible for us to be out here this morning.

"Americans," he said, "seem to put a great deal of emphasis on money, and almost no value on time. They're all in there working so hard that they can spend a week out here in the summer with everybody else." I observed that they were all working so hard so that they could afford to buy expensive photo books about Cape Cod like the one Ralph and I were working on at the time.

"Of course," he admitted, "if they weren't, they'd all be out here spoiling the place for us."

We put in at Quanset Pond in South Orleans about ten thirty. The tide was almost up to the door of the boathouse, and the spit that encloses the small harbor was completely underwater. This is Ralph's country—he grew up along the shores and on the waters of Pleasant Bay, and so I instinctively give in to his guidance in this region—which is one reason we got into the trouble we did.

His twenty-five-horse Johnson balked at first but finally sputtered to life, and we circled the submerged shoal out into the waters of the bay. Pleasant Bay is one of the most scenic water bodies in this country—probably in the world—and I realized at once the hopelessness it must present to the photographer. Carved by an ancient glacial river valley, the bay's essence is shallowness, horizontal surface. This is a wide sheet of water, averaging only six feet in depth (somewhat higher on a moon tide like this one). One must constantly be on the lookout for the yellow bottom of sand to appear suddenly under the boat. The waters that day were a pale, luminescent, silky-blue sheet pulled loosely over the yellow bed of the bay. It radiated out in all directions from our running hull.

Hannah sat in the bow, her favorite place—her face in the wind, her honey-brown ears flapping like wind socks—while Goober, her runty daughter, cowered under a thwart. Even given the mildness of the day, I had put on several layers of clothing—long johns, wool pants, heavy socks, fisherman's boots, pullover, flannel shirt, sweatshirt with a good pile jacket, insulated gloves—and they were just enough. I could feel the weather without suffering from it. I felt like an airborne seal.

"Remember all the bull-raking boats that used to be here?" Ralph asked. "What do you suppose happened to them? What closed down a whole shellfish industry?"

I ventured the obvious. "Overharvesting?"

"You know," he said gravely, "you may well be right"

We started numerous flocks of waterfowl—eider ducks, whistlers, mergansers, geese, brant, black ducks, buffleheads, and a few teal—

but all so scattered and thin on these wide waters that they seemed
to emphasize its emptiness. To the west were the low bluffs of the
glaciated coastline of Pleasant Bay. This stretch in particular, from
Quanset Harbor to the Narrows, still has the settled look of the old
summer culture that flourished here in the first half of the twentieth
century.

These are the places Ralph knew as a boy. He pointed to the Brooks
place, a plain, shingled old farmhouse-style building on the bluff, and
the Cochran place, a larger, rambling-style one right at the Narrows,
and a few others, still widely spaced, the settings not overwhelmed by
the places on them.

"Did you know that Judge Brooks and Granny Cochran were the
first summer residents on Little Pleasant Bay? Both of them were over
a hundred years old when they went. I don't remember which one of
them decided to die first."

We passed a large Moorish-style building, all cream walls and
green copper roofs with arches and white columns that would look at
home in the older sections of Sunset Boulevard, but that, because of
its age, also fits in here

In contrast to these older structures, there is a development of
newer, expensive, more densely packed houses, pretentiously named
"East Egg," that was recently built on the site of Camp Quanset, one
of a dozen sailing camps that flourished in South Orleans in the mid-
twentieth century. The camp was owned by the Hammetts, friends
of Ralph's family, and I asked him whether he and his brothers ever
went to camp as boys. He looked at me, honestly puzzled: "You mean
as campers? No—why would we?"

Normally we would have had to follow the channel between Strong
Island and Nickerson Neck to get down to Chatham Harbor, but
the moon tide gave us options, and so we swung around the north
side of Strong, catching a glimpse of the small Finley cottage on the
back side of tiny Little Sipson Island, which would be flattened by the

"Halloween Gale" two years hence. To the east was North Beach, that shiny thin ribbon of sand, that generous barrier, precious in its fragility, between the bay and too much—topped, like desert mirages, with the softened forms of scattered beach buggies.

"Would you believe," observed Ralph, "that at one time the town wanted to build a paved road down that beach?"

Ralph has a genuine but unsentimental appreciation of wildlife, which comes from having hunted and fished as a boy, and which is frequently a corrective to my bookish opinions. For instance, having just read *Tarka the Otter*, I told him how impressed I was by the effervescent life that otters seem to live.

"I don't know," he replied. "They seem somewhat neurotic to me—like raccoons—always moving."

Ralph, who hunted ducks here when he was a boy, can instantly identify most waterfowl by a kind of gestalt recognition that comes from repeated observation and intimate encounters over time. Once, when he identified a bird as a pintail duck at a distance too great to see field marks, even with binoculars, I asked him how he knew it was a pintail. He replied in a somewhat dismissive tone, "I don't know, it just *looks* like one."

He can admire a flock of brant rising over the marsh, yet comment, "Boy, when I see one of those waddling down 6A, it's hard for me not to do him in." He rates birds for their taste as much as for their grace. Black ducks, he says, can be quite good, but they're unreliable—"They're just as likely to be gamey."

We watched a flock of several hundred geese lift over the inner marsh on North Beach, and I asked Ralph if he thought most goose hunters actually use the geese they shoot.

"Are you kidding? You mean just shoot them and throw them away? It would be like throwing away a juicy fish or a prime steak someone had given you. I doubt if there's one in a hundred goose hunters who doesn't eat what they bag."

The bay was calm, and we made excellent time, reaching Tern

Island (recently reclaimed by terns) within a half hour of setting out. The new cut in the North Beach, created by the "February Blizzard of '87," began just a little north of Aunt Lydia's Cove and continued below Chatham Light. It was hard to estimate its extent from the water, but it appeared to be now well over a thousand yards wide. It did not appear like a "cut" anymore, but as the end of land—the beginning of No-Man's Sea. Though we were close to the inner, mainland shore, all at once the calm bay waters changed to swells of the open ocean, and an element of exposure crept into the boat.

It was strange to see waves washing up against the previously protected beach landing at Andrew Harding Lane. Odder still to see some of the immense new seawalls that have been constructed in front of some of the houses north and south of the breach, including one particularly arcane structure at least twenty-five feet high, composed of stepped tiers of dark rocks caged in wire sheathing.

Given that the tide had probably peaked this far down the bay, Ralph was hesitant about making for South Beach, especially in view of a forecast for the wind to pick up in the afternoon, but in the end we decided to go for it, agreeing to stay only a short while. There was a hook curving in toward land for several hundred feet from the north end of South Beach, and when we swung in behind it, I could see several fishing vessels steaming in through the cut.

"They must be happy to have such a straight shot into the harbor now," I said, but Ralph replied, "No, not really. Oh, on a day like this it's all right, but you get a wind behind you coming back, you can be in trouble. The sea reaches up and curls over oddly now, in random places in the middle of the bay."

Part of the problem, he said, is that the bay is now changing so much. Not just from wave action, which is creating new shoals, even bars, almost overnight, but also because the tides are much higher, and lower, now, which is causing heavy erosion even in the upper reaches of Little Pleasant Bay.

A couple of seals breached like porpoises in the roiling waters.

Seven gray-seal pups, the most ever born this far south anywhere, have now been reported on South Monomoy Island.[*]

We finally beached along a small bight south of the hook, so that the southwest wind would not blow the boat ashore. I waded out and threw the small anchor as far as I could; then we set off, with the dogs, agreeing that we would take, at most, an hour's walk. Ralph, as usual, brought along his "walking hoe," with which he poked and scraped the ground as we went. Like his dogs, he lives in a constant state of expectation, disappointment, and immediately renewed expectation.

I am learning that his knowledge of the land is selective, related primarily to his instinctive interests: waterfowl, fishing, digging. He has for instance, almost no knowledge of beach plants. I introduced him to poverty grass, in which he took an immediate delight. We came upon one patch that was being gradually buried in sand. I remarked that they looked like a frozen army of hedgehogs, but he sees with his own eye and said, "It looks like an entire landscape. You know what they look like? They look like Western forests covered in snow." And he was right: It was a better analogy than mine because the connections were wider and less fanciful. It is good to have your similes, as well as your convictions, challenged from time to time.

Ralph has an eye for the odd detail, the idiosyncratic mystery. Picking up couple of dried horse mussel shells, he said, "Look at these— see how in the light they have that blue speculum effect? I bet I've looked at a thousand of these, and they always have a crack in them here on the right side—see?" I said it might have something to do with the structure of the shell and the drying process. "Well, you'd know better than I would—I never took physics."

We walked along the edge of the long stretch of inner marsh here, starting up a large flock of geese. When we came to the place where they were feeding, Ralph commented on all the goose droppings fouling the marsh. I said that would be a good excuse if you were ever stopped for walking on a private beach: "Just start pissing on it

---

[*] By 2013 their numbers had risen to fifteen thousand.

and say you were there for the purpose of fouling."[*] He laughed for a moment, then stopped and said, "I don't know why I'm laughing—that was terrible."

We spied the head of a great blue heron above the beach grass at the tip of a dune—an odd place, admittedly, for a heron. Ralph wondered if it was hurt, but it lifted off at our approach and flapped south. "No, I guess not," he said, but a few minutes later we saw it again, standing among the dunes. "I still think there's something wrong with it."

As we crossed from the marsh over to the beach, we came upon a large, blown-out bowl containing several weathered wood pallets and several old liquor bottles in the sand. Ralph, an amateur bottle collector, showed me how to date a bottle from its bottom, and how bottles before 1970 have the legend "forbidden to resell or reuse this bottle" embossed on them—a holdover from the Great Depression. By far the most interesting one was a clear whiskey bottle with a note inside it, penciled on a strip of white paper. In faint but legible print it read: "Write to Patty Sullivan – 37 Hillside Rd. – Wellesley Hills, Mass – or phone CE 5 – 6725."

Ralph looked at the bottom and found the code number "56–59," which he said meant "1956 or 1959, I don't remember which." But it was the lettered phone exchange that clinched its age for me. If genuine, it must have lain beneath the sand protected from the sun and wind, for more than thirty years. The wonder it evoked came not so much from finding a "time capsule" as it did from the sense of someone speaking to us over a space of several decades, someone who was likely close to our age now, who might not even remember sending such a message, or what she would say if we located her. Her message was like that science-fiction staple of the twin boys, one of

---

[*]   A Massachusetts coastal resident's insider joke. An old colonial law, still in effect, states that private shoreline owners in Massachusetts, unlike those in most coastal states, own down to the mean low-tide line (a point, in some towns, nearly a mile offshore), and that the public is forbidden to trespass on intertidal lands "except for purposes of fishing, fowling, or navigation."

whom stays on earth, and the other travels at, or near, the speed of light for many years, only to return essentially unaged, while his twin has become an old man, unrecognizable. So Patty Sullivan, whoever she was, was now likely a middle-aged woman, while the message she wrote in her girlhood and stuffed in a bottle had remained forever young. (The next morning I found a Jean and Raymond Sullivan listed at 47 Hillside Rd., (617) 235–8559. I called them and learned that they had lived there for twenty years, on the same street as Patty Sullivan, but oddly, they had never heard of her.)

"You know," said Ralph, "that bottle reminds me of a story that happened about the same time out here. One winter in the late fifties the local Sea Scouts decided to sail to Nantucket in February. I was too young, but my brother John went. It was a big deal, and supposedly *Life* magazine sent a crew out to cover it.

"Anyway, they spent the first night camping on North Beach. That same night Mal Hobbes, the editor of the *Cape Codder,* decided he would go down and do a story on them for the local paper. So he and his wife—that was his first wife, before he married Gwen—drove in their beach buggy down the beach, expecting to find a group of shivering Sea Scouts tenting on the dunes. About halfway down they came on one of the cottages with smoke coming out of the chimney.

"'Those scallywags,' Mal said to his wife. 'We're all told how much they're suffering, and here they are, nice and toasty inside with a roaring stove going. Let's surprise them.'

"So the two of them crept up to the door of the cottage, threw it open, jumped inside, and took a flash photo of Mr. A and Mrs. B, who were in the altogether and going at it. Of course they all knew one another. Everyone did then, but to this day Hobbes has never identified the trysting couple. Can you imagine, though, the last thing you would expect to have happen during an adulterous assignation in a cottage on a remote barrier beach in the middle of winter would be to have the editor of your local newspaper pop in unannounced and snap your photo?!"

We crossed over the beach to the ocean side where recent easterly blows had created a ragged shelf two or three feet high. The shelf and the upper beach were covered with one of the largest deposits of magnetite I've ever seen—a purple layer ten to fifteen feet wide and several hundred feet long. Magnetite is an iron-oxide mineral, heavier and darker than the more abundant quartz, and gets its name from the fact that its grains will stick to a magnet. I examined a handful under my Swiss Army knife magnifying glass and saw that it was not pure magnetite but a rich mixture of minerals, a brilliant array of miniature jewels. Besides quartz there were black magnetite, ilmenite (a darker, iron-titanium oxide), purplish-red garnet (very abundant), tiny green ovals (olivine, or perhaps sapphire), darker green hornblende, feldspar, and a few striking orange-yellow grains (topaz?).

Ralph was at once delighted and discombobulated. He is also an avid sand collector. He has hundreds of small film canisters filled with sand collected from various beaches around the world, not just on his own but with the help of various friends all too happy to contribute to such an eccentric hobby. (Once, just to confuse him, I took a tooth I had recently had extracted, crushed it and put it in a canister, and mailed it to him from Kenya, telling him it was a rare form of volcanic sand known as molarite.)

He scraped at the magnetite layers with his hoe, finding it in places three inches deep or more. Picking up a handful of it, he gestured at the expanse of dark minerals all around him with that confusion of emotions of a finder of treasure made worthless by its very abundance, and exclaimed, "I've taken years to accumulate a small bottle of this stuff, and now look at it!" Still, he could not help but be delighted by it and berated himself for not bringing some plastic film canisters with him. Within a few yards, of course, he found a canister, and said, "See—ask, and it shall be given. . . ."

We had walked to within a mile of the southern tip of South Beach. "You realize, don't you," said Ralph, "that there are five hun-

dred seals hauled out just beyond the next dune." But we decided
that we had better head back. I walked on the beach with Hannah,
while Ralph and Goober walked along the dune line, Ralph poking in the grass with his hoe and Goober jumping voles like a fox.
"Sometimes," said Ralph, "she comes back and all you can see is the
little tail hanging from her mouth." Seconds later, as if on cue, she
appeared with a little black tail hanging from the side of her jaw like
a small thin snake tongue. "I don't believe it! Well, Goober, it's worm
pills for you tonight."

Along the face of the eroded dunes were some classic illustrations
of beach-grass anatomy. Like the bleached tentacles of a giant man-
of-war dangling from a floating fan of blades at the top, the knotted
roots snaked six, eight feet down the dune face. It seemed to me that
we saw and found more on this barrier beach than on most, but it may
have been that things merely took on an added clarity and intensity
because it had become a wild island, cut off from human impact and
strategies. It had fully given itself to the forces of the sea now, and
old beach-buggy ruts, fast filling in with grass and sand but still discernible along the edge of marshes and through the dunes, had that
poignancy and air of self-pity that seems, invariably, to attach itself
to fallen arrogance.

Our own arrogance fell with a thud when we topped the rise and
found the boat stranded on the beach, twenty-five feet from a fast-
ebbing tide. Ralph immediately launched into panic mode, exclaim-
ing, "Jesus, I can't believe it—why didn't I come back? I knew this
would happen!"

It was about four o'clock now—dead low would be about five. If we
couldn't get the boat off we would probably be here until after eight,
in the dark and cold—an uncomfortable if not a life-threatening prospect. I pulled on my boots while Ralph, barefoot, raced down to the
boat and began hauling gear—gas tanks, ice chests, coats, satchels,
removable seats—out onto the beach. We shoved together and managed to slide the hull a few feet. I waded out to see which was the
shortest route to deep water. We didn't have that far to go, but we

were on a shelf, and after a few more tries it became clear that the tide was running out faster than we were gaining on it.

"I still don't believe it!" said Ralph, as he began detaching lines and unscrewing motor mounts. We lifted both the main 25 hp and the auxiliary 5 hp motor off the stern and up onto the beach. Their removal made less difference than I expected, but after five more minutes of coordinated grunting, we felt the wonderful sense of the hull beginning to glide, and in a more few seconds we had it in a foot and a half of water. We look backed and saw that the place where the boat had been was already surrounded by twenty-five feet of wet glistening sand. Ten minutes later and we wouldn't have had a chance.

"I can't believe it," said Ralph. "Would you look at that—it's on a shelf—I picked the highest bottom of the whole damn area on which to beach it!"

I led the boat into as deep water as I could without swamping my boots and threw the anchor out into deeper water while Ralph walked back and began to carry the motors out by himself, barefoot and bowlegged, through the frigid waters.

"You must be freezing," I said as I came to help.

"Well, I'll tell you this—I'm not real comfortable!"

There was another moment of panic when Ralph thought he might have dropped a piece of the fuel line on the beach, but it turned out that in his haste he was trying to connect it to the wrong port. Hannah, who is deaf, had disappeared in the dunes, so I went back and carried her out to the boat (she can no longer hop into the boat by herself).

At last, having packed all the gear, dogs, and us rather chaotically into the little boat, Ralph pulled the cord and the motor blessedly roared to life. We were about to take off when Ralph noticed large clumps of mussels on the bottom. "Want some?" he asked, and—all anxiety instantly forgotten, like an otter—he had me get out of the boat and pull it along as he hooked large, dark, Christmas wreaths of blue mussels off the bottom with his walking hoe, laying them in the stern.

As we rounded the hook below the Inlet, Ralph looked north and said, "I don't believe it!" There, near the lower end of North Beach, were three Jet Skiers bombing around the waves in cutoff wet suits— in the middle of February! Beyond them, at the southern tip of the beach, two ORVs nestled together like huge seals. Ralph, casting a quizzical look at them, observed, "They look like they're mating, don't they?"

On the way back up Pleasant Bay, we stopped at Strong Island, the largest of the islands in the bay. Ralph's full-moon malevolent mojo still appeared to be working, for when he threw out the anchor to beach the boat, the anchor line caught on the loose string of his nylon Windbreaker, pulling the fabric away from the zipper for eight inches ("I just got that in Bermuda at Thanksgiving!"), crushing a translucent amber shell he had carefully saved in the pocket and, whipping around, jerking the anchor back, whose shank point pierced a half-inch hole in the fiberglass hull of his boat, high up by the gunnel.

Ralph, beyond frustration, almost immediately launched the boat again. He let me and the dogs off on the south side of the island and took the boat around to the north, or leeward, side. When we reached him, all frustrations and misadventures seemed once again forgotten. He had come upon the rusted carcass of an old Studebaker Commander, which he was worrying with the relish with which Goober worries vole holes. He pointed to his prize find: a key stuck in the lock of the glove compartment lid. Not being able to extricate the key, he decided to take the whole lid with him. As we headed back to the boat I made some comment about what a good day it had been, and he replied with genuine enthusiasm, "Yeah, I've got an ignition key to a 1946 Studebaker. God, you just never know what's going to happen to you when you get up in the morning!"

February 1989

WRECKING

When Thoreau first walked the Cape's Outer Beach in 1849 he labeled the first person he met as a "Wrecker," and gave a colorful if somewhat condescending description of this individual: He was, says Thoreau, "a regular Cape Cod man . . . with a bleached and weather-beaten face, within whose wrinkles I distinguished no particular feature. It was like an old sail endowed with life—a hanging cliff of weather-beaten flesh,—like one of the clay boulders which occurred in that sand bank. He had on a hat that had seen salt water, and a coat of many pieces and colors, though it was mainly the color of the beach, as if it had been sanded. . . . He looked as if he sometimes saw a doughnut, but never descended to comfort; too grave to laugh, too tough to cry; as indifferent as a clam,—like a sea-clam with hat on and legs, that was out walking the strand."

He was, as Thoreau well knew, actually engaged in a widespread activity—wrecking—which, in those days, formed a large part of the living of many of the local inhabitants. "Wrecking" is a strange term for what was, by and large, a benign and quite legal activity. As used on Cape Cod, Nantucket, and Martha's Vineyard, "wrecking" referred to the practice of salvaging the cargo of wrecked and abandoned boats. But the term has also sometimes been confused with the more insidious, legendary custom of "mooncussing," the practice of luring ships onto the sandy bars on cloudy nights by the use of lanterns that imitated lighthouses. If the sky should suddenly clear and moonlight reveal the nature of the false lights, the perpetrators would "curse the moon"—hence the term, "mooncussing."

Local historians have long claimed that there are no authenticated cases of "mooncussing" on the Cape and Islands, though they allow that the practice took place elsewhere—presumably among less principled seaside dwellers. The historian Henry Kittredge (son of the famed Harvard Shakespearean scholar George Lyman Kittredge) even wrote an entire book called *Mooncussers of Cape Cod*, just to prove that there never had been any—a case, perhaps, of protesting too much.

In any case, the term "wrecking" has a slippery but fascinating lexicographical history. The *American Heritage Dictionary* (1992) does not contain an entry for the practice of beach "wrecking," but "wrecker" appears in both its benign and malevolent forms. Specifically, it defines "wrecker" as "one that salvages wrecked cargo or parts," but also as "one [that] lures a vessel to destruction, as by a display of lights on a rocky coastline." (Apparently this lexicographer was not aware that ships can wreck just as easily on sandy beaches as on rocky coastlines.)

To find a relevant definition for the word "wrecking," I had to go to the unabridged *Oxford English Dictionary* (1971). There I found that the earliest use of the word in print was as an adjective in 1804, when it was used to describe "a wrecking vessel" in the West Indies; but one has to wait until 1868 for its use to describe a legitimate occupation, namely, that "wrecking has become a regular vocation for a considerable portion of the population." What is curious is that in the *OED* the term "wrecking" is described as an "American" term—a peculiarly native, homegrown, opportunistic activity, reflective, as it were, of our national character.

Thoreau recognized something of the same thing when, after bidding farewell to his Cape Cod Wrecker, he asked, "are we not all wreckers, contriving that some treasure may be washed up on our beach?"

January 2003

PRINTS IN THE PEAT

The blow came last Tuesday, without much rain or even wind inland, but it stirred up things mightily on the Outer Beach. When I went out to see it, the tide was just past high, and the surf was in its extreme, foamy-milk stage, with ten- to twelve-foot marbled volutes crashing onto each receding surge. Numerous logs and pilings, some as large as sixteen inches thick and twenty feet long, were being tossed and rolled about in the surf like proverbial matchsticks. It is this *playfulness* of the ocean with large, massive objects that, more than anything, reveals its hidden strength.

I noticed again how the sound of the surf often seems louder, or at least more powerful, at a distance than when you are directly facing it. Perhaps it is the cumulative force of the breakers hitting the beach over a greater span of beach—something like the difference between sitting in the first row at a symphony concert and sitting midorchestra. In the former case the instruments you are sitting closest to sound loudest, but you don't hear the full force of the orchestra except at a distance.

The day after the storm I drove down to Pochet and set out across the little wooden bridge that spans the tidal creek there, full now, flowing out muscularly and shark-green, carrying small islands of muddy foam with it. The sand road behind the dunes was a river of salt water a foot or more deep, which I had to ford to gain the beach.

The day was clear, bright, and springlike, the air crackling with negative ions, full of the heady expansiveness that follows a northeast blow. What struck me most was the vastness and scoured cleanliness of the beach—so open, so new and promising. The surf, still high and foamy, though less than the day before, had withdrawn to an extreme distance, as if to let the beach show off. There were no birds in sight on the water, and only a few gulls on the beach.

There was no driftwood, or even noticeable debris on the beach, and only a few people: a couple of retired walkers, a woman jogger with her iPod plugged into her ears, shutting out the profound music of the surf, and three men with metal detectors, combing the sands for what passes for treasure in these latter days.

I stopped to chat briefly with one of the beachcombers. He was a man in his late fifties or early sixties, I would guess, with gray hair and a long gray-white beard. His jacket was perhaps as particolored as that of the Cape Cod Wrecker Thoreau met on this beach, although in this case by design—a nylon Windbreaker with the maker's logo and stripes in red, blue, and yellow. His metal detector looked like a high-tech version of a diviner's rod, which I suppose in a way it was. He was sweeping the upper portion of the lower beach and carried a long-handled scoop, shaped like a scallop rake and full of holes that seemed to be slightly less than the diameter of a dime. When I asked him what he usually found, he said, "Mostly coins, sometimes rings or pieces of jewelry, though most jewelry is too light and gets carried out into deep water where we can't get at it."

They come out after storms, he said, because that's when things are pulled out of the dunes or churned up on the beach (just as wrecks themselves are). Like recreational fishermen, these modern-day beach-combers seem to pursue their activity more for the sport than the catch. At least I rarely saw any of them bend over and pocket a find. But, as with fishing, there is always the chance of getting the big one.

He pointed down the beach to a long dark stripe in the sand about two hundred yards away. "See that stretch of peat, just below the dune point? I've found some old coins there, and you can see wagon tracks and footprints in the peat."

I had read and heard of this latter phenomenon before, even seen photos in the *Cape Codder* of dents purporting to be hoofprints in peat. I walked down to where a large shelf of peat about a foot thick lay exposed. It was about three hundred feet long and six to ten feet wide. Runoff from the beach above it was seeping seaward over the buried peat and cascading over the exposed peat ledge and its fibrous curtain in small waterfalls. These peat ledges are intact portions of a salt marsh that once grew *behind* the dunes of this barrier beach. The dune line had since migrated landward, rolling over the salt marsh, burying it, but then subsequently leaving the peat substrate exposed on the beach.

Such exposed ledges of peat are not uncommon on barrier beaches, but this one contained an unusual number of signs of past human passage. There were dozens of hoof prints in the peat—some were deep, bowl-like indentations, some shallower, but most showed clearly the perimeter of an iron horseshoe. The prints ran roughly parallel to the ledge, crisscrossing one another, and running beside them was a veritable railroad yard of wagon tracks, three to four inches wide, also tending north to south. I felt as if I had come upon a print made by a mastodon, or a *Homo erectus*, though in all likelihood these prints were only a century or so old.

The history of this particular stretch of beach offers an explanation for the profusion of horse prints and wagon tracks. During the late nineteenth century and into the early decades of the twentieth, the Pochet Life-Saving Station stood just south of here, and horse-drawn wagons were used to ferry crew members and bring supplies to the station down from Nauset Beach to the north.

I took out my penknife and carefully carved out a block of peat about 7" × 7", containing one of the hoofprints. The print measured 4¼" × 5¼". I brought it home and placed it on a dishtowel on the windowsill in my study. As an artifact, I suspect it only has meaning for those who already know its history, and just as the peat ledge will not survive long exposed to the sea, so this fragment will not likely survive as a preserved specimen; already it is beginning to crumble as it dries out.

Nonetheless these are our Cape fossils, if only a hundred years old or so, and we must take them for what they are, for they are all we have. They have that draw of a vanished past made more intense by its transported and transitory nature, the past exhumed in a new setting, already in the process of vanishing once again, this time for good.

February 2005

UNEARTHING THE *MONTCLAIR*

Last November, one of the first of this winter's ocean storms unearthed the remains of the *Montclair*, a sailing vessel that went aground at Pochet Beach in East Orleans in March 1927. The *Mont-*

clair was a big three-masted schooner carrying a cargo of wooden laths. According to the local historian and shipwreck expert Bill Quinn, the *Montclair* was the last wreck of a sailing ship on the back side of Cape Cod, and one of the most spectacular. The battering of the waves broke the ship in two, and five of the seven-man crew drowned before the last two were rescued.

The *Montclair* is only one of hundreds of ships and boats that have wrecked on the Outer Beach from Monomoy Point to Race Point in Provincetown over the centuries, but this wreck has gained a modicum of literary immortality because Henry Beston described it in his classic book, *The Outermost House.* His vivid description of the breakup of the ship and the drowning of the crew members is one of the finest pieces of journalistic prose I know. It's even more remarkable because it is a secondhand account. Beston did not visit the site until a week after the wreck. He pieced together his description from the reports of others, but so powerful is the writing that you feel you are reading an eyewitness account.

I felt a personal connection with the wreck of the *Montclair* because some years ago the Chatham Chorale, a local chorus in which I sing, commissioned the New England composer Ron Perera to write an oratorio based on Beston's book. One of the movements is called "The Wreck of the *Montclair*," and it uses Beston's words to marvelous effect. One of my fellow basses, Dick Griffin, a native of Chatham, told me that it was his father who found one of the drowned crewmen:

"My father found the cook. There were only two survived, you know, and they only found two of the five bodies. My father was out there collecting laths. There were laths spread up and down the beach for miles. He was kicking the sand away from a pile of them with his foot, and suddenly he uncovered this eye staring up at him. He shied away from it like a spooked horse, but it was the cook. One of the stern sections was carried down the beach and came ashore just about opposite the Chatham Lights. I remember as a lad going out there and playing in it. You could climb right inside."

Beston called the wreck of the *Montclair* a "primitive tragedy." It was that, of course, but there's another side to the *Montclair*'s story. The old Cape Codders had a mixed attitude toward shipwrecks. They were not only human tragedies, they were also business. Cape Codders would willingly risk their own lives to save the crew of a wreck, but once the fate of the crew was settled, they would also exploit the same wreck, stripping an abandoned ship not only of its cargo but of all usable material, including planks and beams and cabinetry from the ship itself, with as much alacrity and efficiency as a school of piranhas stripping the carcass of a cow.

There is another account of the *Montclair*'s fate, one less well-known than Beston's, that effectively portrays this other, less tragic side of shipwrecks. In his book *Mooncussers of Cape Cod*, published in 1937, the historian Henry Kittredge recounts the adventures of one Albert Snow of Orleans, who was on the beach shortly after the wreck of the *Montclair*. When Snow climbed on board one of the two halves of the ship's hull, Kittredge says:

> He found himself in the company of the best people in Orleans, twenty-five or thirty of them, young and old, who had come over to make a Roman holiday of it.
>
> Snow made his way into the cabin where a jovial group were making free with the stores, especially tea, ham, and condensed milk; almost everyone he saw had a five-pound ham under his arm. Snow soon had one too, as well as a set of four or five deep drawers and a half a dozen cabin doors.

One of my favorite passages in this account illustrates how, in Kittredge's words, "The beach sharpens men's wits while it dulls their scruples":

> A man was standing beside the wreck of the *Montclair*, pausing for a breather, [and] leaning against a big pile of laths, still neatly tied in bundles that somebody had collected.
>
> "That's a good-looking lot of laths you've got," remarked a

passerby to the man who was resting against them. "What'll you take for them?"

"Five dollars," he replied.

"You sold some laths," said the other, and handed over a five-dollar bill.

The tired man put it in his pocket and sauntered off, leaving the purchaser of the laths to come to terms with the man who collected them as their natures might dictate.

This wryly appreciative account of the native Cape Codder's pragmatic and sometimes less than honest dealings with the cargo of a wreck isn't at odds with the pathos and "primitive tragedy" of Beston's account. They are two sides of the same coin, from a time and place where consistency was less important than survival, where heroism and opportunism could exist simultaneously in the same breast.

I had never seen the wreck of the *Montclair* before, though winter storms have unearthed it from its sandy grave several times over the decades. When I heard about this most recent exhumation of its wreckage, I decided to go see it. Late one January afternoon I parked at my friend Audrey Robb's house on Pochet Road. She told me she had last seen the wreck about ten days ago in the washover area about four hundred yards south of the Pochet access. It had been lifted and carried into the dunes and was rapidly being covered by the drifting sand.

I walked across the wooden footbridge at Pochet Creek and out into the winter dunes in all their frozen nobility. The receding landscape resolved itself into a series of distinct rising bands, highlighted by the intense light from the setting sun: first the tall, golden marsh grass, succeeded by the low, white-gold-tufted line of dunes, then by a dark band of fogbank offshore, and finally overarched by the clear, pale-blue winter sky.

The temperature was in the high twenties, with a light northwest wind. It was a classic winter beach, full of light and nobility, but devoid of life—only the ghosts of dead men, whose solid wooden repository I was hoping to find. Eventually I came to the overwash area, some five hundred feet wide now, with tufts of beach grass plastered down into the wet sand from a recent overwash. Though there was nothing obvious at first, I was somehow certain I would find the wreck, and I did. With the sun still two or three fingers above the horizon, I came upon it at the very southern end of the washover area, about thirty feet into the dunes. One full oak rib and a second broken rib protruded above the sand, and several oak planks were partially exposed around them. These fragments of a once-proud ship were still held together by a dozen or so wooden pegs, or trunnels—tapered cylinders of locust wood that were preferred to iron spikes or nails by boatbuilders because of their flexibility and resistance to corrosion.

And that was all. I took a few photos and stood there in the golden light, thinking about the tragedy that played out here on a violent night eighty-four winters before, and the countless other dramas that have taken place over the centuries, most of which, unlike that of the *Montclair*, are unrecorded or long forgotten. I wondered not how many times this ship had been unearthed and reburied, but how many times it had been "wrecked"—in that good old Cape Cod sense of the word—by others like me over the decades? I pulled out a loose trunnel and took it with me as I started back along the beach in the dying light, the wet sand laced with a garland of marsh grass that glittered in the final rays of the sun, like straw that the ocean had spun into gold.

March 2011

JOB AND THE
BEACH-COTTAGE TENANTS

Over the past several months I, along with many others, have been following the controversy over the ultimate fate of the remaining beach cottages on Chatham's North Beach. The controversy stems from the National Seashore's decision to demolish five of the remaining cottages that it owns, and which it has been leasing out to summer tenants, some for nearly half a century. The position of the Seashore is that, in the judgment of coastal geologists it has hired to assess the situation, the cottages are in imminent danger of being swept away in this winter's storms. The Seashore would rather remove them in an orderly way rather than having the cottages' debris pose a potential hazard to the waters of Chatham Harbor, and they have now served eviction notices on the cottage tenants.

The tenants, on the other hand, dispute the Seashore's estimates of erosion rates, and believe that the cultural and historical significance of the cottages should allow them to remain as long as possible, especially since next year is Chatham's three-hundredth anniversary. To this end they have applied to have the cottages placed on the National Register of Historic Places—a process that could take several months. By that time, of course, the sea itself may have decided the issue, so unpredictable is the ocean's fury.

This is hardly the first time the cottages on North Beach have found themselves in harm's way from the erosive forces of the sea. The so-called Perfect Storm, or Halloween Gale of October 1991, destroyed about fifteen of the remaining cottages on North Beach, and I remember being impressed by the attitude of those whose cottages were lost. Most expressed a bittersweet resignation, sad over the loss of their cottages, but resigned to what they had known for some time would be their ultimate fate. Part of what allowed them such equanimity was the fact that, in material terms, they were not losing that much. This contrasted greatly with the more substantial houses in Chatham center, which, after a similar northeaster in 1987, were suddenly open to the full fury of the ocean and fought expensive legal battles to build permanent bulkheads to protect their valuable waterfront property. So much of our attitude toward natural destruction, it seems, depends on what we have at stake in it.

The most interesting thing about the situation for me, as a disinterested bystander, is that neither the Seashore nor the cottage tenants dispute the ultimate fate of these cottages: The real questions are when and how. "When" is a relatively minor one. The Seashore feels the cottages could go at any time, whereas the tenants feel that at most they might get "a few more summers" before the ocean takes them. The real issue seems to be *how* they will be destroyed. The Seashore's superintendent, George Price, believes that it is better to tear them down now than to risk the hazards of natural destruction later. The tenants, according to a recent *Boston Globe* article, would "rather see the homes swept away by the sea in a poetic surge than dismantled by the government." One tenant, Susan Carroll, put it this way: "If the ocean took it tomorrow," she said, "as long as the Seashore didn't take it, I'd be happy."

The question for me is, Why? Why such a difference in attitude between natural and human destruction? If, as even the tenants acknowledge, the cottages will soon be taken by the sea, what difference does it make to have a beach shack destroyed by the ocean as opposed to a government agency? The result, after all, is the same. Is it just a romantic preference, the appeal of a "poetic surge" over a government edict? Is it a basic distrust of any government agency? Or is it something simpler, merely the fact that, in the face of natural forces of a certain magnitude, we accept that we really can't do anything about them, but that we somehow feel that human force, human agency, should have done more? In other words, Does natural destruction have an inevitability that human action lacks?

I'd like to suggest one more possibility: Perhaps our acquiescence in the face of overwhelming natural destruction comes, at least in part, from an unconscious recognition that the forces of wind and wave are part of an infinitely larger system of interconnected natural forces, the same forces that created us. In our more secular age we tend to ascribe to nature what we used to ascribe to an all-knowing divinity: a basic trust that, however inscrutable its reasons or purposes, it works on a profound level of connectedness and continuity—as opposed to merely human decisions, which tend to be seen as arbitrary and shortsighted, based on political, economic, or legal considerations rather than human ones.

When Job asked God why he, a good man, should suffer so much, Jehovah replied: "Where were you when I laid the foundations of the earth . . . when the morning stars sang together and all the sons of god shouted for joy? . . . Who shut in the sea with doors, when it broke forth from the womb . . . and said, 'Thus far shall you come and no farther; and here shall your proud waves be stayed'?" Perhaps, hearing the roar of those waves, we—like Job, like those cottage tenants— assent to the mystery and majesty of a creation we have not made.

December 2011

4

....

Nauset Beach

A TALE OF TWO PLAQUES

In the fall of 1971, when I first moved permanently to the Cape and was living in Orleans, I made my first visit to the Aran Islands, three large limestone rocks set in Galway Bay off the western edge of Ireland. The Aran Islands are rugged and rockbound islands, rising three hundred feet above the open ocean on their western sides. They have been inhabited for well over a thousand years and were made famous more than a century ago by the great Irish playwright John Millington Synge, who used them as the setting for several of his plays, including *Riders to the Sea* and *The Playboy of the Western World.* They were also the setting of the classic staged documentary, *Man of Aran,* filmed by Robert Flaherty in 1934, which portrayed the traditional and hazardous fishing life of the residents. Even in the early 1970s most of the residents still spoke Gaelic, and the men still went to sea in small, fragile rowboats with tarred-canvas hulls known as curraghs.

The ferry from Galway docked at the village of Kilronan on Inish-more, the largest of the three islands. As I came off the wharf I saw anti-British graffiti spray-painted on the walls of buildings. These were signs of the "troubles," or terrorist violence, between the British army and the IRA, still rocking Ireland at the time.

At the end of the wharf was a tall stone monument with a brass plaque set in it. The writing was almost entirely in Gaelic and therefore totally indecipherable to me, but at the bottom of the plaque, inexplicably—startlingly—in English, were the words "Orleans, Massachusetts."

I was completely nonplussed. Here, in a foreign land, more than three thousand miles from home, what should I see on the first sign I encounter but the name of my recently adopted home town! It took me a minute or two to recover my wits, and when I did I realized that I knew the *twin* of this plaque. I had come upon it several times in my walks around Nauset Harbor. It is bolted onto a large glacial boulder that sits in shallow water at the south end of the harbor. That plaque, in English, reads as follows:

A Fighting Chance
John Ridgeway and Chad Blyth
Rowed Atlantic in *English Rose III*
From Orleans to Kilronan Aran
Ireland. 4 June 1966 – 3 September 1966
NAR LAGA DIA IAD*

Suddenly it all made sense. Both this plaque and the one on the dock in Kilronan commemorated the first successful row across the Atlantic, and it was by pure chance that I, a visitor from Cape Cod, happened upon the landing place in Ireland of the voyage that those two Englishmen had set out on from Orleans a few years before. Instead of the graffiti of political and religious separation, these plaques spoke of the spirit of connection. The two plaques, one in Orleans and one on the Aran Islands, separated by an ocean, were connected by a remarkable feat of maritime skill and courage so rep-

---

* Roughly, "God strengthen them!"

resentative of the history of both places—which I had coincidentally encountered here, far from home.

September 1971

THE NEGLIGENT BEAUTY
OF THE OUTER BEACH

At 5:30 p.m., after a very businesslike day (and expecting little more), I drove down to Nauset Beach, where I had not been for several months. The bunches of bleached beach grass and their dry tasseled seed heads still dominated the dunes, but at their bases one could see sharp little green-pointed blades starting up, four or five inches tall and very tough, like cactus spikes. One rounded dune in front of me resembled a porcupine's back. There is an aggression and territoriality in this plant, a hard thrust rather than a soft spring, as though to say, Whoever would disturb my growth had better be hard-soled indeed. The beach grass, compass grass, stands, its seed head held high and straight, its long bent blades fingering in the sand the bold and ancient act of circumscription—See, here I am!

Flocks of sea ducks floated offshore, just beyond the breakers, which fell softly in long, glistening, unbroken curls, like giant unfurling strands of kelp. In further, a loon dived and rose, again and again, just as I would fix on him, as if he could sense the movement of my eyes at a hundred yards. The sea itself, though coming in, was strangely calm and peaceful, as though, if it knew, it was giving no inkling of the human tide that would soon descend upon it. Only a half dozen other walkers were spread out across the mile or so sweep of beach, a good human distance from one another, relieving us from any obligation or semblance of purpose or expression, leaving us merely to gather if we could the bloom of this incipient season, here in the light of the dying sun.

Suddenly the beach hit me again in all its unimaginable simplic-ity of grandeur, the rolling and tilting planes of sand, so tenacious and so yielding. Nothing, not even its naked, casual cruelty, shows nature's indifference to us as much as its negligent beauty. I walked back to the parking lot on the inside of the dune line, more than satis-fied, even asking for no more. Yet the sun slanted across the sand as if stalking me, shadowing my tracks with a light blue-gray tint and giving the dunes above me a rosy luster. Once again I experienced that purposeless, lavish overflow of nature's abundance, a symptom of its healthy disposition that tells us to look on any misfortune or disappointment as insignificant, as a spot too heavily focused on. No other place I know sears the heart with such a constant juxtaposi-tion of pleasure and pain, of beauty being born and destroyed in the same moment. Sometimes I wish I could contemplate the Cape with detachment; it would be so much easier if I could simply write off its fate. But still it groans and sings its ancient, aching song, and I know that, if necessary, I would beg to live here.

March 1972

"WHEN IS IT OVER?"

We were recently visited by a couple who moved from the Cape to Vermont several years ago. Their three young sons had been born off-Cape and had never seen the ocean. We took them all down to Nauset in the afternoon, where a heavy surf clawed away at the sum-mer berm, creating a sharp shelf two feet high, while an offshore wind blew back the crests of the waves like the manes of a thousand horses. The boys watched for several minutes in silent awe, until finally the eight-year-old turned to his father and asked, "Dad, when is it over?"

November 1973

WITHERED GUARDS

Last night after an Orleans Historical Society meeting on old water mills (they were mostly tub-wheel, not paddle-wheel, driven), I went down to Nauset for the first time in months. An old man in the booth at the parking lot stopped me. Like the Porter in *Macbeth*, he seemed slightly inebriated and comically cantankerous. He told me I had till midnight to get off the beach (when, presumably, the ocean turned into a pumpkin).

The beach, as is often the case, was not real. A very gibbous moon hung up above the waves, casually drifting south as ripped and ragged masses of cloud raced north against it. The waves came in silhouette, low black forms, like great fish swirling in on the moon-crusted surface of the sea. The beach went light and dark, light and dark, as though with sheet lightning under the pulsing moon. To the north Nauset Light sang its triplets, and Chatham answered twice from the south. A man stood calf-deep in the surf, doing exercises, or a dance, I could not tell which. I walked north on the beach for a ways, then came back on the back side of the dunes, where the beach grass, in the season's fullness, glistened darkly like the pelt of a healthy beast.

Back in the parking lot, I was waved down again by the old fool with his light, like a clown in cap and bells, for not observing the 15 mph speed limit at midnight in an empty lot. How could I tell him the torrent was still in me, the thundering music of sky, wind, wave, and moon, the urge to ride a black mare naked under the stars that gave vent in excessive pressure on the gas pedal of my clunky VW bus? What would he care? Our passions are held more and more in check as we voluntarily give up our right to destroy the things that feed them. We must, we know, hire withered guards to erect barriers between us and what our hearts starve for.

September 1974

HUNTERS ON NAUSET SPIT

I was taking an early morning jaunt on Nauset Spit recently, walking south along the inner side of the dunes, when a trio of Canada geese came winging in from the ocean. They began to cross over the beach some distance ahead of me, when suddenly they veered off and headed back out to sea. I soon saw why.

A few minutes later, among the dunes, I almost stumbled on two hunters with shotguns crouched down in the beach grass. One was very large and fleshy, the other thin as a rail, like Laurel and Hardy. They looked very cold and very bored, and, rather than resent my intrusion, they seemed to welcome me as a diversion.

I recognized them as the pair of hunters I had seen in the coffee shop in town about an hour before. I had overheard one remark to the other that he "never realized there were so many ponds on the Cape." The other said that last fall he had seen his first deer here in nine years. I figured that such hunters were no great threat to local wildlife.

Now, out here on the beach, I asked them what they were after.

"Eiders," the thin one replied.

"How do you get them after they're shot?" I asked, since they didn't have any dogs with them.

"Oh," the large one said. "We get them when they fly over the beach into the Town Cove. Only when we're here, they stay up at the other end of the spit. We don't really fool them, I guess. There's lots of geese out in the marsh too. Season closes tomorrow, though. C'mon geese—c'mon over *here*."

I've never tasted eider, but experienced duck hunters I've spoken with say they taste something like boiled hunting boots—only not quite as tasty. And it didn't seem likely that these two men were after eiderdown to stuff pillows with. Like most duck hunters I've met, these two seemed fatalistic and not unkind about their endeavors, almost embarrassed that they needed such a serious excuse to get themselves outdoors. Many people, it seems, need to have some earnest purpose or socially acceptable reason simply to be outside in natural surroundings. The eiders would have welcomed this pair just as well without guns, but without guns they would not have been here. Still, whatever one's ultimate judgment about hunters and hunting, these two were at least quiet and attentive—more than can be said for most beach visitors.

We watched a flock of red-backed dunlins sweep in and land on the beach near us. The hunters looked at them, and then the large one, as though for lack of anything better to do, *shoosh*ed them away. I felt I was making him self-conscious and so I said good-bye, leaving him muttering, "C'mon geese, *c'mon* ducks," and checking his watch.

January 1979

A NEW YEAR'S DAY WALK

For years now, on or about New Year's Day, I have found myself taking a walk along Nauset Spit in Orleans. This is no conscious ritual on my part, though I find myself doing it with almost migratory regularity. I can account for this in part because in January this beach, though deserted by sunbathers and boaters, is, from a naturalist's point of view, at its liveliest. There are always reliable multitudes to be seen: great rafts of eiders on both sides of the Inlet, enormous congregations of resting gulls on the flat sand plains to the north, and herds of harbor seals moving through the dark channel waters or hauled out on New Island.

But I am also drawn here, I think, because it was on this beach, half a lifetime ago, that I first encountered the mystery of the ocean and its peculiarly human relationship with this land. Since then I have come here hundreds of times, at different seasons and for different reasons, but at this time of year I come for a sense of renewal, of new beginnings. I have never been disappointed.

This year I arrived at the beach on New Year's morning at 6:00 a.m. It was quite cold, about twenty degrees, clear, and still dark. The lightest of breezes flowed out of the northwest, due to turn northeast and bring in some snow by late afternoon. Offshore a high bank of smoky clouds delayed the coming of dawn. Three lighted ships moved slowly and smoothly north along the horizon.

The sea was calm and flat and gray, a sheet of shimmering metal. The tide was low and rising with small breakers purling and curling in, spreading out from the middle in both directions, like the final, quiet, repeated chords of Samuel Barber's *Adagio for Strings*. I took a last sip of coffee, pulled up my hood, and got out of the car.

Setting off north from the parking lot toward the Inlet, I hugged the inner edge of the dunes. The sand trail was firm enough for easy walking, but too dry to be really hard. My bones were still cold from sleep, but steady movement soon warmed them up. The back dunes wore a winter-blasted look: Ragged, wiry, gray mops of poverty grass dotted the colorless sand between irregular, brittle mats of lime-green reindeer lichen. In the sand patches between broken clumps of beach grass I found rabbit spoor and the tracks of other small animals that must fight for survival here year-round.

The wind scythed through the wheat-colored winter beach grass, stirring dry stands of old cattail reeds and setting them to rattling like sabers. Weak yellow light began to seep in from the east. The only bright spots of color on the landscape were the shriveled Chinese-red rose hips, dangling like forgotten Christmas ornaments from the bare, rounded, spiked clumps of beach rose.

I circled around the small brackish pond that lies between the barrier beach and the bluffs of Nauset Heights—all that remains of a navigable channel that once ran behind Nauset Beach. (A woman I know, now in her late eighties, remembers sailing as a young girl from Nauset Harbor to Little Pleasant Bay through this channel.) Its northeast shore was frozen solid where winds had piled up the ice in rough waves. Near the edge of the pond among the locked reeds I found the body of a black duck, encased in ice.

At length I came out on the beach at a trail-widened break in the dune ridge, just where a group of glacial boulders lay a few yards offshore—the last visible remnants of the eastern edge of the Sandwich Recessional Moraine. There is always something momentarily purifying, a sudden but brief surge of the soul on first gaining the beach that no amount of repetition, anticipation, or inner dullness can completely block. That first moment of entrance, like that of love's, is always one of newness and promise.

Now I stood on the broad, flat, frozen plain of Nauset Spit, where piping plovers and least terns nest on the hot summer sands. I began to walk north, with swiftness and ease, on the wide ice track left by the preceding tide. Men have used this "ice path" on the upper beach for winter walking for generations. (Beston remarks on its convenience for the Coast Guard patrolmen in *The Outermost House*.)

I came eventually to the end of the dune line, which so far has suffered little damage from the storms this winter, and cut across the sand plain to the harbor side. Here the frozen beach was even wider. Large masses of exposed mussels lay among the ice. Why is it that mussels, with their relatively thin shells, can withstand freezing better than most shellfish? In many ways these underrated mollusks seem to be creatures of extraordinary tolerances, able to withstand not only unusual temperature extremes, but chemical pollutants, disease, and other environmental stresses. They bear watching, as well as eating.

All at once the frozen landscape became littered with the dead bodies of birds, half covered with wind-driven sand. There were several eiders, a headless cormorant and a headless brant, two large Canada geese, and numerous gulls in their characteristic smashed or slapped-down postures. Many of these bodies looked as if they had been worried by dogs or coyotes.

At first I dislodged each of these dead birds, inspecting them for possible causes of death: traces of oil, shotgun pellets, emaciation, infection. I was trying to determine whether they had died by some human agency or were just part of nature's great mortality, but the distinction between human and natural death begins to blur and lose significance in such a place, and I soon stopped examining the stiff forms. This wide, open, gravelly plain is surely one of the great natural stages of this or any other land. It possesses a kind of submissive power and integrity born of its naked exposure. Here, on the first morning of a new year, among a graveyard of birds serving as their own half-hidden markers, it spoke of bare survival, without benefit of human flattery, whose only mercy is the driving cover of the wind.

January 1980

5

....

Nauset Marsh

MEAT FISHING

Flounder fishing, as anyone who has tried it knows, is meat fishing, not sport. There is no fish that is less of a challenge to lure to your hook, or that will give you less of a fight once you do.

On the other hand, what this fish lacks in fight it more than makes up for in amiability. I am talking now of the winter flounder, *Pseudopleuronectes americanus*, also known as the black-back or lemon sole. Just when many of the summer game fish are beginning to leave our shoal waters, the winter flounder arrives, almost, it seems, so that we will not feel deserted. Widespread and at home in shallow waters from Newfoundland to Georgia, the winter flounder requires little expense or effort to catch, and is so easy to land that a small child can do it—and often does, better than his or her adult companion. Being a bottom scavenger, the flounder will take almost any bait— sea worms, night crawlers, clam feet and necks, fish scraps, leftover chicken—and once it does it will obligingly lie there quietly so that a colleague may swim up and take the other hook. (Flounder are normally taken on double-hook devices known as spreaders.) They lack

the numerous sharp spines found on many other game fish, enabling
you to disengage the hook without fear of impaling your hand. They
also rarely swallow bait, so that three or four fish can be landed on
a single hook without rebaiting. Because of their flat shape they also
stack neatly and efficiently in the bottom of your bucket or fish box.

Once brought home, flounder are, if anything, even more obliging.
They do not need to be cleaned, but are easily filleted. They need
only to be scaled or skinned on the top side. ("Top side" is a reference
to the flounder's strange morphology. The adult fish is vertically flattened and swims along the bottom on its side, with both eyes on one
side of its head.) And smaller fish, the ones that suddenly metamor-
phose into keepers at the end of an unproductive day on the water,
seem to be purposely shaped for pan-broiling. They are, in fact, the
Shmoos of the marine world.

In the last afternoon of October, during a sweet stretch of balmy
weather, my friend Ralph and I set off in his Boston Whaler with a
couple of dozen nightcrawlers to spend a few hours flounder fishing on the calm and clear waters of Nauset Harbor. Anchoring off a
sandy point, we each threw in two sets of baited hooks and waited for
signs of gratitude from below. When fish are biting well, there is usually not much time for anything but hauling in line, unhooking fish,
and resetting. But the run of the tide was beginning to slow and the
flounder with it, so that we had time to jig our tarred lines between
thumb and fingers before pulling them up. (For some reason, though,
I have never hooked a flounder by playing it; it has either been there
or it hasn't. I suspect jigging lines is just something flounder fishermen do to keep from feeling totally useless.)

Even without such a practical justification at the other end of your
line, Nauset Harbor is a wonderful place to spend an Indian summer
afternoon. A few lobster boats ride placidly at anchor. Hundreds of
pots are heaped in mounds on the lower part of the beach. Partially
submerged in the rising tide, they look like skeletal reefs, rising men-
acingly out of the water. A cormorant fishes in the shallows, diving
with little fillips and emerging again.

To the east the long white arm of Nauset Spit stretches northward longingly and empty. At its far end we can just make out some turbulence in the water, indicating the Inlet channel entrance from the ocean, and beyond that the truncated arm of Coast Guard Beach.

New Island (which, though formed nearly twenty years ago when the southern end of Coast Guard Spit was cut off, will probably be called New Island until the flounder forage over its dunes) is much closer to us on the north, with a couple of more recently formed shoal islands trailing off behind. Beyond the islands, to the northwest, the bare grassy crown of Fort Hill lies shining in the October sun, prominent not only for its lack of trees but even more for its lack of houses, for it is there that the National Seashore begins to take in the mainland as well as the beaches. The phrase "nick of time" applies more vividly to the Fort Hill area than most, for when it was included in the National Seashore takings in the early 1960s, the hillside meadows had already been subdivided and marked with lot stakes and bulldozer tracks.

I seem to see the encircling scene more clearly than I do in summer, partly because the low sun lends contrast and shading to each feature, so that shapes resonate rather than blend. I realize, with something of a start, that relative to the winter solstice this afternoon is the equivalent of late February. How the tides of the season lag here, casting lengthening shades of reluctance and regret over all endings and partings. It is a wide and flowing place, and flounder fishing, not requiring much concentration or effort, is a perfect activity during which to contemplate its history and pleasures.

It is a lovely and a peculiarly empty day, as we sit in our small boat jigging our flounder rigs in the clear green waters. Not only are the summer crowds missing, but many other recent noises and sights as well. Gone are the screaming clouds of common and least terns that nested all summer on the sandy plains of Nauset Spit and on the grass-covered dunes of New Island. Gone, too, are most of the shorebirds of late summer and early fall; only a few black-bellied plovers, a lingering yellowleg or two, and flocks of bright sanderlings forage on the disappearing flats and along the tidal wrack. The migrating swallows that cruise the spartina prairies and the wandering monarch butterflies that straggle down the beaches in late September have all flown.

On the other hand, the large flocks of eiders that regularly feed on the estuary's mussel beds have not yet arrived, nor has the herd of young harbor seals that spend the winter months fishing its waters and hauling out on the frigid beaches of New Island.

It is a slack time of year, a time between seasons and currents of life, between the growth of more salt marsh behind the dunes and the attrition of the Outer Beach in the face of winter storms. Like the flounder that we assume are hooked, waiting to be pulled up and turned into fish dinners, the year seems to be lying quietly at the bottom, waiting for some sea change.

For more than three hundred years European settlers have fished the waters of this estuary, and still the fish are here. That seems to me an incredible fact, even after the simple explanations of biology. Perhaps it is the more remarkable because of the increasing number of once-rich estuaries that are no longer productive, or because of the always-imminent threat of oil spills along these shores. Somehow the flounder, the winter flounder, coming into our cooling waters to feed and spawn through the dead months, seem a symbol of the renewable and undying—though not inexhaustible or indestructible—riches of a place like this.

Ralph, who has a more pessimistic nature than mine, wonders if the offshore dragger fleets have, over the past several decades, affected the number of flounder available to us here in this protected embayment. It is difficult to determine such things, although the total flounder catch for New England has decreased more than 30 percent over the past half century. It is a typical question from him. He is instinctively much more aware of the loss of fish, birds, other wildlife, and open land than I am. In contrast I have to fight against an almost constant sense of undeserved richness and unexpected beauty. We have similar sensibilities, but it is a matter of differing backgrounds. He grew up here, took the land's abundance as his natural birthright, and so, in this era of the rampant blind development and exploitation of this land and its waters, he has developed an ingrained sense of diminishing resources and expectations.

I was born in an urban setting, on the glass-littered banks of a dead river whose dark waters glistened with the rainbow hues of oil slicks. I grew up expecting no more, so that when I came here, like most washashores I found myself in the midst of unwonted plenty. Overwhelmed by the improvement of my surroundings, I did not, at first, sense the eroding forces at work. Since then I have become only too aware of the vulnerable nature of this natural richness and the implacable forces at work to rape it for short-term profit and short-sighted benefits. Yet, even after all these years, I still have to make a conscious effort to overcome this initial sense of undeserved riches, must force myself to know and to feel how much I am missing, might have had, and will have taken from me, lest I become just another pathetic refugee from the city, grateful for whatever scraps the developers might leave us, taking a kind of morbid comfort in what we have not yet become, aspiring only to stretch out what is left over my own lifetime. Even the flounder, carrying next year's generation in their bellies, have higher aims than that.

This evening, as I fillet them under sink light on the cutting board, I find rich, yolk-colored roe or pale white milt along the ventral openings of almost every fish—a promise of continuity, like the leaves and flowers of next spring's trees, already formed inside the tight bud scales on the stripped branches of November's woods.

October 1979

A DAY ON NAUSET MARSH

Tides, along with the seasons and the diurnal rhythms, are one of the few dependably regular reciprocal rhythms in nature. One can journey into summer, or midnight, knowing one will be returned, in time, to winter and the light of day. With the tide, it takes a conscious timing and positioning, but a round trip ticket on one of the Earth's great forces is equally available.

It was on an early day in June that I took my first canoe trip on Nauset Marsh. I borrowed a canoe from a friend,* an eighteen-footer, loaded it into the back of my VW bus, and drove to Hemenway Landing, on the northwest side of the marsh, at about eleven o'clock.

For companionship I took with me my paperback copy of Wyman Richardson's *The House on Nauset Marsh,* first published in 1952. Richardson is a genial and well-informed guide. He may be a less impressive stylist and less consciously literary writer than Henry Beston, who chronicled of this same stretch of the Outer Beach a few decades earlier, but his perceptions and reactions are no less true and valid. Moreover, since those perceptions and reactions come out of not a few weeks or even an entire year but a lifetime of extended visits and vacations, he expresses his experience more expansively and familiarly, and with greater affection and perspective. In addition, there is an abundance of practical observations and information on tide, weather, navigation, fishing, crabbing, bird-watching, and other topics that comes out casually, as if in conversation. With Beston one wants to sit and listen to him, exalted and enthralled, but with Richardson, one wants to travel and converse with him. He is a man sensitive to the majestic, but also with a strong practical sense, a generosity in sharing his experience, and a desire and capacity for the pleasures of hearth, table, and bed.

Nauset Marsh is unusual among large Cape Cod salt marshes, because, as Richardson points out, there is more water than marsh in it, with the deep and navigable creek around its perimeter and large bays at its upper end. In most large marsh systems, as in the

---

* Thoreau gave great license to all borrowers, having borrowed his "neighbor's" [Emerson's] ax to cut down his neighbor's trees to build his little house, in which he squatted for two years on that same "neighbor's" land.

Great Marshes of Barnstable, you can enter a main harbor or estuary and paddle up any one of a branching network of gradually narrowing, dead-end creeks, or paddle on the outer edges of long "fringe marshes" bordering the inner sides of the barrier beaches such as those in Pleasant Bay or on the back side of Monomoy.

But Nauset is younger than most major marshes on the Cape (some peat corings put its age at five hundred years) and so has not yet taken on the classic configurations of a mature salt marsh. Here the marsh grass is divided into several large blocks and many smaller hummocks, forming a kind of peat archipelago, around which one can navigate in a canoe or a small boat even at low tide. Such a configuration invites voyages of exploration and investigation. It also invites local names for the various bays, inlets, creeks, marshes, and hummocks, as well as various geographical analogies with the larger world outside the marsh. All of this is to be found on the maps on the endpapers of Richardson's book, which document his half-century acquaintance with its various features and lives.

I intended to circumnavigate the largest of the contiguous marsh islands: a wide crescent-shaped peat island known on Richardson's map as "Porchy Marsh" (no doubt a variant on "Pochet"). Well over a mile in length, Porchy Marsh is shaped roughly like the South American continent, a similarity obviously noticed by Richardson, who named its tapered southern end "The Horn" and the narrow passage at the very tip the "Straits of Magellan."

The tide, when I arrived, looked about an hour past high. I figured I had about four hours to paddle down the outside of the marsh, visit the tern colonies on New Island and Nauset Spit, and take whatever side trips might present themselves. The tide on the outside of Nauset Inlet was scheduled to change about two forty-five, and I estimated that the currents on the inside would begin to turn about a half hour later, allowing me to return on an incoming tide. I walked the canoe out of the van and carried it on my back, like a lurching terrapin, down to the water's edge and shoved off. There was a light wind, maybe five to eight knots, that had been west-southwest at ten o'clock and had now shifted into the northwest, so that I had both wind and tide going out with me.

It was a perfect day to be out on the marsh, warm but not humid, early enough in the season to avoid the greenhead flies, and with a wind light but strong enough to keep away whatever insects there might be. The sky was clean and new, unglazed by summer yet, washed by high horsetails and embroidered with fair-weather clouds. I was accompanied by small pale butterflies that tumbled along lightly through the air. The peat banks of the creeks were exposed and riddled like brown head cheese with the burrows of fiddler crabs. The creeks were lined, as were broader channels, with numerous lobster pots. I drifted with the outgoing tide a hundred yards or so down the inside border of the marsh to the little twisting cut-through that Richardson calls "Northwest Passage"—a quite navigable route twenty to thirty feet wide, with little current. I stopped at one or two inlets to explore the marsh and examine the "salt pans," small depressions in the marsh that are clear of grass and contain shallow pools of salt water full of convocations of periwinkles.

Though the map in Richardson's book is over thirty years old, I was struck at how little the marsh configurations had changed. The main marsh blocks, creeks, and channels, as well as most of the smaller hummocks, have remained nearly unaltered—this despite strong tidal currents. Nor does the extent of the marsh seem to have increased significantly in that time. Perhaps marsh buildup and sea-level rise have reached equilibrium.

The wind frequently pushed me up against the peat bank on the south side of the channel or threatened to ground me in sand shallows, where I had to push myself off with the paddle. Eventually I emerged into the main channel, glanced at the flats to the north, but was immediately lifted and carried southward along the east coast of the main marsh by the broad, gentle sweep of the ebbing current. The marsh is smooth and rounded on its outer side, a testimony to the trimming power of the main tidal currents on that side. I put my paddle down and enjoyed the beauty of the marsh.

The great green islands of the marsh slipped smoothly by: high, flat, raised grasslands whose creeks and configurations were completely hidden from my angle of view. Their smooth fringed bank suggested the shore of unknown, untouched coasts above the grass. The white breasts, necks, and heads of gulls appeared, looking at me with the passive curiosity of natives. Once, when I picked up the paddle to push off a bank, they all took off and dispersed in total silence, except for a great rustling of wings. Far to the south I could see a great cloud of common terns rising from some disturbance in their colony on New Island, emitting an electric storm of alarm calls.

As the curved coast of Porchy Marsh slipped by, I watched out for the mouth of Broad Creek, the largest creek that winds into the marsh's interior, the miniature Amazon (to elaborate on Richardson's geographical analogy) of this miniature marsh continent. But when I entered it, I found the outflowing current so strong that, even with the most strenuous bottom poling, I could make my way only a few rods up the creek. Exhausted, I wedged the canoe between the peat banks and stood carefully up to survey the marsh surface. Far to the west several white snowy egrets and a pair of tall great blue herons dotted the marsh, preening or standing motionless over some hidden creek or pool. Despite the gulls, terns, and herons, there is a lack of ducks and shorebirds on the marsh this time of year. Aside from a pair of blue-winged teal I startled, and later on, several immature black-bellied plovers in with the terns, I saw no other waterfowl. Almost all were still on their northern nesting grounds, though by the first week or second week in July, the "fall" migration of shorebirds would be well under way.

There was a noticeable lack of other people as well, except for a few fishermen in small commercial skiffs and lobster boats. Whether behind a wheel or at a tiller, all stood up in their boats as they powered out toward the Inlet in that classic pose of the fisherman, a position that looks somewhat precarious, but which I suspect allows them to spot bars and rips in the dangerous inlet shoals.

I had now drifted and paddled down to the lower third of Porchy

Marsh and decided to make for the north end of Nauset Spit on the Outer Beach. Though I was already past the Inlet, I knew enough to get well below it before attempting to paddle across to the beach. On a fast ebb the outgoing current near the Inlet is surprisingly strong and easily capable of sweeping a small unmotored craft, with or without an anchor, out through its opening into shoal water and breaking surf.

Paddling hard, I ended up on the inside of the barrier beach, about a hundred yards south of the Inlet. It was a little after noon, a passage down of an hour or so. I beached the canoe on the rounded, humped sand spit, and, unpacking my binoculars, spent the next hour and a half or so exploring the least tern colony from outside the perimeter, posted with signs.

It is a large colony here, a half mile long by about six hundred feet wide, with nests scattered over wide areas. I saw only eggs, no chicks, always two to a nest, but varying greatly in color from light to dark brown, sea-green, fawn, and soiled ivory. Only a few of the nests were close enough to observe without going inside the posted perimeter—as it should be—and these were difficult to spot. A brooding least tern seems to leave its nest when you approach within thirty yards, though distances are notoriously difficult to estimate in such places. One has to take what few coordinates there are at hand to judge relative distance: a short line of beach grass, a leaning post, an occasional small stone—guessing at perspective, distance, depth. A shadow, caught by a slight depression in the sand, may help, though there were few of these at midday since terns nest at the height of the solstice.

In a true sense the least tern's nest's protection lies in its very exposure, its lack of definition, its pure anonymity. It does not so much conceal itself, like, say, the yellowthroat's small, conical nest woven invisibly into the center of a viburnum bush, as it shares the lack of concealment, the constant exposure, that characterizes its surroundings. Like the beach, the nests stare back blankly at the observer, and so are not seen: brief, tiny, silent, hollow words on this wagging tongue of a sand spit.

I did not stay long at any one point, not wanting to keep the terns off their nests, for exposure can also be lethal to the eggs or young chicks. Though the air was relatively cool and breezy, the sand burned my feet, and I had to burrow them in several inches in order to stand in one place for more than a few seconds. (The next day the upper parts of my feet and ankles were bright red and itchy, as though sunburned, or as a post will rot first, not above or below ground, but at the point of contact between earth and air.) I placed my palm down into a nearby beach-buggy track, where young chicks often seek refuge if disturbed, and found that the compressed sand of the track was much hotter than the surrounding sand.

Least terns flew up at my approach and made gentle assaults as I passed, uttering their high *keevee* calls, but remained too spread out to mass. I saw one, at the center of the colony, with a large sand eel, five or six inches long, held crosswise in its beak, nearly as long as itself. It didn't seem to know quite what to do with it. It shook it, like a hawk shaking a snake, put it down on the sand, picked it up again, and finally flew off with it.

I watched other birds diving into the channel west of the Inlet, hovering seven to eight feet in the air on whirring wings and fanned-out tails, then dropping like arrows beneath the fast-sliding currents, emerging a few seconds later like born-again angels.

Terns are not perfect hunters. For that matter, nothing is. The birds I watched took an average of three dives for each catch, which may say nothing definitive about their success rate, but their method and form tend *toward* perfection; their grace of motion has an almost mathematical purity about it.

Sand eels form one of the principal food sources for our local terns. I have watched these graceful birds many times diving into creeks and offshore waters and coming up with coiling silver ropes in their mouths that flash in the sun. Their vision, in this respect, is much more refined than mine, since they not only have to pick these fish out beneath a sparkling, broken water surface but also to correct for water refraction in their dives. It is not surprising that these two organisms—tern and sand eel—locked in an elemental relationship

for ages, have each become such sculpted, refined representatives
of their respective mediums. Over the ages the sand eel's form has
become less and less discernible in the water, the tern's eye keener,
the eel more supple and elusive, the tern more adept and skillful in
pursuit, and so on, until—what? Until the tern can catch light itself
and the fish move in the grip of wind and sun.

I cannot help but wonder if anything else besides increasing competence and perfection of form has evolved between tern and eel
in their long and mortal relationship. Do they, for instance, "recognize" each other as anything more than a matrix of sensory signs,
signaling respective automatic behavior—pursuit in the one, escape
in the other? Is it possible that on some level they actually "talk" to
one another?

The idea is not as absurdly anthropomorphic as it might sound.
In one of Barry Lopez's early essays, "The Conversation of Death,"
he suggests that wolves and moose engage in a complex ritual of
communication in which a moose may to signal to a wolf pack that
it is "available" as prey. Though a seemingly far-fetched theory, it
nonetheless helps explain certain anomalies in the process of pursuit
and capture between these two animals. Most prey-predator relationships are, in fact, much more complex than the simple, straightforward flight-pursuit-escape-capture scenarios usually portrayed in
wildlife films.

"Conversation of death." Can such an idea also be applied to bird
and fish? Admittedly it seems a stretch, and yet, like many provoca-
tive speculations about animal behavior, it does not necessarily imply
anthropomorphism as much as it demands an expansion of what we
mean by such human conceptions as conversation, sacrifice, acceptance, and dignity. The falling of the last barriers between ourselves
and animals, like those between mankind and machines, does not
mean we must throw human values to the wolves of science, but
rather that we must extend them to the science of wolves, terns, and
computers.

Even if there is no "conversation" in the sense we understand it between terns and sand eels, there seems to be at least some implicit pact, some ritualized approach, chase, and final assent, as formal as the elaborate courtship rituals between the terns. Is it in fact possible to have a purely impulsive or instinctive act in the natural world? Isn't ritual, as Beston thought, at the heart of the world?

What pact does the tern make with its prey to ensure its renewal? We have no pact with anything. Perhaps this is why we cannot catch anything without one-sided technological artifice. It is an exploitative stance, an obsessive approach that we impose on other animals. Perhaps this is the real draw of wild animals: We will never equal the cheetah, for there is more to its competence than raw speed. It involves the cheetah's understanding of its prey. We are the only creatures who regard all other creatures as either potential prey or potential enemy.

As I was musing on this, a small piping plover emerged from the dunes, running out on the sand on short little feet, uttering its short, clear, sweet, plaintive note, like the whistle of a friendly, gentle policeman, to draw my attention. It went into its injured act, not only dragging its wings, calling alarm, and weaving away, but actually flopping over as though dead several times. The plover, the only nesting shorebird on the Outer Beach, is frequently associated with tern colonies, since it nests in the dunes near the surf line where it feeds on the upper beach, and is easily disturbed. Later I saw a pair feeding, and calling on the flats behind New Island. This year's Audubon report says only 125 nesting pairs are left in the state.

It took me about one and a half hours to circle the colony and return to the canoe. The wind was now northeast. I took my lunch, book, and beach chair to the northern tip of the sand spit and sat there to wait for the tide to turn.

North Point is one of the great watery meeting places of this coastline. I sat at the Inlet, watching the turbulent, grating, pulling ebb of the tide sucking out through its gap, and spreading out again to meet the low curling waves coming in over the bars. I could literally see the bottom shifting at my feet, new sandbars forming under the water as I watched, moving like dunes to cover a pebbly slope. The Inlet can move north or south dozens of yards in a single storm, and the barrier spits north and south of the Inlet retreat or elongate hundreds of feet in a year: two sandy fingers not quite touching, with an electric current constantly running between them.

At low tide there the Inlet appeared to be about a hundred yards wide. Seal herds bob and swirl here in winter; now a few lazy fishing poles arched out from the beach on either side in hopes of hooking bass or cod. The inside of the Eastham spit is bordered along its wide length by a fringe marsh that grows quite wide on its upper end. At the very tip of the ocean side, exposed ledges of peat emerging out of the dunes attest to the retreating nature of the beach. To my left the outflowing water flowed swiftly, but smoothly toward the channel. It ran in distinct patches several yards across, like plates, or floes of ice in a river.

It was pleasant just to sit, reading, watching birds, watching the water drop slowly around me. Three o'clock. Three fifteen. Still the current ran swiftly out the Inlet. Still the waters dropped around me, leaving me higher and drier. Three thirty. Still the fishing launches and skiffs allow themselves to be swept out through that impossible turbulence with no sign of slackening. I began to wonder if I had read the tide tables wrong, or had not corrected for daylight saving time or something. Then, as though I had asked a friend, I came on the answer in the "Tide" chapter of Richardson's book, one I should have read the night before.

"The tide inside the marsh is not easy to figure," he writes. He goes on to explain how "rise and fall" differ from "ebb and flow," how the height or the time of tide may vary by the constantly changing width of the inlet, and so on. Then: "The flood inside the marsh takes from 4 to 5 hours, the ebb 7 to 8 hours."

What?! He does not elaborate on this point, and at first I could not see how it could be so, but I began to work it out in my head. In other words, on the outside beach, where flood and rise tend to coincide, the tide might indeed turn at 2:45, as I had calculated. But inside the Inlet, in the marsh, the waters might continue to run out, or ebb, for another two hours even as the sea level itself was rising. In other words, I might have more than another hour to wait before the current began to run up into the marsh again. Still, I found some comfort in Richardson's own admission that "in spite of many years experience, one day last summer, I found myself six hours out of the way!"

I decided to spend the extra waiting time by visiting the tern colony on New Island—actually two small islands connected at low tide by tidal flats. I towed the canoe down inside the spit so I would not have to fight the current, then paddled across to the northern end of the peat flats that spread out north of the island. It is a curious area—obviously once a marsh, now with little grass growing on it. There are numerous tide pools, and on the northwest shore an extensive raft of blue mussels, about one hundred yards long by twenty feet wide, all attached to one another like knotted ropes or strings of rock candy. Say there were one hundred mussels per square foot—a conservative estimate. That would equal six hundred thousand mussels on a little more than an eighth of an acre!

I first explored the back island, a little sand tuft a hundred feet long, eroded, like its larger companion, on the north side. There were no gull nests this year. I saw immature black-bellies and a pair of piping plovers on the intervening flats, and then moved on to the common tern colony on the larger front island. As I approached the back side of the tern colony, the birds rose in a cloud, screeching and diving at me and my straw hat. It was a strong attack, deliberately mounted from a distance. An alarmed colony has a high, hard sound, like ten thousand knives being sharpened in the air above you, screaming as they dive. Some birds attack more frequently than others. One bird swooped down at my head regularly and rhythmically for several minutes. I could watch its shadow swinging down at me on the sand in an arc, echoed by its scream, then swing up and float back into position a few yards behind me, then swoop down again. Once I looked up as the bird dived and saw an open-beaked mask of defiance and wrath, a white, spread-winged avenging angel, and had for an instant a sense of what a sand eel or sea worm might see in the second before oblivion. But mostly I kept my head down, watching the shifting pattern of sweeping bird shadows on the sand in front of me, feeling a beak occasionally tickling my hat, their well-aimed droppings spattering my shirt. (Hitchcock missed a great opportunity by not filming *The Birds* in a tern colony.)

The nests were more concentrated here than in the least colony on the beach. They were higher up in the grass, though several spilled down to the upper beach outside the posted signs. These all had three unhatched eggs, and were better defined by rings of beach grass and other debris.

I spotted a small short-tailed, warm brown vole hiding among the patch of beach grass. This "wee, . . . cow'rin g, tim'rous, beastie"—how came it here? On this island less than a decade old, was it a descendent of one of the voles trapped out on the tip of the Eastham spit when it broke off to form the island? Or did it somehow swim that treacherous channel? Aside from myself, it might very well be the only species of mammal out here at this season. How does it exist out here, cowering now at the base of a bunch of beach grass, exactly as I've seen tern chicks do? If there are others of its kind on this island, and they survive and procreate, will they eventually evolve into a separate subspecies of vole, as they have on the small island of Muskeget in Nantucket Sound? I snapped several close-ups; then he made a dash for it, a little running scuttle, a brief brown shot of panic across hot open sands, as the birds shrieked and rent the air above him, and shadows of their wings passed and crossed over him like gray gloves, until he reached the safety of another bunch of grass.

I walked on to the tip of the eroding north end of the island. There I stood nose to nose with several common tern nests balanced at the very edge of the eroding bank, about five feet high. They were decorated with dried grass, bits of shell, some gull bones, and a long, curved white strip that, when I picked it up, proved to be the spine of a very small mammal. So our lives candidly weave out here, life mixed with death so openly and casually that the distinction lacks the harshness of contrast one finds in more sheltered places.

I set off back across the peat flats to the canoe, a single tern following, dipping and screaming at me the whole way. I took my dip net and shoved it, handle end first, into the muck at the very edge of the tide, then sat in the canoe to wait for the prolonged ebb to finish. Every five or ten minutes I got up and moved the net another foot or so down the gentle slope, as the boats anchored in the channel continued to point their sterns toward the Inlet. The current seemed to run out unabated, until, at four thirty, having slipped the pole some five feet farther down the slope, I saw that the waterline had stopped its descent. At last: Dead low.

Though the current still ran out, it seemed somewhat slowed now. I decided to shove off, hoping the flood would catch me before long. As it turned out, I had nothing to worry about. The wind had come round nearly full circle, so that it was south-southwest, eight to ten knots, and I soon discovered that a canoe, sitting so high in the water, is more subject to wind than current, if the two are reasonably equal. Thus I had the curious sensation of being carried, without paddling, upstream *against* the current a good part of the way back. I passed through the "Straits of Magellan," then headed north, hugging the southwest shore of Porchy Marsh. I passed close to the Tonset shore with its collection of monuments to modern architecture; stopped briefly at "Stony Island," which unlike the other sand and marsh islands in the marsh, is a small but true glacial deposit, a little hump of till with more than a dozen good-size barnacle-fringed boulders on it, looking as though someone must've placed them there as a rude fort; then up through the deep but narrow channel between the west side of Porchy and Fort Hill, past the latter's blessed sweep of undisturbed hillside meadow, where the anomalous notes of song sparrows and prairie warblers drifted out over the salt waters, the land rising slowly to the dark thick ridge of cedars, past the interpretive shelter as I rounded Skiff Hill, and finally back to Hemenway Landing by six o'clock. Gnats were thick and everywhere, going into my eyes, ears, and mouth. I had to haul the heavy canoe over a hundred feet of marsh flat and wrestle it back into the car. I was exhausted, hot, grungy, and hungry, but strangely exhilarated. Wyman, you keep a good marsh!

June 1981

6

....

Coast Guard Beach

BUZZ HUTCHINS MOVES HIS ROCKS

The other day I drove up to Coast Guard Beach, where I found Buzz Hutchins in his large yellow John Deere front-end loader hauling granite boulders off the beach below the bathhouse. When he saw me he put the machine in idle and stepped down to talk. Buzz is a native from an old Brewster family, one of those Cape Codders who seem to have inherited a certain perspective from his seagoing ancestors, adapting to changing conditions without too much questioning. He seemed amused at his situation, and when I asked him he said, "Well, this is the third time I've moved these rocks. First the Seashore paid me to place them up at the Gut in Wellfleet, but that didn't work, so they paid me to take them out and haul them down here. Course that didn't work either—just made things worse—so now they're paying me again to haul them off. Wonder where they'll pay me to put 'em next?"

October 1975

THE CAPE AS THE RIVER OF TIME

Thoreau's beach—or most of it, or the site where it was—is more than a hundred yards out to sea. The Cape's outer shores are a solid metaphor for the river of time, into which we can step only once. So wedded is their character to the forces of time that, when we try to stop or "control" those forces, we either fail absurdly, like the disaster of a woman's face repeatedly kept surgically young, or create something perhaps pleasant, but essentially different and static, cut off and preserved from all the processes that once fed and nursed and destroyed it. The more mobile we become, the more immobile we demand nature to be, as unruly children demand stability in their parents. Nothing in nature is ever finished. Beston's pronouncement that "Creation is here and now" is only true because destruction is also here and now. The Judeo-Christian God, in creating day, did not banish night but balanced the two, and we are the richer for it. Everything proclaims the global give-and-take—the diurnal rhythm, the seasons, the tides. When my neighbor complains that "it would be sad to lose that nice natural sand dune" in front of her house, she does not recognize its source in destruction elsewhere, or that it itself is a source of future nourishment. We see Earth's movements as a threat to our mortality, and our own fevered shuttlings as attempts to escape it. For that matter, all of our beaches, sand spits, bluffs, hills, valleys, and plains are the work of destruction. The Cape itself is a monument to the death of many a mountain range.

August 1977

THE WEEK BEFORE

Intrigued by the recent controversy over the causes of the erosion on Eastham's Coast Guard Beach in front of Nauset Marsh and the proposed banning of beach-buggy traffic on the barrier beach there, I decided to go out and see for myself just what has been happening.

I arrived at the parking lot a little before seven on a clear and bitterly cold morning in late January, just in time to catch a magnificent winter's sunrise flooding the beach with intense purples, deep pinks, and ringing golds. A withdrawn, curling sea pawed impatiently at the low-tide line, bridled momentarily by wind and tide, leaving a clean tilting plain at the base of the dunes.

The beach had indeed lost much this winter. The foredune walls were sheer, as though a giant knife had sliced vertically down through the entire length of the spit. Signs of recent washovers were visible in several low places where the sand had a churned, cratered look, and lines of posts have been erected to keep beach buggies from deepening the breaches.

Last fall there had been a large dune at least fifty feet wide in front of the contemporary beach house belonging to Conrad Nobili. Now only a dozen feet of low bluff remain in front of its porch. A set of wooden steps that had led up over the vanished dune stood at the edge of the bluff, now leading up to empty air, and I climbed them for a better view of the ocean and beach.

Although this expanse of beach takes the brunt of northeast storms each winter—as does the entire Outer Beach—most of this year's severe erosion took place three weeks ago during the ferocious gale that hit the Cape a few weeks before. According to Bob Prescott, educational director of the Cape Cod Museum of Natural History, the offshore bars here normally shift and line up parallel to the prevailing northeast swells during the winter, thereby acting as a buffer to the storms' force. The surprise southeast gale of January 9, however, slipped up through the "alleys" between these bars, like a tight end dashing up between the forward line and the defensive backs, reaching the shore with undiminished force. In some places as much as fifty feet had been torn from the beach in seventy-two hours.

I began to run along the wide hard beach to keep warm, and, as I jogged, I noticed the top of a blue pickup above the crest of the dunes going down on the marsh side. Farther down the spit I found a galvanized well point sticking straight up and still firm in the sand at the low tide line. I walked directly back from the well point to the base of the dunes and peered over the low wall. Sure enough, there, in its little bowl-like hollow on the marsh side of the dune, sat Henry Beston's beach cottage, the Fo'castle, as he called it—the "Outermost House" to the thousands of readers of his book of that name—as unpretentious as ever.

I wondered if the well point were indeed that of the house's original well, sunk some fifty years before, when Beston's beach cottage sat on a dune "scarce twenty feet above high-water mark, and only thirty in from the great beach," as he measured it. Since then the Fo'castle has been moved back twice, and the distance between its present site and the well point on the beach is about 150 feet. At an average rate of erosion of 3½ feet per year (though it has been much greater than that of late), the well point would indeed seem to mark the house's original position.

Whatever its past or present position, it looked as though the Outermost House would soon have to be moved again. Only a thin wedge of dune is left between the beach and the hollow in which it now sits not more than a few feet above sea level. It may, in fact, have to be moved off this beach entirely this time if it is to be saved—perhaps to a site somewhere up on the hill beside the Coast Guard Station.

I wondered if Beston would have approved of that, or if he would have preferred to have it swept away some night in a winter's storm, its legacy already established for future generations on unerodable foundations. Whatever its ultimate fate, it must surely be the only traveling National Literary Landmark in existence.

As I approached the inlet, I saw the pickup truck, with two people in it, come around the end of the spit. A young man got out and began to walk back up along the ocean side. As the other man turned the truck around and began to head back on the inside sand road, I hailed a ride. The driver, a genial red-haired man with a face that had seen at least a half century of winters, had a slight local accent, a genuine rarity these days. He told me that he was a native "Cape Cawdder," that his grandfather had served at the "Eastum" station when it was part of the old Life-Saving Service, and that his father had been born there and used to ride his horse on this beach when he was a boy.

He was beachcombing with the younger man, his son, perhaps, and his truck itself was a veteran of the beach, a 1957 Chevy pickup that had been used for years by the Massachusetts Audubon Society on Monomoy, which he had purchased from them and rehabilitated: "Best truck on the beach—it's never failed me."

We made our way up the marsh side, stopping at the cuts to meet the younger man and see what finds he had made. Most of the good wood, he said, had been taken off the beach by the last high-course tide, but we loaded a few items, including a sound eight-by-ten-inch beam fourteen feet long. I picked up for myself a yellow fisherman's jacket in good condition except for tattered cuffs, and tried not to think too hard about where it might have come from.

I have no doubt that beach vehicle traffic, even when confined to the established sand road on the marsh side, helps to create accelerated erosion of a barrier spit like this by interfering with natural processes. A barrier beach normally maintains itself by building up its back slopes as the front dunes erode, retreating into the marsh or inlet behind it in an orderly and long-adapted manner. Constant vehicle traffic on the marsh side impedes this building up of sand on the back slope, and over the long run can result in the entire spit's becoming unnaturally thin and increasingly vulnerable to storms.

Indeed, the lowering of the inner road by heavy summer traffic has apparently allowed encroachment of the marsh on that side, forcing the beach buggies to create a new road higher up on the back side of the dunes, thereby destroying existing vegetation and further accelerating the attenuation of the spit. The danger is not that this road will eventually disappear, or even that these beach cottages and shacks may be swept away, but that the centuries-old marsh behind the spit, with its rich food factories and estuarine populations, will lose its natural protection.

The beachcomber, however, had that cheerful resignation of the

native about beach erosion. As we rumbled and bumped along the
sand road between the old shacks on the dunes and the colorful derelict boats in the marsh, he remarked casually, "Well, well, looks like
they moight have to move the Outermost House again. . . .That fella
moight get another summer or two out of his place if we don't get any
mo-ah bad storms. . . . Hear this place lost thurty feet durin' the last
blow . . ."—and so on, in a manner that suggested he was commenting
on the condition of their paint.

I asked him what he thought of the beach-buggy question, expecting to get a spirited defense of his "God-given" right to drive where he
wanted. Instead he shrugged his shoulders and said he didn't know,
but he suspected that the ocean would "settle the matter."

Three, maybe four generations of his family had walked, ridden,
and driven along this stretch of beach for the better part of a century.
Although I never asked his name, he might have been a descendant
of one of the same Coast Guardsmen Beston had entertained in the
Fo'castle on their night patrols during the 1920s.

Vehicles or not, one settles into a certain relationship with a place
over such a span. He seemed to me, in fact, as much a part of the continuity of this spit as the horned larks running along the winter beach,
the marsh hawk swooping low over the line of dunes, and the starlings
circling the marsh that the occupant of the Outermost House had
recorded in his time.

January 1978

AFTER THE STORM

When, along with hundreds of others, I arrived at a barricaded
Coast Guard Beach the morning after the storm, the air was
full of metaphors of war. The beach, people said, looked as though it
had been strafed and bombed. The line of wrecked cottages reminded

some of the older men of Dresden and other European cities after World War II. From one of the remaining cottages, just beyond where the parking lot had been, the owners were hurriedly loading boxes, blankets, and furniture into a waiting jeep. Someone said they looked like a family of refugees, or a small army unit retreating from a Pacific islet. Over the beach shack a tattered flag still flew bravely. The general consensus was that the scene was one of total destruction.

The images struck me as exaggerated and inexact, though they certainly expressed the sense of awesome power conveyed by the effects of monumental tides and massive surf. But why, I thought, this emphasis on destruction? Great storms, after all, are nothing new on this beach. In 1928 Henry Beston, describing his own stay on this beach in his classic book, *The Outermost House*, wrote of "the great northeast storm of February 19th and 20th" which, like this one, produced record tides and severe cuts in the dune walls of the barrier beach, islanding Beston's Fo'castle.

This storm, it is true, had extraordinary credentials. We were viewing the effects of what was termed "the Storm of the Century" and "the Great Blizzard of '78" by the media. Two days before, on February 6, an unprecedented winter storm, a hurricane in all but tropical origin, had struck southern New England, dumping thirty inches of snow on eastern Massachusetts, forty inches on Rhode Island, stranding twelve hundred commuters on Route 128 outside Boston, whose abandoned cars remained buried for several days. Car travel was banned in half the state for nearly a week, leaving many visitors marooned in expensive motels. There were several storm-related deaths, and more than thirty million dollars in damage to shorefront structures in the South Shore communities of Hull and Scituate.

On the Cape fourteen-and-a-half-foot tides were measured in Provincetown Harbor during the height of the storm on Monday, and ninety-two-mile-per-hour winds were recorded at the weather station in Chatham. But except for the ever-precarious beach cottages and some heavy flooding in Provincetown Harbor, we escaped relatively unscathed, compared with the wholesale inundation, loss of life, paralyzing snowfall, and severe damage inflicted on communities elsewhere on the coast.

Only on these outer barrier beaches, open to the full force of the storm surges, had the destruction been so complete. On Monday the storm had broken through the upper end of the beach, smashing apart the large National Seashore parking lot located there. The tide caught a Volkswagen lingering in the lot, swamped its engine, and floated it (minus its owner) out into the marsh, where it sank. The enormous waves heavily battered and undermined the public bathhouse, but the structure survived the first onslaught. The following day the massive surf rammed it again and again, while a crowd on the hill cheered with each crashing wave. (The building was finally torched by park rangers, afraid it might float off and become a navigational hazard.) The mile and a half of barrier dunes, having been weakened and set up earlier in the year by a series of powerful autumn storms, was virtually flattened. Storm surges cut sheer twenty-foot-high gouges in the dunes, and from Fort Hill across the marsh the long spit looked like a series of small mounded islands. Five of the eight remaining beach cottages were carried off. Some were totally destroyed, some had floated out and were sitting now like houseboats in the marsh. One had been carried all the way across to the town landing on the mainland side, a mile to the west.

One of those destroyed was the Outermost House. I first heard about it Tuesday morning when a friend called up and asked, "Did you hear the Outermost House perished?" All at once the storm turned serious, creating a loss that mattered. His choice of words was curiously appropriate. Its passing somehow deserved a term usually reserved for souls, thoughts, and principles of human liberty.

Now I stood with the crowd, looking down the changed beach, thinking of that house, whose remains had been scattered and swept out to sea through Nauset Inlet. Henry Beston would have understood and assented. Twenty years after his stay there "the little house, to whom the ocean has been kind," had already been moved back once from the beach. He had no expectations for its immortality. The house had been but the shell for the book. He knew where it was he lived.

At the end of *The Outermost House*, Beston makes his famous statement, "Creation is here and now." Its converse, of course, is that destruction is also here and now, and in this moment it seemed to be the stronger truth. But they are really two sides of the same coin, or rather, a single indistinguishable process that human beings have divided into "creative" and "destructive" forces to express its effects on their own interests.

It seemed to me that the beach, looked at dispassionately, might have suggested either. The major victims of the storm appeared to be the offshore beds of sea clams, tens of thousands of which had been dragged off the ocean bottom and now lay smashed and strewn along most of the spit. As far as the gulls now picking among them were concerned, the storm meant a bounty past reckoning.

Aside from the clams, however, and a half dozen lobster pots visible down the strand, the beaches were remarkably clean, a thousand times healthier than the lingering air of desolation and degradation that hangs over areas of human despoliation even before final abandonment and decay set in. Wide, clean plains of sand stretched across from ocean to marsh where walls of dune had stood the day before, spilling out in thick fans and pools into the marsh itself. It reminded me of old construction sites cleared away before new building began, a kind of marine urban renewal.

Often, after storms like this, the earth remembers itself. Out on those newly created sandy plains on the beach beyond the fragmented remains of the parking lot, I saw the curious shapes of a dozen or more galvanized well pipes sticking up out of the sand. They looked like strange periscopic life-forms, some with long black noses of plastic pipe hanging from their tops, such as might be imagined on a Martian desert. Several of these well pipes belonged to the cottages that had been swept away in the storm, but others represented former abandoned wells of the same buildings, or of others, which had been moved back or removed completely years ago.

There was also considerable evidence that erosion of the beach is not as straightforward or linear as we sometimes like to think. In one place, at the base of an eroded dune wall, a rusty old hand pump had emerged, indicating that the beach had built up some eight to ten feet since the pump was originally set. The storm had thrown up some large logs onto the beach, but it had also exposed others that had been buried in the dune wall and now stuck out from its face like huge cannons, suggesting that here too the beach had been much lower in a previous epoch.

An even more curious thing happened. On the way out to the beach, I had stopped at the Fort Hill overlook and scanned the Outer Beach across the marsh with binoculars. At the far end of the spit I spotted the blackened ribs of a small boat. It must have been exhumed by the storm, for it had not been there a week ago when I had last walked the beach. The following morning I walked the ruined beach again and could find no sign of it. Resurrected for a day, it was apparently broken up and carried off by the next high tide.

By far the most remarkable manifestation of previous lives here was just under our noses as we crowded the barricade on the road above the former parking lot. For years the asphalt bordering this road on the ocean side has been gradually crumbling away during storms. Beneath the asphalt is the surface of an earlier parking lot and, below this, several feet of beach sand. Underlying the sand is a ten-to-fifteen-foot bank of clayey glacial till, reddish in color and capped with a black sticky material, stepping down in layers to the beach.

Early on the morning after the storm, in the top layer of this clay till, the clawing surf had exposed the remains of two ancient Indian fire pits, about three feet across, containing rocks, charcoal, flint chips, bits of bones, and other artifacts. Normally such a find would have precipitated delight and a prolonged, careful archaeological excavation with sieves and toothbrushes. In the face of the rising tide, however, no such approach was possible, and the reaction was one of controlled panic. For an instant the sea had opened up a deep chapter in the earth's memory and would close it forever in another. Park rangers and volunteers shoveled the pits out pell-mell, hoisted their contents on boards up to the road surface, and threw chunks of prehistory into a government pickup while the diggers jumped out of the way of the crashing surf. When I arrived late in the morning, the round, excavated pits, sheared cleanly into cross-sections, were still visible, but when I returned two days later to show them to a friend, even the outlines were gone.

What are we to make of these fossils and artifacts, well pipes, pumps, logs, buried ships, and Indian pits? It is true that in the long run the Cape is losing ground, or at least attenuating, century by century. But along its edges, at least, the processes are not so simple. Average rates of erosion are just that: averages. Some beaches, especially at the extremes of the Outer Cape and along the bay shores, are actually accreting and extending. But on barrier beaches such as this one, its dunes riddled with present destruction and pieces of our forgotten past, there is an oscillation that should make us wary of classifying them too quickly as either retreating or building, for they have done both before and are likely to do so again.

Finally, there were impressive examples of the sea's insistence on revealing not only human history but its own geologic past. At Race Point in Provincetown, for instance, the sea broke through the dike that was built decades ago across the inner side of Hatches Harbor, flooding the valley behind it, on whose floor the municipal airport had since been built, submerging the runways and advancing to within a few feet of the terminal building itself. By doing so it reasserted its claim to the original extent of "Race Run," a long, narrow tidal estuary that flowed there in the early part of this century.

So humans make cosmetic changes on the shoreline, building dikes and sea walls, filling in swamps and marshes, dredging harbors and rechanneling streams. But the older, deeper currents continue to run in the daily tides, like the schools of alewives that are said to swarm and beat each spring against entrances to ancestral spawning grounds that we have blocked off for generations. These currents carry a deep, insistent earth memory that sometimes breaks out during major storms into sudden consciousness. And when the waters finally recede we are left staring across an unfamiliar landscape to redefine our human world as best we might.

February 6–8, 1978

THE WRECK OF THE *JOSEPHIA*

At about four this morning the *Josephia*, a thirty-nine-foot scallop vessel out of Stoughton, Maine, went aground just north of the old Eastham Coast Guard Station, breaking up and forcing its two-man crew—Michael Darragh, thirty-four, and his brother-in-law, Ian Orchard, thirty-two—along with Orchard's one-year-old pug, Leo—to swim for shore in high seas and thirty-eight-degree water. Miraculously all three made it ashore alive.

Darragh was found by Sgt. Robert Schutzer of the Eastham Police Department, who was patrolling the beach in the predawn dark, after having been alerted by the Coast Guard of a vessel in distress. Schutzer said he spotted Darragh by the reflection of his flashlight on Darragh's life vest "less than a mile away." He was "soaking and freezing," but alive. Darragh was holding Leo, whom he had found safe, though "with a bit of water in her lungs."

A search for Orchard then ensued, involving the Coast Guard, the National Park Service, a helicopter, and emergency personnel from Orleans, Eastham, Wellfleet, and Truro, but after four hours there was no sign of the missing man. Then Sergeant Schutzer noticed a broken window just to the right of the porch of the empty former

Coast Guard Station. The rescue team went inside. There they found Orchard, who had broken in, stood under a hot shower "for a long time," wrapped himself in a window curtain, and "passed out from exhaustion." Ironically, the Coast Guard Station, though decommissioned more than a half century ago, had nonetheless played a direct role in saving one of the men by serving as a kind of oversized charity hut with running hot water.

The police called Orchard's wife (who is Darragh's sister) in Maine. She said that when she heard her husband's voice, "He sounded awesome, he said it was really scary." Darragh was described in the *Boston Globe*'s account of the wreck as "an urchin diver."* He had gone south into Cape waters with Ian in search of scallops, hoping to make up for a poor urchin season in Maine that had resulted from "bad weather and overfishing," according to his mother, Dawn Gray. At that time Chatham scallopers were getting from nine to ten dollars a pound.

Curiously, this was Darragh's third life-threatening accident in the last few years. Two years earlier he and his wife, Laura, were forced to jump into the ocean when his boat went aground at Bar Harbor, and the previous winter, according to the story in the *Boston Globe*, "while he was sleeping in his house in Maine, a wood-burning stove caught fire. He managed to crawl out his bedroom window as the fire engulfed the house." A photo accompanying the story showed him and Orchard, "presumably" at Orchard's wedding. In the photo Darragh is a good-looking chap with a clean-shaven face, but, given his history, he doesn't sound like a good bet for either seafaring or domestic life. Still, his mother said that both men are likely to return to the sea. "I'd rather they didn't, but I'll just pray them through."

March 2006

---

* A curious word, "urchin." In this case it's short for "sea urchin," a spiny echinoderm. It is also a term for a hedgehog, and a "mischievous child or scamp," though the origin of this last definition remains obscure.

NIGHT CASTING

On Sunday my friend Adam called me up and asked if I'd like to go surf fishing for striped bass that evening. I said sure and met him at Coast Guard Beach about five thirty.

It was a calm, overcast day in the high sixties, and I was surprised to find the overlook parking lot nearly full and people still down on the beach in sweaters. There were one or two other fishermen getting their gear out, including a somewhat grizzled character who wore thick glasses and shorts that revealed very white legs with thin tattoos running down the outside of his ankles. He accosted us amiably, saying, "No point in you fellas goin' out—I aim to catch 'em all." Then he went on to tell us how green he was, so green he put a trout leader on his line the other night and the fish broke it. He tried to hold onto the leader, while a friend tried to gaff the fish. A wave knocked him down and started to draw him out, and but he was hauled in by a surfer. I told him I didn't know a trout leader from the glee-club leader. He was carrying a vintage red Bernzomatic white-gas pump lantern, which he said was as old as he was. He looked like Demosthenes searching for an honest man.

We walked down the outside beach, and I realized how long it had been since I had been out here. The dune line seems no larger, but a wide forebeach of more than 150 feet stretched out in front of us. The surf was fairly high and barreling into the shore, though high tide was still more than three hours away. We walked quickly past most of the beachgoers, who were beginning to head in, and stopped about one-third of a mile down the beach near a few other casters.

In nearly thirty years of living here I had never been surf fishing, but I soon got the hang of it. We used two-hook leaders, each rig about eighteen inches apart, with a three-ounce pyramidal lead weight on the bottom. Adam was using "live" dead sand eels—slender, eel-like fish about six inches long. Each baitfish was hooked through the eye and its body slid along the curve of the hook until the point and barb emerged through the anus. The idea is that the weight sits on the bottom, and the motion of the waves moves the baitfish about, attracting feeding stripers. (Some fishermen, Adam said, use actual live eels, hooked through the lips, but this seemed somewhat cruel to him.) The aim is to cast your line beyond the breakers, about 100 to 250 feet out, set the drag to a light pole, set the butt of the pole into a plastic sleeve set in the sand, and wait for a strike.

The stretch of beach we cast from had a strong longshore current running south that quickly pulled the line sharply to the right and into breaking surf, so that we had to recast regularly. It was already dusk and growing dark, and soon we could no longer see the cast hit or the angle of the line, but played it by feel. We got no strikes, and our bait seem to be tumbling in the surf, ripping it up somewhat, so we decided to move down the beach.

We continued down past the last of the low dunes and out onto the broad, flat sandy plain that was even more expansive than I had remembered it. The evening was nearly completely calm, and dark enough so that things appeared and disappeared as dark shapes. A large flock of gulls flew by coughing huskily, and I could hear a few yellowlegs whistling among them. Then a large black shape detached itself from the rim of a tidal lagoon and spread huge wings into the dark evening sky—a great blue.

To the west, across Nauset Marsh, a thin line of lights appeared on the far shore. I thought of Henry Beston out here, looking at the scattered lights of Eastham village from his little dune cottage seventy years before. The lights are different now, more numerous and brighter, and the flattened dunes are a mere suggestion of what the lifesaving crew saw when they walked down the night beach on patrol from the old Coast Guard Station, but the essence, and the effect on us, was the same: a sense of vast exposure, and visible distance from the haunts of men, a freewheeling, circulating life, a place of primal gestations.

We cast over and over into the calm, glassy swells, getting no strikes, so we set our poles and sat at the top of the berm. Adam broke out some lamb stew, and I shared my glass flask of Laphroaig. We sat there, two writers, sharing shoptalk.

After a while we reeled in and walked farther down the outer shore, near the inlet, where the waves seemed to be rolling in with increased force. Adam said the stripers feed closer in to shore at night, and even come into the inlet and the marsh, "scooping up everything in sight" at slack high tide. Now the moon had broken through the clouds and shone with a full hazy light down onto the rolling surface of the sea. We stopped at a spot with a steep berm down to the surf and what appeared to be a deep pool between the outer bar and shore, and cast out. The tide was coming in fast now, so that every five to ten minutes we had to move our poles and gear farther back up the slope of the berm. At one point Adam reeled in a striper, a twenty-four-incher, but the minimum size had been raised to twenty-eight inches, so he threw it back. Another time he got an even heavier strike, the pole bending strongly, but the line broke as he tried to bring it in. He shouted, "Dammit!" knowing it was a keeper.

I got nothing, but the line stayed out straight here, and after a while we sat on the top of the berm. The whole surface seemed more agitated here, near the inlet, a great multifarious river of overlapping sounds, like Beston's "people of the sea."

At last the waves began topping the berm, sliding down the tilt of the sandy plain toward the marsh—great foamy sliding rafts of water rumbling about our ankles and calves, slithering and disappearing into the dark sands. We were washed and washed again in the foamy overflow of the waves, "like being on the rim of a champagne glass," as Adam put it, and indeed there was something tippling and intoxicating about it. There was a softness, a gauziness to everything here such as I had never known on the beach before, so that the presence or absence of fish did not really matter, as it shouldn't. It seemed as if we stood on some far shore, desultorily engaged in one of the few interactions with the wild that still requires little effort or skill. Our black poles sat in their black sockets, and only a slight bend and rocking of the tips registering the movement of the weight along the bottom let us know we were tied by an invisible filament to the tumult of the waves beyond.

At about nine we reeled in, pulled up pole holders, and headed back. There was no one else left on the beach. Across the marsh the soft lights still shone, and only their faint reflections in the flood tide let me know where sand left off and water began. We were now on a fairly thin wavering tail of sand, only one hundred yards wide or so, and in the dark air above the water there was a familiar cloud of sound. It was, I realized, the bristling chirping of tree swallows, migrating, as many land birds do, at night. (A friend of mine told me that he has observed gulls at sea forcing migrating land birds down into the waves, and then gobbling them up.) The sound filled the air, adding an excitement to the marsh that the agitated surf did to the shore.

Ahead of us the bright shaft of Nauset Light punctuated the night, followed by several burps of white and red before slashing out again, and I thought that I was now in a minority of those who remember its former triple beam, which was itself a tribute to the original "Three Sisters," the three small separate lighthouses that Thoreau remarked on when he walked this beach. And thinking of Thoreau, it occurred to me that the difference between Walden Pond and the Outer Beach is that Walden was made extraordinary by the book that recorded Thoreau's attachment to it, whereas, although Coast Guard Beach is certainly enhanced by Beston's book about it, it is not defined by it. It is extraordinary in itself, so that many generations of celebrants can and do drink from it.

September 2011

AN UNNAMED COAST

Few things on the Outer Beach last long enough to acquire a name. Unlike, say, the coast of Maine, the sea here tends to erase quickly all physical evidence of specific sites and events. As a result the number of names associated with the Cape's Atlantic shoreline is relatively few. There are perhaps a dozen or so large natural features on the Outer Beach that have acquired familiar and accepted names. These include Long Point, Race Point, Head of the Meadow, the Clay Pounds, Long Nook, Pamet, Newcomb, Cahoon, and LeCount Hollows, Coast Guard Beach, Nauset Spit, North Beach, and finally the constantly shifting incarnations of Monomoy Island.

And that's about it. Beyond these geological macrofeatures, little endures on the beach long enough to be officially labeled. Sand castles, messages in the sand, little stick figures, the charred remains of beach parties, last only until the next tide. Whales beach and, if not removed, are usually reclaimed by the sea within days or weeks. Their bones do not remain exposed for decades as they do on rockier or more protected shores. Farther up the time scale, summer beach sculptures and edifices made from driftwood and other found material may last a season or more. Beach cottages, if they're lucky, may remain for decades, but not much longer. Oddly, the well pipes of these vanished cottages often do last much longer, protruding from the cliff faces and dunes, sucking air now instead of water. Lighthouses last, but only by being relocated farther inland from time to time.

Ironically, the structures that may last the longest of all on the beach do so only after they have ceased to have any function. I'm talking of the carcasses of old wooden ships that were wrecked on the Outer Beach and subsequently buried in the sands. Years, decades, even centuries later, they are occasionally uncovered by wind and wave and show their old bones to new and wondering eyes

But the beach itself remains largely nameless. In fact you cannot even step onto the same beach twice. It is literally a river of sand, always changing, always moving. The most we can do is to impose our own personal nomenclature on its featureless length. Over the years I've done this, attaching invented names to the various places, objects, and events I've encountered there. I have no illusions that these names will last any longer than hundreds of other names that once attached to its shifting sands. Already many of the features and structures that have been part of my history here no longer exist, or have changed beyond recognition, but no matter. The Outer Beach may not support the rich assortment of historical names that decorate more enduring coastlines, but it is *our* beach nonetheless, and I find it fitting that it has become a National Seashore. For it is so axiomatically American, this beach. With each night tide it wipes out our history, providing us with a clean slate in the morning, our sins and soiled lives washed clean, with its corollary that nothing here lasts much beyond the day.

June 2012

7

....

Nauset Light Beach

CULTIVATING ECSTASY

When I arrived at the ocean beach the other day, a southeast gale had been blowing all morning, warm and welcome after a week of cold northerly winds. It had been raining earlier, but now it had turned into a drying wind. I stood on the edge of the bluff overlooking the beach, the sand stinging my eyes. At the very edge the wind was so strong that I could lean ten or fifteen degrees into it, resting my body on its strength.

Below me, running across the face of the cliffs, were wide bands of muddy brownish clay alternating with narrower strips of hard blue clay. At the bottom of the slope the softer sand spread out into wide deltas, while at the top a matted growth of grass, shrubs, and weeds grew a foot or two out over the undercut rim, suspended in air, and the wind tore at the exposed and salt-blackened roots.

Dark surf and somber clouds marched in together from the sea like complementary armies. The tide was still low, exposing a few rocks, but was starting to climb. I made my way down to the beach, which had the look of an abandoned frontier. No remnant of summer remained; the beach had cleansed itself, and there were fresh, raw gouges at the base of the cliff.

The waves themselves seemed to be held or pressed down by the weight of the wind, and I walked calmly down to the edge, fancying myself one of the winter shorebirds, slipping easily in and out of the seethe.

For an hour or more I walked north, indifferently beachcombing, while the tide crept in. I picked up a small coil of copper wire, a beautiful, highly-striated piece of black granite, and what appeared to be a small piece of whale baleen. Earlier this fall, on another beach walk, I had picked up a small surf clam and stuck it in the pocket of my windbreaker, intending to have it with dinner that night. But I forgot about it and, four weeks later, on another walk, I reached into my pocket and found it there, still alive (a Jonah among clams!), and threw it back into the surf.

Farther along, the beach became wider. The previous high tide had chewed away a four-foot-high cut at its front edge. Now the tide, rising again, began to throw waves up over this barrier of its own making, making lakes and rivers of an hour on the upper beach. Here was time-lapse geology, where river mouths and spillways of Cascadian proportions formed and dissolved again in a matter of minutes. I saw large logs tossed about and lost in the muddy tumult. Loose lines of geese hurried south directly overhead, their beaks into the wind, long necks undulating.

At one point the rising tide was reaching the base of the scarp, so I climbed up the face of it, about twenty feet or so, and as I did I felt the whole slope move beneath me. At the bottom there was nothing but air and water, no firm footing beneath me. I shook and grabbed some of the salt-blackened branches of beach-plum bushes that had already slid halfway to death. Slowly and with a few more false starts, I picked my way across to safety. So often only a slight slipping of our standing undermines our whole perspective.

Farther north, where the glacial scarp curved westward out of sight, I could see the black outline of a tree, suspended over the edge of the cliff, frozen in the act of falling. Below it all was a whirling yellow haze, blurred by wind and sand. In that strange apocalyptic light, I seemed to be watching creation falling into oblivion, only to be refunded again into new creation. Once again I found myself standing on the edge of mystery, and I felt that in such a place as this it was both possible and fitting to cultivate ecstasy.

October 1973

BEACH GRASS SPROUTS
ON THE CLIFFS

I saw a remarkable phenomenon the other day out on the eroding cliff face near Nauset Light. Halfway down the slope were clumps of beach grass that had been growing there or had been cut under and dragged down from the ridge above. These clumps now rested in loose, moving soil in a kind of limbo, neither firmly fixed in nor totally exposed by the earth. What was remarkable was that in the center of each clump of leprous-brown bent blades that characterize the grass this time of year, was a center of new sprouts—hard, thorn-tipped, bright green spears of growth. It was almost as though the plant could sense that it would never see another spring, and, instead of accepting death passively, was sending new growth out and over the brink of oblivion. Who knows what gestures the beach grass is capable of? Perhaps these plants would survive the slide toward death and recolonize on another stretch of beach? Who knows the prosaic answer? We call plants fixed, but how many of us would undertake such a journey with such green hope in our hearts?

November 1973

AN OLD FRIEND VISITS

Over the holiday weekend I was visited by an old friend from the Berkshires who at the moment is undergoing a crisis of sorts, both personal and professional. He recently lost his teaching job in a local high school, his marriage is deteriorating, and he seems to have lost his bearings. In short, his life seems to have gone awry. But he wanted to talk, and so late one afternoon, in descending dark and light snowflakes, we drove up to Nauset Light Beach in Eastham and walked along the barrier beach. The sea kept us ceaseless company.

As we talked, he seemed to be fighting for a sense of individual significance in a world focused on abstract mass crises. He seemed to be looking for someone to tell him that he'd made some of the right choices, that his existence had mattered and had some form to it. He was, as we all are at times, close to being overwhelmed by life. I reassured him as best I could, but I knew I could not really solve anything for him.

He is from the hills of western New England, the mountains of the Berkshires and Vermont. He was formed by them, as were his father and his father's father. He belongs to that place in a way I can never belong here. I got to know him when, for a few years, he lived and taught here on the Cape. But even then he was always mocking us as "flatlanders," and he returned to the hills as soon as he could. He trusted their laconic solidity and unmoving expanse, and now that trust seems to have failed him.

I think I took him to the beach that winter's day to show him that it offered a truer image of the human condition. One's foundations continually shift here; the sea regularly breaks through in new places, constantly forming new inlets, closing off old ones, running in new currents. The beach teaches us the need to adapt continually to change, always to be watching for undertows and rogue waves, to dance nimbly along its edges. If I have learned anything from living here, it is that this world is not geared for large answers, and certainly not for final ones.

I didn't say any of this to him, of course. Most men tend to speak indirectly, obliquely, about such matters. But I knew he understood what I was trying to show him that day on the beach, as I knew that he would reject it. For it is, after all, the place where we live that gives us the metaphors we live by, whether we're born to a place or choose to make it our home. If I were to live by aesthetics alone I would probably live where he does, among mountains, for I actually prefer them to the low grandeur of the sea. But the sea tells me more about myself, as the hills do him, and so that is why each of us chooses to live where we do.

He left the next day, and seemed glad to be going home. We both knew that he'd have to continue to take his chances in an uncertain world. The hills may temporarily seem to have failed him, but he would never leave them. They are *his* hills, they belong to him as he belongs to them, and, just as I seek solace and reassurance from the beach, it is from the hills that he will have to find new patterns for his life.

January 1974

THE HOUSE ON THE BLUFF

The U.S. government now measures change from bluff erosion at Nauset Light Beach by means of a newly installed concrete brass benchmark set fifty feet or so back from the cliff edge about a quarter mile north of the parking lot. My own personal erosion benchmark in this region is a small beach cottage located along these same bluffs, just north of Nauset Light and about fifty feet above the beach.

I first discovered the cottage after a December northeaster five years ago and was struck then by its proximity to the cliffs and the rapid erosion taking place there. I measured the distance from the seaward side of the building to the edge of the bluff that day, and I have measured it every day since. In 1971 the distance was fifty-one feet; in 1973 it was forty-three feet; this year it is thirty-five feet.

There are any number of places along the thirty-mile stretch of the Cape's Outer Beach that provide more dramatic examples of the ocean's power, but this small cottage remains my personal yardstick of destruction, perhaps because the effects are so immediate and on such human terms. It's one of the older cottages in the area and has probably housed several summer generations. I would guess they've been the same family, too, for the humble structure has a settled, cared-for look, a comfortable informality and an affectionate aversion to modernization.

Worn paths run from the house across a small yard and out to the cliff. I wonder how far out these paths once ran, onto what is now empty air. When I first came here there was a crude bench placed at the cliff edge, but it was gone the following year. Recently a protective railing has been erected, but it doesn't look as if it will last the winter.

I have never met the family that summers here, for I only come here in winter, nor do I even know their name. Yet I feel I know them well and that we share a common interest or concern. I sometimes wish I could leave them some cheering message, something like, "Watching out for your interests, late winter 1975. All is as it is." Perhaps I only choose this place in order to have something constant to return to each year on this restless shore. At any rate, with only twenty-two feet left, its own lifespan now appears increasingly coincident with those of many of my friends and acquaintances, perhaps even my own. (We fool ourselves with "average" lifespans the same way we do with "average" rates of erosion, thinking they apply to specific cases.)

Peering over the brink I can see the insatiable fury of the breakers ending in patient nibbles at the base of the cliff. Loose lines of geese hurry south directly overhead, and a few gulls fly up like ashes from the sands.

One can plainly see that the days of this cottage are numbered. Its back is already up against the wall—or rather, the cliff road—and there's no place left to go. The well house in the yard now sits no more than ten feet from the edge of the precipice; soon it will be sucking dry air, or, at most, salt spray. The east windows, empty eyes of the house, can even now look down into the storm surf.

No amount of zoning regulations or No Trespassing signs will keep the sea from its own brand of development on this spot, or from its eventual taking of the house by an incontestable eminent domain. Surely, a diligent tax assessor would be kept busy here, adjusting his books, trying to strike a balance between increasing land values and decreasing land. And yet this cottage's family, whoever they are, will at least know its evictor well by the time the mortgage falls due in another dozen or so bittersweet years.

November 1975

SAND SPOUTS

Not far from Nauset Light in North Eastham, there is a section of beach cliff dramatically scored and pitted by erosion. When I arrived there recently, a southeast gale had been blowing all morning. It was warm and welcome after several days of cold, wet weather. The rain from earlier that morning had now turned to a drying wind, so that my eyes were stung with beach sand before I got within thirty yards of the bluff. At the very edge the wind was so strong that I could lean several degrees into it, resting my body on its strength. At the bottom of the slope the sand had spread out into wide deltas, while at the top a mat of grass, shrubs, and weeds grew a foot or two out over the undercut rim, suspended in air, while the wind tore at the exposed and salt-blackened roots.

I carefully made my way down the face of the ancient cliff to the beach. From there, looking back up toward the top, I observed a phenomenon I had heard of but had never seen: the so-called sand spouts of the Outer Beach. These are produced when strong, dry easterly winds blow fine sand up the face of the scarp. From a few feet below the rim, small geysers of sand seemed to materialize, whirl like dervishes for a few seconds, and then shoot up over the edge and stream away in the wind.

Ordinarily this fine sand is stopped and collects at the top of the slope, trapped by the overhanging lip of plant roots. This supply of "purified" sand eventually dries out and begins to flow down the face of the cliff like water, creating those interesting sand rivers and sand falls one often sees during a calm dry spell following an easterly blow. Sometimes, however, these pockets of sand will dry out while the wind continues to blow strongly from the east. When this occurs, as it did now, a stream of fine sand will begin to descend from just under the rim. When it reaches a light lip or irregularity in the cliff face, however, the wind will flick it up into the air and over the rim, so that it appears to erupt or spout out of the cliff itself. Over time, in certain places, these sand spouts can deposit substantial amounts of beach sand on the upland behind the cliff, actually creating a band of low sand dunes fifty or a hundred feet above the beach. One of the best places to see this phenomenon is the stretch of sand barrens between Marconi Beach and the Marconi Site in South Wellfleet.

So the tides do not always end at the edge of the surf. The waves move sand up onto the beach, where the wind may take over, sending beach sand flowing up and down the face of the cliff itself, breaking through at times where even the highest storm tides never rise, spouting and showering the upland with sprays of gale-winnowed sand.

October 1977

THE LESSON IS ALWAYS CHANGE

I arrived early one winter morning at the Nauset Light parking lot, where a handful of draggers that had already been out for hours showed clearly a few miles offshore in the predawn light. Farther out, and much larger, were the hulls of ships with what looked like lighted towers atop them. Tankers? Ships carrying oil rigs? Will we one day look out from these bluffs and be able to see permanent towers along the horizon on some of the proposed oil tracts less than twenty miles offshore? I felt for a moment as one of the Nauset Indians might have felt, nearly four hundred years ago, spotting the first English or French towers of sail off the empty coast.

The reflectored lights of Nauset still whirled their patterns of three into the dying night. The seashore plaque at the head of the stairs, telling of its history, was nearly buried in winter-driven sand. The stairs themselves were heaped in snowlike sand drifts as I waded down through them, past the Facilities Closed sign on the washrooms. As I came to the bottom of the stairs the dawn broke upward through a rose funnel of clouds, flooding the stairs and the beach so suddenly with clean, bright light that I grabbed onto the railing as though a wave had struck.

But the tide was low, the bluffs gave shelter from a stiff northwest wind, and a wide ice path invited walking. I headed south, toward Coast Guard Beach, beneath a gradually descending headland. The cliff face wore a ragged look of recent erosion, exposing clear the cocked strata of glacial till with wide alluvial fans spreading out at the bottom. These layers lie in different planes from the ones in which they were originally deposited, twisted, crushed, and uplifted by the force of subterranean pressures and subsequent glaciers.

A few small boulders, recently fallen out of the cliff face, lay on the upper beach, along with several large chunks of iron conglomerates, curious rust-colored masses of gravel and pebbles loosely cemented together with leached iron oxide. This is not the bog iron of our swamps and peat bogs, but seems to occur where a layer of gravel has been laid down on top of an impervious layer of clay. Surface water leaching down through the upper till carries iron-oxide particles down to the clay-gravel interface, where they precipitate and bind together the pebbles, creating these conglomerates, which gradually erode out of the cliff face.

There were, as well, chunks and ledges of the underlying blue clay lying about the base of the cliff. In places the iron-oxide mixture had coated them with a thin layer, like a sheathing of rusted sheet metal that I could pull off in crumbling plates. Some of the clay chunks had rounded, sculptured edges where it had melted and flowed in the rising surf, but now it lay frozen and hard, like dumped concrete. No homogeneous "sand cliff," this.

The tide was now quite low, and the beach berm rather steep, so that I was surprised at one point to come across a thin gully of tidewater apparently draining back down across the upper beach. Then I saw that the small stream was not seeping out of the beach but issuing from a spot some six feet up the face of the cliff. It was a spring—a freshwater spring, flowing here on the Outer Beach!

I cannot explain why I was so surprised, so strangely and disproportionately cheered at the appearance of this spring on the ragged, ancient, dry face of the cliff. The phenomenon in itself was not hard to explain. The groundwater was no doubt collecting above a layer of clay in the bluff and finding release at this point. There must be many such springs, from time to time, issuing from different parts of this retreating bluff, though I like to think that perhaps, at this moment in time, this one might be the only source of fresh water flowing openly into the Atlantic along the entire length of the Outer Beach from Long Point to Monomoy Point.

Though thirst was among the least of my discomforts on the beach that morning, I took off my glove, cupped my hand into that freezing water, and drank. It was—sandy! I looked up, and there, directly above the spring, a small sand fall was trickling down the cliff face and mixing its Aeolian grains into the flowing water.

Leaving the spring, I continued walking south along the beach from Nauset Light. About a quarter mile before actually reaching Coast Guard Beach, there is an abrupt change from coastal bluff to coastal dune. This is signaled in part by a sudden drop in the height of the cliff, from about fifty feet to twenty, but also by a less obvious change in appearance and vegetation. Compared with the twisted, ice-tilted glacial strata on the cliff face, the windblown layers of sand on the dunes' seaward side are in a roughly horizontal plane. The vegetation on their crests and back slopes is sparser, too, mostly beach grass and poverty grass.

Though they are lower and less firmly covered, these dunes look less "destroyed" than the adjoining bluffs. This is due to a further, and even more important, difference between them, though one that is harder to see over short periods: a difference in their behavior in the face of the advancing ocean. Dunes "give." That is, they slope themselves more readily, assuming what is called a storm profile, to disperse the force of large waves. Bluffs, on the other hand, are relatively static features, and so receive the full brunt of the winter surf directly. In addition, a healthy, undisturbed line of primary (sea-facing) dunes tends to keep a fairly constant shape as it retreats, similar to an advancing wave but in reverse, building up in back as it wears down in front.

In this sense, then, the barrier-beach system of Coast Guard Beach really begins here, a good quarter mile north of the public beach access, though there is a section of low glacial cliff still farther along, on which the old Coast Guard Station sits. Anyone who looks at the topographical map, however, or simply peers over the top of this first set of dunes, will realize that the station actually sits atop a glacial island, or clay "wart," connected to the mainland by a low line of fluid dunes, a tenuous road, a wet swale, and a fringe of Nauset Marsh.

This last low section of clay bluff and the beach it fronts are infused with millennia of human history. Seaward, below the high-tide line, lie large pieces of concrete, the remains of an abortive attempt at erosion control by the Cape Cod National Seashore several years ago. On the upper beach, sections of asphalt from the large parking lot destroyed in the Great Blizzard of '78 are scattered among chunks of broken clay. Toward the top of the bluff I could see an exposed layer of another, older parking lot, a slightly undulating tar-black ribbon three inches thick, covered by a thicker layer of windblown sand, so that now it looks like just another glacial stratum.

Turning from the beach, I climbed the road to the top of the clay hill, and stood in the lee of the Coast Guard Station to get a good look at the barrier beach stretching south. A Seashore plaque next to the building informed me that the first Nauset Life-Saving Station, built in 1872, lay "350 yards southeast of this site"—a spot long under water. Encroachment of the sea had forced it to be moved inland, but in 1937 the second location was so endangered that the present building was built on the top of the hill. (It was last manned by the Coast Guard in 1947.)

I had watched this spit being battered during the '78 storm, two years ago, and had walked it several times since, but somehow I was not prepared for what I saw that morning, in the clear winter sunlight. Perhaps it was the foreshortened perspective, decreasing its attenuated length even more, and emphasizing the extent of the overwashes into the marsh. Perhaps it was because, with the ban on motor traffic since the storm, we have been told repeatedly that this beach is "recovering" and "rebuilding."

But expectations and perspective aside, it looked, in the dawn light, as though almost nothing were there. Along its entire mile-and-a-half length only a single, token chunk of dune ridge remains, isolated in a pooled vastness of flat sand, reaching far back into the marsh, flecked here and there with bits of human debris: chairs, bricks, a gas stove trimmed with marsh grass. Nothing else.

The effect of desolation was heightened by the recent removal of two of the four remaining beach cottages. At one time there were a dozen cottages and hunting shacks along its length. Several, of course, were swept off during the 1978 storm, including Henry Beston's Fo'castle. One of these still lies, white and hollow-eyed, on a hummock halfway across the marsh. Of the two removed last month, one was carted off on a flatbed trailer, to be relocated inland. The other, so I read, was severely damaged and was deliberately demolished, with the hopes of rebuilding it later on some remaining bits of the owner's upland property.

But now only two cottages remain, both near the north end of the spit. I viewed them through my binoculars, one heavily boarded up, as though under siege, the other open and looking more resigned to its fate. I could not quite bring them into focus, however. There was a fuzziness to their edges, and I wondered if something was wrong with my glasses or whether the cottages were in fact real or only ghost houses. Then I realized that the fuzziness was the effect of a small sandstorm on the barrier beach, set in motion by the wind blowing across the exposed marsh. Two winters ago the sea rose in violence and washed tons of sand out onto the marsh. Now the wind is taking it, grain by flying grain, back out to sea again. How, in such a place as this, do we know which way to lean?

As I pondered the fate of this beach and its remaining human habitations, I was suddenly surprised to hear noises, doors banging, and sleepy voices in the building right behind me. I had forgotten, in my preoccupation with the barrier beach, the old Coast Guard Station's new role these days as the Seashore's Environmental Education Center. I walked around to the back of the building where a yellow school bus, with "BROOKLINE PUBLIC SCHOOLS" painted on its side, sat in the parking lot. Through the windows of the old station, frosted with the condensation of human breath, I could see the clouded forms of young schoolgirls in flannel pajamas lying on the bunk beds from which Beston's rugged "surf men" had risen at all hours at all seasons, to patrol the beach.

Where, and what, I wondered, would all this be when these girls are grandmothers? Still, in this changing succession of human use and human possession—with one foot on the bus, so to speak—are we not closer to the spirit of this place, to the custom and habit of the old Cape, than those who argue either for permanent occupation or total abandonment? We possess best by knowing when to let go, and when to return.

I left them and started back toward Nauset Light by way of the shore road, walking between stands of bayberry and bearberry, salt-burned cedar, and circumscribing blades of beach grass. Rabbits and flickers, with their white rumps showing, ran through the underbrush and flitted across the dunes, while a small flock of myrtle warblers flashed spots of winter yellow as they wheeled over the bushes.

At one point I came upon a pitch pine, more a spreading bush than a tree, about eighteen inches high and more than ten feet across, clinging to the back side of a dune. One of its lower branches had been snapped off in a recent storm. I cut the branch clean with my knife and counted the tight rings. There were nearly thirty, on a branch a little over an inch thick. This tree, not all that much younger than myself, would endure here but would not remain. This is no place for permanence. Only those things that come and go, that change, or are allowed to, can remain: the ocean, the dunes, the dancing myrtle warblers, and, if we permit it, ourselves as well.

January 1980

THE THREE SISTERS

In 1839, three brick lighthouse towers provided protection along the North Eastham coast. Henry David Thoreau, during his rambles on Cape Cod, noted that the three lights identified Nauset, but thought this "costly." In 1892, all three toppled into the remorseless sea. So strong was custom and habit that they were replaced by three wooden towers in 1911, and in 1923 this red and white sentinel was moved here from Chatham.

—NATIONAL SEASHORE PLAQUE AT NAUSET LIGHT

This morning I drove down to the parking lot at Nauset Light, wide and bright and completely empty. An offshore storm had passed by a couple of days before, and a stiff southwest wind was blowing, so that large horse breakers with tossing manes plunged toward shore. The surf appeared completely foam-white, almost dry, for several hundred yards out, so that in its slow slide toward shore it had the appearance not of water but of snow, not of surf but of an avalanche slowly gaining speed, powerful, majestic, and white.

When I descended the stairs to the beach, it was completely flattened and cleared by the storms. A wide, flat, undisturbed sheen of water stretched more than fifty yards from the base of the cliff to the surf's edge, marked only by isolated fragments of sea clams. Because of the beach's flatness and slight incline (the summer berm removed, the winter berm not yet formed), the surf rolled in more than a hundred feet with each surge, keeping the sand wet and firm to walk on.

I walked north until I came upon a large object on the beach below the light, and a man standing examining it. It turned out to be one of the old Three Sisters foundations, exposed from time to time, which I had not seen for several years. The "Three Sisters" was the name given to the original trio of brick lighthouses, built in 1838, that stood on this bluff when Thoreau passed here in 1849. His reaction is frequently cited to confirm his reputation for miserliness: "There were so many that they might be distinguished from the others; but this seemed a shiftless and costly way of accomplishing that object." These original lights fell into the sea in 1892, and despite Thoreau's criticism, three more wooden lights were constructed to replace them. These were replaced by the current Nauset Light in 1923, which itself had been moved from Chatham, where it had served as one of the twin towers there. After the Cape Cod National Seashore was established in 1961, the former Three Sisters wooden towers, some of which had become private cottages, were tracked down, acquired, and are now on display on Cable Road about a quarter mile behind the existing light.

Every few winters one of the brick foundations of the original light towers is exposed by winter storms. This one lay about a hundred yards from the base of the bluffs, which must roughly mark the spot where the cliff it stood on was undermined nearly a century before. The deep-red bricks, slick and black with algae and seaweed, glistened in the morning sun as the surf soused and washed over them at roughly thirty-second intervals. The foundation was round, about fifteen feet across, with three or four rows of bricks exposed above the

sand, so that it looked like the root of a large reddish tooth, rotten
but stubborn.

The remarkable thing about this foundation is not just that it slid
down the face of the sixty-foot scarp intact, but that the brick- and
mortarwork was so strong that at low tide the 150-year-old base is
still watertight, brimful of murky green water like a backyard swimming pool.

The man who was standing over it as I approached was, I would
guess, about sixty years old. He was standing in an attitude of inarticulate awe and astonishment, though not at the endurance of the
exposed foundation.

"Man, this fucking beach . . . It was . . . I was here a week ago
and . . . ," he stuttered, gesticulating helplessly with his hands.

He knew what the foundation was, but insisted that it must originally have stood at beach level, rather than having slid intact down
the face of the scarp. I had to admit that his explanation seemed
more plausible, however incorrect. He had been coming to Eastham
for forty summers, he said, and remembered "lots more" cottages on
the bluffs between Nauset Light and Coast Guard Beach, where now
there are only a half dozen—a change attested to by the number of
leaching pits, well pipes, cables, and so on, that protrude at various
heights from the cliff face along this stretch of beach.

Near the foundation was a long outcropping of iron conglomerate.
We easily worked a couple of stones out of this natural mortar and
raced down to the foundation, like a couple of boys, trying to knock
out some of the bricks as souvenirs. But the bricks held. We should
have guessed as much, since the continuous buffeting of the waves
had not dislodged any before our coming. The next surge chased us
back, high up onto the upper beach. In such a situation the surf literally keeps you on your toes. We walked companionably together
back to the stairs and climbed them up to the parking lot. I left as he
ransacked his van for a cold chisel.

December 1988

SEEING NOTHING AT NAUSET LIGHT

For the past seven days I have been shepherding a dozen or so students from Williams College up and down the Outer Cape as part of a winter-session course in Cape Cod Literature. We have been staying in the old station at Coast Guard Beach, which now serves as a hostel for educational groups like this one. They are an exceptionally bright and curious group, and my time with them has been both exhilarating and exhausting. But I have also been struck by how, leading them on walks, showing them events, processes, and perhaps a few mysteries, I myself have seen nothing. They have made me feel somewhat brilliant in their eyes, illuminating my homeland for them, giving them some landmarks by which they might navigate and explore on their own. But I have seen only what I had already seen, repeating what I knew over and over.

Last evening I left them to themselves and drove up to the darkened and empty parking lot at Nauset Light Beach. There, for the first time all week, I was aware of the landscape speaking to me in its own voice, unfettered by my presentations of it. I saw, as if for the first time, the Dopplered beam of the light—first white, then red—an image that one of the Williams students would later describe as the flashing light of an ambulance, but that for me was a bright blind beacon, stabbing again and again out into the dark universe, serving as a landmark for ships at sea, seeing nothing.

January 1992

8

....

Marconi Beach

BEACH FOAM

The day after tropical storm Noel strafed the Cape, I went out to the ocean to check out the news. I began to walk north beneath the unconsolidated bluffs of the Outer Beach. The wind had abated but was still strong out of the northeast. Looking up, I could see the utility poles that line the cliff road there. Even down on the beach, I heard the wind howling and whining through their wires. In places the road now swings quite close to the edge, and at one point a guy wire on one of the poles had come loose and was flapping wildly in the storm wind. The crossed poles appeared to be moving along with me, just above the trembling, hairy lip of the crest. Their linked, swaying wires wailed as I walked, and a spooky yellow sun glowered behind them, as though behind frosted glass. The metaphor of ships' masts and rigging was inescapable.

For the next third of a mile the signs of storm damage gradually increased, Here and there along the cliff face, old well casings and fiber waste pipes from former dwellings stuck up or protruded from the slope. Most of the vanished houses to which they once belonged were moved back before destruction overtook them. On the Outer Beach you won't find any abandoned cellar holes, slowly filling in and closing over with mounds of salt-spray rose. Out here a house keeps moving, or else it sinks swiftly out of sight without a trace, like a vessel going down at sea.

Eventually I arrived at an area of unusually active erosion: The vegetation on the cliff face was sparse and ragged. Rivers of sand twisted down the banking, leaping up over the more resistant outcrops of clay and splaying out at the bottom in wide deltas. In places whole sections of bluff twenty feet high had shelved off.

Occasionally I had to leap up the slope a few feet to avoid a shattering slide of muddy, green surf. The tide continued to come in, and with it came great crashing seas tumbling over one another. They carried rafts of brown mud floating and sliding among milky foam. The curled volutes of the waves themselves were veined with white vertical bands. They look like curved, moving walls of jade.

I've noticed that it's when the wind is of "moderate" speed like this, say thirty to fifty miles an hour, that beach foam seems to reach its greatest concentrations. When it does, it becomes a plaything for the wind. The upper beach was strewn with this fluffy wreckage of the sea. It scudded along in large clumps like broken clouds, then flew upward in small bits, like small birds. It lay on the sand in large, quivering masses flecked with innumerable tiny iridescent bubbles. It came slithering in, like fat, muddy lips at the leading edges of the waves. It slid along the wet sand on a film of its own deliquescence, like ice melting on a hot stove. I picked up great weightless armloads of beach foam, tossing it into the wind like autumn leaves to watch it scatter and fly ahead of me on the beach. I strode through banks of it without resistance, leaving my boots covered with insubstantial dirty snow. Up against the base of the cliffs, gray clumps of foam huddled in cracks and crevices, like wads of old newspapers, filled with yesterday's news.

September 1977

BARREN GROUND

Perhaps it is best approached in misery of soul, because then
it stands out in all its cryptic mystery as the raw room that
owns us, the desert without illusion.

—JOHN HAY, *THE GREAT BEACH*

One day last month, before the rains fell again, I thought to escape
the darkness of the afternoon by taking a walk on the Outer
Beach. I drove to a spot near LeCount Hollow and headed toward
Marconi Beach, about a mile and a half south.

For some reason, this is a stretch of beach I rarely walk. The bluffs
here are largely unvegetated and notably level in height, averaging about
fifty feet. The scarp showed signs of recent severe erosion. Its face was a
steep slope of intersecting facets composed of thin horizontal layers of
very sandy, light, varved clay, with seams of iron oxide, the color of dried
blood, running through it. The steep angle, the faceted patterns and the
rusty stains gave it the aspect of an ancient sandstone wall—Jerusalem's
Wailing Wall, perhaps. Its sand layers looked momentarily stable, but
when I walked up to it and looked closely, I could see that the entire
face was alive with trillions of minute sand grains flowing down its
face, like multitudes of tiny mites.

About a half mile south of LeCount, I passed beneath the site of
the Marconi Station, where America first sent a wireless message to
England in 1903. Since then half of the site has eroded into the sea,
and the massive square concrete foundation of one of the four original transmission towers lies exposed, cracked, but still remarkably
intact, on the sloping sands of the beach.

Offshore, beyond the breaking swells, several dozen black scoters
bobbed in the shoals. Farther out, hundreds of yards offshore, I could
see the large white forms of gannets feeding actively, closing their
streamlined bodies like umbrellas and plunging like javelins into the
dark sea, sending up sprays of water as straight and narrow as them-

selves, as if their unfocused reflections had emerged from the water as they entered it.

As I continued south, the composition of the bluff changed from glacial drift to pure, homogeneous, wind-driven dune sand, with here and there a long-buried log protruding from it. It was beginning to grow late now, and so, at a place where the angle of the cliff face gentled out, I climbed to the top of the bluff and began to walk back along the flat and curiously barren shelf of land that borders the beach here.

Though still in Wellfleet, this part of Cape Cod is geologically in the northern part of the "Plains of Eastham" that Thoreau described as "an apparently boundless plain, without a tree or fence," when he walked across it 150 years ago. At that time most of the Cape was a treeless landscape, but this particular area has long been recognized by Cape Codders as unusually barren. For reasons that are not clear, this stretch of the Outer Cape is covered with inland dunes, thick layers of sand overlaying the glacial deposits and extending more than a thousand feet in from the beach. It was traditionally called "Goody Hallett's Meadow," a reference to the quasihistoric "Witch of Eastham," exiled by the good people of Eastham to this barren stretch of ground, where, it is said, she lured unwary sailors to their death or, in some cases, fates worse than death.

Whatever the cause, long after most of the Cape has reforested or at least revegetated itself, this fringe of tableland remains curiously bare and stark in appearance. Its flat sandy surface is mottled with thousands of small stones, most undercut by the wind and perched on miniature sand pedestals, with tails of sand stretched out behind them, driven by the north winds of winter. This time of the year it is a waste of darkened humps of poverty grass, with small stands of bare bayberry and beach-plum twigs, an occasional bright-green, bristly eyebrow of a pitch pine hugging the ground, withered gray seaside goldenrod with blown cottony seed heads, and the whitened drooping sculptures of dusty miller that stand like miniature melting ghosts.

As I trod this ground, a chorus from Brahms's *German Requiem* came unbidden into my head: "Denn alles Fleisch es ist wie Gras . . ."

Behold, all flesh is as the grass,
and all the goodliness of man
is as the flower of grass;
for lo, the grass with'reth,
and the flower thereof decayeth.

I had been rehearsing the *Requiem* with a local choral group for several weeks, and I realized that the rhythms of this chorus, stately and insistent, were those of the sea beating endlessly against the shore.

At one point I saw what appeared to be some green fabric and black wire emerging out of the top of the dune. The fabric was quite rotten, and tore easily as I tried to extricate some, but one swatch I pulled free was unmistakably the right front section of an army fatigue jacket. There were still four metal buttons, heavily rusted, down the front, and another button held shut a flap pocket. Above the pocket, on a sewn white canvas strip, were the faint but legible block letters: SOUSA.

This unexpected artifact brought to mind an aspect of this place's past I had temporarily forgotten, an era not as old as Goody Hallett's legend, or even the Marconi site, but one that had more of an effect on the local populace than either. During World War II this featureless plain was part of Camp Wellfleet, an antiaircraft emplacement, and, after the war, an offshore firing range. Sousa is a common local name at this end of the Cape, and most likely this jacket belonged to one of the dozens, perhaps hundreds, of local boys who spent all or part of the war here. It was tempting to think that this was some old bivouac site or gun emplacement, but more likely it was just one of the numerous small dumps that pocked the area.

Now, half a century later, nearly all the visible signs of Camp Wellfleet—the watchtowers, bunkers, gun emplacements, and barbed-wire fences—have vanished. Instead, a huge benign blue water tower looms over the beach, and to the west the outlines of the faux-colonial buildings of the Cape Cod National Seashore headquarters. The few remaining corrugated-metal barracks, now used for storage, are hidden from view.

It is curious that, while the Marconi site and its remaining artifacts have been carefully preserved, labeled, and memorialized, there is nothing to point the casual visitor to the more recent and less benign uses to which this place was once put. One needs a certain knowledge of local history and a willingness to weave the past out of such tattered threads: a patch of stained fabric, some corroded buttons, a faded name strip. But they stand for a life lived here, or perhaps one put on hold, depending on how its owner viewed war and his part in it. A child of luck and timing, I have no personal knowledge of war, but like this anonymous soldier, I too have stood in desert places, waiting for something to jump-start my life again.

December 1994

A QUICKIE AT THE BEACH

One evening a little before seven o'clock I pulled into the vast empty parking lot at Marconi Beach in South Wellfleet. I had just come from Russ's Marconi Beach Restaurant, a place I like to go two or three times a year for ribs. I always enjoy Russ's Elizabethan-innkeeper banter, the way he seems to know every customer personally, his hearty and infectious good humor that seems to rub off on everyone there. I had ordered my usual: the half-slab barbecued ribs dinner with coleslaw, baked beans, and smashed potatoes with gravy. I was on my way to the Wellfleet Cinemas to see the 7:25 showing of a high-gloss trashy action movie in 3-D and, since it was such a lovely evening and I had a few extra minutes, I decided I had time for a quickie at the beach.

So I drove into the empty parking lot and stood on the wooden platform halfway down the stairs. It was one of those classic early-spring evenings on the beach, which looked more like a stage set than something real. The moon, a few days shy of full, hung high in the clear sky, its orange reflection torn into fragments by the agitated

ocean. The scene was infused with lingering twilight, a charged setting where I could easily imagine both a beach murder and a beach
romance taking place.

Once again I was struck by how *cinematic* the Cape's landscape is,
especially the Outer Beach. It's always seemed odd to me that more
movies have not been set here. Of the few that have, the most famous,
of course, is *The Thomas Crown Affair*—the original 1968 version, that
is, not the 1999 remake—starring Steve McQueen and Faye Dunaway. There's a scene in that movie where McQueen takes Dunaway
on a wild joyride in a dune buggy through the Provincelands (a scene,
I later learned, that was shot with the blessing of the National Seashore). I was an impressionable twenty-something when that movie
came out, and that scene remains an indelible romantic fantasy in my
imagination, impregnable to later environmental awareness.

But I was alone that evening, the beach was empty, the surf was
low, almost inaudible. The salt air lightly rasped my nostrils, the cold
wind off the ocean shivved through my light jacket, and the low, dark
vegetation stretched out sparsely across the russet plain to the south
and north. And that was all.

This beach is one of the most evocative landscapes I know, rich
in both human and natural drama. Over the years, in innumerable
encounters with it, it has spoken eloquently and mysteriously to me.
This evening I had it all to myself, and I waited, a little impatiently,
I think, for it to give me something. But it remained mute, withheld.
The earth, I think, closes in on itself when we do not give it our full
attention, when, for instance, we're still savoring a big meal and looking forward to mindless entertainment. The beach refuses to be a pre-
view. Nature does not offer itself to one who would slip it in between
trivial events, between gluttony and lust. It will not hold counsel with
us when we are already going someplace else as we arrive.

So I walked back to the car, closed the door, and drove to the
movies.

March 2014

9

....

LeCount Hollow
to Cahoon Hollow

CENSUSING THE WRACK LINE

One of the constantly changing aspects of the Outer Beach, and one that has its own series of telescoping mysteries, is the feature known as the "wrack line." On a sandy shore like this one, the wrack line is the more or less continuous line of debris left on the beach by a previous high tide. (In this sense it may be viewed as miniature reenactment—in both dimension and time scale—of the terminal or recessional moraines left by the retreating glaciers.) If the most recent high tide is a moon or spring tide, higher than the ones that preceded it, it wipes out all the previous wrack lines, leaving only its own thin line of debris at the high-water mark. If it is a neap tide, lower than previous ones, the beach presents a series of wrack lines, looping and intersecting with one another over a width of many yards.

Like many terms associated with the shore, the definitions of "wrack" are curiously varied. According to the *American Heritage Dictionary*, the primary definition is "Wreckage, especially of a ship cast ashore"—as in "wrack and ruin"—but it is also defined as "Dried seaweed" and, with odd specificity, as "Marine vegetation, especially kelp." The word's etymology apparently goes no further back than the Middle Dutch *wrak*, reflecting its consistently primal, Teutonic sound. Its first English appearance in print, in the sense we are using it here, was in 1513 in a Scottish translation of the *Aeneid* by Gavin Douglas: "Rent me in pecis, and in the fludis swak, / Or droun law vndir the large seis *wrak*" [italics mine].

There seems little point in delving deeper into the origins of such an adamantine and unyielding word. Still, it is clear that the phrase "wrack line" is flexible enough to include anything thrown up and deposited by the waves and tide, large or small, human or natural, animate or inanimate.

The first time I deliberately looked at the wrack line and tried to get an overview of its contents was in the spring of 1980. Several of my friends that year had taken part-time jobs as fieldworkers for the U.S. Census Bureau, and it occurred to me that it would be appropriate to do my own informal census—not of people, but of things thrown up on the beach after a storm. So one March day, following an easterly blow the night before, I went out to LeCount Hollow and began walking north. It was an hour past high tide, and raining lightly. The waves, all foam and milk for several hundred yards out, had the hollow, grinding roar of a receding storm surf.

As I walked north, the beach was densely littered with debris thrown up by the storm. I pulled out my notebook and began jotting down a casual record of objects, natural and human-made, that had been stranded in the tidal wrack from LeCount to Newcomb Hollow, a distance of about three miles. I ended up with an inventory of items almost three pages long. Many were generic; for instance, there was a long list of "Plastic Bottles" of too many different types to be categorized. There were at least fifty lobster buoys, all Styrofoam. There were also numerous pieces of lumber, netting, and a few creosoted wharf pilings. The most common animal remains were starfish and the shells of sea clams. Among the more unusual objects I found were the following:

Item: A one-gallon plastic jug of milk (nearly full, but salty and
  sour) from the "Oakhurst Dairy, Portland, ME 04101."
Item: An eight-inch-diameter gray metal float with "Made in
  Spain 1A Corina" embossed on it.
Item: The bottom half of a refrigerator.
Item: An official wooden National Park Service sign that read:
  "DO NOT THROW ANYTHING OVER THE CLIFF."*

The amount of plastic bottles, jugs, six-pack rings, tampon applicators, bags, and other debris was staggering. In places the beach
looked like some urban shoreline. At the same time it retained its
primitive simplicity, inviting me to a different and larger level of experience I could not quite reach.

Out of old habit I began to comb as well as census the beach, picking up some of the more offensive or desirable items, sticking some in
my pack, tying others to my umbrella, and holding still others under
my arms. After a while I began to take on the aspect of a large walking
decorator crab. I carried one of the steel floats on a piece of line that was
attached to it, occasionally dragging it behind me like a ball and chain.

---

* For any reader who might be interested, here is a complete list of items I
censused on my beach walk from LeCount Hollow to Newcomb Hollow in Wellfleet on March 11, 1980: Kelp—fucus—sea clams—razor clams—plastic bottles,
jugs, and bags—plastic shelving—wire rolls—glass jars—bottles—jugs—tampon
applicator cases—nylon line—lobster buoys—Styrofoam cups—driftwood—
creosoted wharf pilings—cap visors—lightbulbs—spotlights—gas cans—propane
containers—cardboard containers—a spruce tree 15 feet long—orange peels—
cobblestones (up to 6 inches)—dead herring gull (mature)—concrete block—moon
snail, large— a gallon plastic jug of milk—flip-flops—wooden sandals—6-inch
corrugated pipe—paintbrush—mermaid purses—Jonah crab—skate—doll
torso—Styrofoam floats of various sizes—spray cans—birchbark—flashlight—
tennis ball—plastic net bag—4-foot fluorescent bulb—spruce trunk 30 feet
long—two 8-inch green metal floats—one yellow onion—food locker tops—
paint cans—plastic net bags—oak barrel—moccasin—jogging shoe—tire—hair
curler—a wooden oar—several signs—a wooden ladder—boat planks—electric
motor—fishnetting—leather shoes—one pencil—boat seat—fish crates—lower
half of a refrigerator.

I seemed to swing between extremes of perception: one moment plodding with my head lowered in intense examination of the multi-colored river of wrack and litter at my feet, toting up the items among it like some drudge of a littoral inventory clerk; the next moment feeling as if I were embarked on some unplanned pilgrimage, chasing haltingly after some vision of the eternal present, caught somewhere between the clean, sleek, shelving slopes of the immense glacial scarp to my left, the continuous, gathering, overlapping, hollow roar of the breakers on my right, and the tilting, curving beach ahead of me, where a flock of gulls rose continually and repeatedly into the air at my advance toward the misty destruction in the far distance, a place where novelty and perception would become unnecessary, and abiding, constant grandeur might suffice.

But novelty and perception kept their hold. I soon became aware that there was little else to see: no boats on the water, no ducks in the surf, no shorebirds on the beach. The slopes seemed remarkably bare of vegetation on this passing, as though nearly this entire stretch of bluffs had undergone some active erosion since I had last been out.

As I approached the landing at Newcomb Hollow, I saw a couple—the only people I saw all morning, making their way down the bluff. The man was stocky and middle-aged, and wore a plaid jacket. Several yards in front of him was a much younger woman in a London Fog raincoat, with kerchiefed hair and sunglasses. She strode confidently down the beach toward me, and as she did the breeze carried the scent of her perfume to me. It caught me with a sudden, unexpected pull. All at once I was intensely aware of what an absurd and pungent figure I must have presented, adorned and odoriferous with the assorted pickings of three miles of beach walking attached to my body. But she spoke cheerfully as we crossed paths, as if she were alone and I were not ridiculous. Perhaps, like me, she was simply not surprised at anything she found on this outermost shore.

March 1980

BETWEEN DREAMS

There's a dense fog on the beach this morning. The visibility to seaward is only a hundred yards, if that. This sea is muscular but calm. Gray-green swells three or four feet high move landward in powerful pulses, but do not break, or even show a definite form, until they trip on the gravelly ledge at the bottom of the beach. The point at which they break is determined in part by their height and in part by the position of the previous retreating breaker, which seems to be clawing at the beach in a scatter of gravel, as if resisting being drawn into the maw of the next oncoming wave. The waves that break farthest in seethe and slide high up onto the beach, making me skip and scuttle up out of the reach of their lacy hems.

It is on foggy days like this that the beach most nearly resembles our movement into the future. We look ahead toward the constantly retreating edge of the beach, not quite able to see beyond the next bend. We walk along in the soft bubble of the present toward some increasingly cloudy and obscured next phase of our lives—lives whose meaning seems to be whispered into our ears with a soft, rhythmic susurrus by the constant breaking of the waves. Only by noticing the subtly changing texture of the cliff face, which rolls like some huge canvas diorama loop above us, can we sense any progress on this strand—though never our position, and never our ultimate destination. Always we are trapped in the dreamlike trance of the present, whose dissolving boundaries shift with us, so that what we were traveling toward is suddenly already behind us, where we were is already lost, and where we are is where we have always been—sojourning on an empty beach between dreams.

May 1999

NIGHT WALK AT WHITE CREST

One night last week, after chorale practice, I stopped off at White Crest Beach on my way home. We'd been rehearsing Ralph Vaughan Williams's great antiwar cantata, *Dona nobis pacem*, which was written a few years before the outbreak of World War II. Much of the text is taken from Walt Whitman's poetry. That evening we had been working on the section, "Dirge for Two Veterans," based on Whitman's poem of that name, with its haunting lines, "Lo, the moon ascending, / Up from the east the silvery round moon, / Beautiful over the house-tops, ghastly, phantom moon, / Immense and silent moon."

I think, in fact, it was the moon—a waning gibbous moon just lifted over the ocean—that drew me to White Crest Beach that night. There is no better place to watch the moon rise over the ocean than White Crest, with its soft white flanks of sand curving down to the white beach and the dark waters beyond. I followed its contours down to the beach, where there is a sharp but still gentle drop-off. The tide, though low, was coming in fast over a wide, flat, clean beach, rushing up to my feet like a crowd in a hurry, making me dance back a few steps.

Because of the bright, silver backlight of the low moon, the advancing breakers had the inescapable look of black caves moving toward shore. The sea between them ran like molten metal, and the backwash was a mesmerizing weave of soft silver rivers running against themselves, occasionally throwing up a ghostly silver arm.

The swash of each wave ran rapidly back into the black, cavelike maw of the next advancing breaker, leaving a sheen of wet sand covered with little foamy pads, like legless crabs crawling slowly after it. It was a wonderful chiaroscuro of grays, blacks, whites, silvers, and the yellowish tinge on the surface where the reflection of the old moon was torn apart like taffy in the waters. I turned around and looked up at the steep but soft walls of sand that stretched from south to north as far as I could see. In the soft moonlight all the footprints on the beach were erased, and I could see only the dim outlines of the sands, blanketed in soft beige flannel by the light of the fading moon, as if sight itself were growing old and shutting down. Behind me I could still hear all the variegated talk of the sea—all its modulated, irregular rhythms broken across the regular lines of the surf, the way the rough rhythms of human speech break across the meter of a memorable poem. Before me there were only the soft, stark, serene, and silent walls of the cliffs, surmounted by a moon-faded star.

I turned once again to the sea, and there, to the northeast, out on the dark horizon, I saw a single light—one low, dim, orange ship's light—some trawler, perhaps, heading home late. It reminded me of a human presence in a world that otherwise seemed to bear no trace of us, a world that as yet took no cognizance of us. And I thought, How many places, as intensely occupied as this thin peninsula is, can give you this experience of an open world, with no visible sign of man, except a single fading light at the edge of vision?

March 2000

OFF-HOURS

The other evening we drove out to White Crest Beach—well named with its high, bare, white shoulder of a dune cresting the hill, and several foot trails creased into its flanks leading down to the shore and the surf.

It is a mystery to me why there are not more people on the beach at this hour (in fact, most seem to be leaving just as we arrive). As far as I am concerned, this is the best time of the day to be here, for it is now that the human presence recedes and resumes its proper proportion. This is the time when the rounded contours of the bluff begin to throw their soft gray shadows across the baked sands like a benediction; when a few surfcasters appear and heave their heavy lures in steep arcs out beyond the breakers, the repeated, arching casts of the lines forming a human counterpoint to the rollers coming in endlessly upon themselves.

Compared with the display of human flesh here earlier in the day, people are not only much fewer in number now but seem to be friendlier, less contained, and with a sense of sharing, rather than defending, their stretch of beach. At high noon we are like dense colonies of nesting gannets—raucous, defensive, aggressive, bristling at intrusion, irritated at the common lot. In extreme cases these birds kill one another's young and defecate on one another. We don't, of course, do that, though sometimes we behave as if we would like to.

Now, amid coolness, quiet, and space, we are more like the shorebirds that flock leisurely and feed up and down the beach: the dark, ring-necked plovers with their necklaces of white staying below the high-tide line, the lighter-colored sandpipers with their long, dark, chisel-like bills patrolling both the slant of the upper beach and the rumpled terrace of sand behind.

We saunter down over the white brow of the hill. A boy of about ten, slightly chubby, is showing off for his mom, cartwheeling and somersaulting with careless, imperious abandon down the face of the bluff. We descend more soberly, along one of the slanted footpaths, an improvised trail worn into the sloping sand as if by a camel train in the Sahara. We walk only a few yards south of the base of the trail, but it is enough—space is generous this time of day. We go down almost to the high-tide line to catch a few minutes of the westering sun before the shade of the cliff engulfs us. Then we spread out our gray wool blanket, beach chairs, towels, and wicker picnic basket and simply sit, unwinding, falling outward into the rhythms of this hour of grace, this hour of day yielding to shadows and the soft sounds of evening.

The beach still seems to ring, vibrate, and tremble with the vanished energy and cacophony of the day. That, in fact, is part of its pleasure—the sense of noise and frantic activity recently dissipated, the peace of a classroom just emptied. The tide rises languorously toward its climax in soft, sand-saturated surges to smooth the wrinkled, foot-furrowed brow of the summer berm. The surges are dark-jade, marbled, miniature Alleghenies, ridge after ridge, sometimes breaking with a muffled crash, sometimes with a luscious, voluptuous seethe thick with the grate of gravel. Sometimes the overlapping lines of breakers along the shore fall into a momentary alignment, their sine curves merge into phase, and there is a series of wonderful half seconds of pure silence between the crashes.

It is this, probably more than anything, that defines this time of day: that the soft pulse of the surf has once again become the dominant sound and presence on the beach, the metronome to which everything, including us, sets its tempo. Terns sail like silvery origami sculptures offshore and suddenly plunge into the dark-green bulges of the sea for sand eels. Gulls rock indolently in small rafts offshore like sea ducks, or plant themselves in front of us, arrogantly demanding chicken bones, which I dutifully throw them, just to watch their naked greed and aggression. Flocks of shorebirds now reappear, reinhabit this stretch of beach, from which they had been exiled all day by the press of human presence. A few dogs are allowed to run free, despite the regulations we all know, and no one complains. There is room for all of us now.

Every now and then a much larger wave—the "seventh wave"—hurls itself in and reaches, with a hundred foam-laced fingers, just up and over the high-tide break in the beach, then recedes. It will go slightly higher in its flood, but only slightly. All things are regular and contained this evening, steady; all things know their territories and respect boundaries. Even the unbounded power of the sea is sheathed.

The shadows of the bluff have enveloped us for at least twenty minutes when suddenly there is a sharp, palpable drop in the temperature, as when a low-pressure system moves in. Something has suddenly shifted, some turning in the evening's clock has occurred, and it spurs us to think of talking a walk.

The beach to the north, a series of undulating cusps, is slightly backlit and wears a thin mantle of mist, giving it a somewhat mysterious look. In the distance, a mile or so off, we can see the foreshortened stick figures of the larger evening crowd on the beach at Cahoon Hollow, anchored there by the presence of the Beachcomber nightclub.

We put the food back into the basket, zip up our backpacks, and leave everything there, something we would never do during the day. Even trust is somehow more apparent now. As we walk north, I watch the ghost-sheen on the slanted lower beach as each wave recedes: the luminous shadow of moisture in the sand that traces in slow motion the retreat of each wave like a lingering, unsubstantial caress.

A mother and daughter, preceded by a nervous, yapping, yellow Lab-mix, come toward us. They stop and chat, make us formal introductions to "Chloe," who relents some, but remains suspicious.

We pass two young girls, perhaps ten and twelve, the taller one with incipient breasts, romping in the surf, totally relaxed with each other and themselves as only young girls can be—playing with the waves and screaming to each other in mock terror as a surge side-swipes them, then going right out for more. And we ask, what does society, or hormones, do to young girls to rip their self-confidence away at the onset of adolescence, to make them so desperately self-aware, desperate for peer approval and to find a boy who will like them, validate them? Teenage boys, of course, also experience inadequacy and anxiety, but seldom, it seems, to such extremes.

We pass some of the broken harsh debris of the day—the wrecks of beach chairs and plastic trays, shards of broken jars and glasses, odd bent painted metal poles with concrete weights molded around their bases. There are also more benign signs of the day's occupation: a large rectangle outlined in eelgrass, probably demarcating a volleyball court.

Coming back we pass a woman sitting in a beach chair: heavy-set, with jet-black hair and a bright-red jacket draped over her shoulders. She is sitting alone, looking peacefully out at the sea. Beside her, near her hand, is an open pack of cigarettes. She isn't smoking.

For us and for all these people, this time of day allows us to reconnect ourselves to what is around us, to engage our senses, our bodies, our imaginations, our propensity to story, with this elemental seascape.

It is now, right now, at this time of day, when the allure, the enduring mystery, of the beach creeps and insinuates itself into our perceptions and our memory—when it makes our day, speaks to us in recollection, and when, because it is no longer exclusively ours, it becomes truly ours.

August 2000

WATCHING SURFERS

To paraphrase an old joke, I love surfing—I can watch it for hours. I've never actually been on a surfboard. The closest I've ever come is so-called bodysurfing, which, to paraphrase Mark Twain, is to real surfing as lightning bugs are to lightning. Still, I've always been fascinated by surfers and will stop my beach walks to watch them any time of the year.

What makes watching surfers so fascinating? Well, for one thing, like fishermen, they appear to be doing nothing most of the time, simply sitting there on their boards, just beyond the breakers, watching the incoming swells. Perhaps I identify with this, since, to most people, that's also what writers appear to be doing (that is, if writers were watched) most of the time, simply sitting there, staring out into space, doing nothing. But like writers, surfers are actually doing something even when they don't appear to be. What they are doing is *reading* the waves. To the uninitiated the swells may all appear to be uniform, nearly identical. But to the surfer they are as different as poems, each with its own distinct shape, height, alignment, speed, curl, and potential for a ride. Each wave speaks its own watery sentence, which the surfer has to parse. Floating there, holding his (or, increasingly, her) board, he hangs on the lip of every wave, listening to its every word, until finally he discerns one that fits his needs, clambers up and onto the board, and paddles furiously to be in exactly the right place when it arrives. The thrill of watching a surfer catch a wave and ride it is so exciting that I often feel as if I would, still could, do it. Then I see one of them wiped out by a breaker, and I settle back, resigned to the pleasures of simply observing.

More than most people who use the beach, surfers learn to respect the power of the ocean. Yet one's understanding is always imperfect, and, even on this beach of relatively gentle waves, one is often just a single misstep from obliteration. I remember one September day after Hurricane Isabel had kicked up a monumental surf at White Crest Beach. When I got there I saw a half dozen or so wet-suited surfers standing on the beach looking out. Following their gaze, I saw a pale-yellow surfboard far out among the distant breakers, being tossed over and over again like a little toy. The tether rope was loose and thrashing about, and there was no rider in sight. I felt a slight sense of the emotions that men from an earlier generation must have had when they watched shipwrecked sailors clinging to the rigging or suddenly disappearing in the surf. Then the lone board caught a wave by itself and rode it, almost perfectly, in toward shore and up on the sand.

One of the surfers went down to retrieve it. Still, there was no sign of the board's owner. I asked him if he knew who the board's owner was.

"No idea," he replied.

We waited for several minutes, and then finally saw an indistinct figure far down the beach, wading ashore. He was not hurt, it turned out, but had become separated from his board and "couldn't get in."

Of course surfing is not the matter of life and death that fishing was to the old Cape Codders. It is optional and purely recreational. Still, surfers, more than any contemporary figures I can think of, pit themselves directly against the might of the ocean, with only their skill and a little synthetic board between them and potential disaster. Perhaps that is part of the fascination of watching surfers: They keep alive at least a pattern of that vulnerable individuality with which we all must ultimately encounter the universe.

September 2003

SHADOWS ON THE BEACH

Yesterday afternoon about two thirty, I drove out to White Crest Beach and walked north for a mile or so on the lower slope of the beach. On this portion of the ocean shore the glacial cliffs are composed of nearly pure sand, and here they seemed to have undergone significant recent erosion. An incoming tide washed the beach in low, gentle curlers, coiling and uncoiling themselves at a slight angle to the beach.

This time of day at this time of year is one of those moments when the character of the Outer Beach shifts palpably. Long, finger-shaped shadows creep down the face of the cliff before gradually solidifying into the dark curtain of afternoon shade that envelops the beach and eventually crawls onto the waves. These shadowy fingers seem a counterpoint to the waves themselves, which push up the foreslope of the beach in surges, as if with perceptible effort, gradually slowing and reaching their limit before sliding back and sinking into the sand, like retreating armies cut off from their supplies and reinforcements.

These two superficially complementary extensions—one of shade and one of surf—seem to embody the difference between the two borders of the beach. The shadow fingers creep down the cliff face in a steady, measured, predictable fashion, day after day, following an unchanging solar rhythm, and are ultimately insubstantial and inconsequential. The surf is also superficially rhythmic and steady, rising and lowering with the tides, but it is full of surprises and variations and follows a lunar cycle that perpetually falls behind the solar cycle roughly an hour every day. And, unlike the shadows, it ultimately eats everything in its path.

There is always this lesson in front of me—well, actually, on either side of me—as I walk the beach. It's such an obvious, primal, constant and plain lesson that I see it clearly everywhere but can't seem to articulate it satisfactorily. The shadows emphasize the muteness of the cliffs, their stoic, infinitely patient silence. Separated from the sea at low tide by this wide, smooth, highway of sand, the cliffs and the sea seem to have nothing to do with each other—or at least they seem to have agreed to a temporary truce, with the beach serving as a kind of DMZ.

Of course I know this is an illusion. This is no case of an immovable object meeting an irresistible force. Far from it. The cliffs are eminently movable, the sea insatiable. Still, there is something in the way that these glacial cliffs passively surrender to the sea that seems to give the sea its full expression. By giving themselves so unreservedly to the ocean, they allow it to be most itself. For this reason I cannot help but think that in some more-than-sentient way, the land must love the sea that destroys it, as the sea must love the land that it destroys.

October 2007

MOVING AN OLD BEACH COTTAGE

Last month, while walking the ocean bluffs in the southern part of my town, I came upon an odd sight. Well, it didn't seem odd at first. Near the edge of the bluff was an old wooden two-story beach cottage of a style predating World War II. It was modest in size and materials, and its days were obviously numbered. A small deck already leaned slightly over the lip of the crest. In its current location the cottage probably had no more than five years to live.

Next to the cottage, and towering over it, sat a large red crane. It was a heavy and expensive piece of machinery, and its purpose was clear. Thick steel cables were wrapped around the cottage, and the crane was poised to move it to a new and safer location.

So far, this was not an uncommon sight on the Outer Beach. In the past modest structures like this one were usually allowed to fall into the sea. But as these beach cottages became more valuable and more substantial, owners have engaged in increasingly strenuous efforts to save, or at least prolong, their lives. Since erosion control is not a feasible option on the Outer Beach,* the strategy is usually to move the structures back from the edge of the cliff, if there is room on the property to do so. If the structure is within the boundaries of the Cape Cod National Seashore, the Seashore itself has often offered to "swap" land farther inland with the cottage owner. This has always seemed remarkably generous of the Seashore, since it is essentially giving up land that is not currently threatened for land that is rapidly disappearing.

In this case, though, moving the cottage back was not an option. A dirt road ran directly behind the cottage, preventing a retreat. Instead, a new and very substantial foundation of concrete posts and pressure-treated pilings had been built immediately *to the side* of the cottage. Thick wire cables were wrapped around the cottage, and it seemed clear that the intent was to have the crane lift it off its old wooden-post foundation and move or slide it sideways onto the new one.

Now, normally a horizontal move like this would not gain the owners anything. But in this case the edge of the bluff currently swings out substantially in front of the new foundation. The site where the cottage currently sits is about fifteen feet back from the edge of the ocean bluff. On the new foundation it will be about forty-five feet back from the edge. That will give them a net gain of about thirty feet. Okay, I thought, let's do the math.

Traditionally the erosion rate for the Outer Beach is given as three feet per year, probably a conservative figure. Given that the shoreline tends to even out over time, chances are that the protruding portion of the bluff to which the cottage will be moved will erode at a more rapid rate in the coming years. But let's be generous and stick with

---

* Though that didn't keep Wellfleet from commissioning a study by the Army Corps of Engineers back in the 1950s to determine if the entire length of the Outer Beach might be armored with rock riprap to prevent erosion. The corps, to its everlasting commonsense credit, concluded that such a project was "not economically feasible."

the figure of three to three-and-a-half feet per year. Still, that means this move will give the cottage owners *at best* ten extra years. The cost of such a move must be substantial, surely far more than the original cost of the building and the land on which it sits.

It's easy, of course, to feel a smug contempt for such futile and expensive attempts to escape the ocean's relentless advance. But in this case I didn't. Instead, I felt a certain sympathy, even a grudging admiration. Perhaps it was the modest nature of the building, or the fact that by moving sideways, rather than backwards, the owners seem to be acknowledging that they cannot avoid their fate but only postpone it for a while.

Or perhaps it was because the whole enterprise seemed to express something fundamental about our attitude toward the inevitable. How we scramble and scheme to purchase a few more years for both our buildings and ourselves! Money is no object. We know that the ocean will not stop, that the land will soon give way in spite of all our stratagems and expense. Oh, but give us but a few more summers to see and taste the beauty of life, to stand on the lip of the earth and drink in its pleasures—then we will go, if not gladly at least willingly, with a sense of a bargain made, accepted, and kept.

December 2007

FAMILY FUN

This weekend I had a visit from my son, Christopher, and his two older children, Anna and Henry, who live outside Philadelphia. Anna is ten and Henry seven, and during their visit I had the pleasure of introducing them to two of the Cape's iconic summer experiences: whale watching and a beach party.

Actually, I'm not sure that either of them would describe the first one as a pleasure. I took them out on one of the Dolphin Fleet boats in Provincetown. The weather was iffy—overcast, with a stiff northeast breeze, and as we left the harbor it began to rain—hard. As we rounded Long Point and left the harbor the rain let up, but the water became rougher and the sixty-five-foot boat began pounding into the teeth of the wind and six- to eight-foot seas. At first Henry and Anna found it a thrilling ride, and they were excited when we came upon a mother humpback whale and her calf lobtailing off the port bow. But in a short while, despite the Dramamine that had been handed out beforehand at the snack bar, many of the passengers, including my two grandchildren, began to get seasick, and Henry and Anna spent most of the rest of the trip slumped miserably against their father's side, oblivious to whales. Still, they weren't as miserable as several of the adult passengers, who stayed inside the cabin the whole time, hunched over plastic bags and groaning, "I paid forty-five dollars for *this*?"

I was afraid that the whale-watch trip would become one of those negative memories my grandchildren would always associate with this visit, but I hadn't counted on the resilience of the young. By the time the boat returned to the wharf, they were feeling much better. Henry announced that he was "92 percent recovered," and Anna was already recasting the experience as a narrative that she would tell, asking, "Remember the guy who puked in his hat?" We walked down Commercial Street to find pizza and ice cream.

That evening we had a beach fire at Cahoon Hollow with more family and friends. The weather seemed to be trying to make up for the rough morning. The day had calmed down, and a gibbous moon, trailed by Venus's bright glow, drifted in the southern sky. A bank of stationary clouds hung several miles offshore like a shelf in a department store. While some of us got the fire going, Christopher played with the kids in the surf, and then clambered up the high sand slopes with them. As evening descended I wired forks to lengths of pinewood, which Anna and Henry used to roast hot dogs, and after that we made s'mores—Henry's first.

The trajectory of the day, which had started on a low note, ended on a high one. As we sat there, feeding the fire, watching the liquid flames, listening to the beat of the rising breakers, and telling stories, one of our group reflected on the magic of a beach party: "You don't need much: a fire, a few hot dogs, some beer and soda, and people who like one another—the rest pretty much takes care of itself."

At about nine thirty Christopher gathered the kids up, and I was pleased see that Anna was reluctant to leave the place I had made for them. "I want to see the fire die down and help to put it out," she said. Her father, running his fingers through her hair, assured her that there would be many more beach fires in her life. And she, with irrefutable ten-year-old logic, replied, "Yes, but not *now!*"

August 2008

DEAD SEAL ON THE BEACH

Last Sunday, as I was walking the beach, I came upon the body of a small young harbor seal, its soft gray coat mottled with black fingerprint smudges. It lay on its stomach, parallel to the beach, with its front flippers and rear leg appendages splayed out from its torso. Its small catlike bewhiskered face had a peaceful expression, like that of a young child who, unconsciously exhausted from play, has fallen asleep on the floor of its playroom. There was the hint of a smile on its face, as if it were continuing to play in its dreams, that uncannily humanoid face of seals that prompts and gives such credence to the legends of selkies and mermaids. Its body was completely unmarked, even the eyes, except for its anal cavity, which had been ravaged, harrowed into a red, raw hole by something fierce and unrelenting.

Oh yes, the beach is an unseemly place. It frolics and indulges in creating scenes and objects that seem to cater to and confirm comforting or reassuring human concepts and images, only to smash them to smithereens with the slightest naked hint of merciless violence. The beach is not a place for reassurance or affirmation, but for revelation and correction. It is the easy juxtaposition of beauty and violation that strikes us, that draws us to these narrow strands, that says, These are the terms, take it or leave it—oh, right, you can't leave it.

March 2010

PLUS ÇA CHANGE

By sheer chance, I happened to be at LeCount Hollow in South Wellfleet on the day the Murphy cottage was demolished. The cottage was the latest, but by no means the last victim of oceanfront erosion on the Cape's Outer Beach. A storm tide on December 27 had undermined the front of the house, and left the porch cantilevered out over the bluff. The porch floor had subsequently dropped out, scattering chairs and other household items down the cliff face and onto the beach.

When I arrived at the landing most of the demolition had been completed, except for some foundation blocks. Two large Mack trucks idled in the dirt driveway as a large crane was finishing the job. I didn't know the owners—Kathryn and Paul Murphy of Mansfield— but I couldn't help but feel sympathy for them, though the outcome had long been obvious and inevitable. The family had bought the house in 1976, when it sat nearly 100 feet back from the bluff. It was, as most of these oceanfront cottages are, a fairly modest structure— two bedrooms, 770 square feet. As Ms. Murphy put it, "It was never a trophy house. We could go down on the weekends, and my kids grew up there. It has a lot of memories."

To add to the poignancy, the Murphys apparently don't have enough land to build another house farther back. The property is currently valued at $1.18 million, though the house was valued at only $108,500. Now that the house is gone, and the owners can't rebuild,

I wondered, How much is the remaining land worth? How much is it worth to sit on one's land in a beach chair and watch the sun rise over the ocean?

But since these problems and questions weren't mine, I was struck by something else in the final stages of the house's demolition. With the house itself mostly gone, the crane appeared to be clawing at the edge of the cliff. I maneuvered closer to the edge and saw three workmen standing on the beach thirty feet below. They had gathered together a pile of debris that had fallen out of the house and onto the beach—plastic chairs, broken wallboard, an old air conditioner, wooden planks, and a couple of windows. The crane was lowering on a chain what appeared to be part of an old oil tank, with one end cut off, forming a large black metal bucket. When the bucket reached the men at the bottom, they filled it with the beach debris and the crane hauled it back up the cliff—quite dexterously, I thought—and dumped it into one of the waiting trucks. The cliff was so steep that the men had to haul themselves back up by climbing a thick rope.

Watching all this, I had a strange sense of déjà vu—well, not déjà vu exactly, since it wasn't something I'd actually seen before, but rather read about—vicarious déjà vu, I suppose. In any case I realized that the whole thing reminded me of the old wrecking business on the Outer Cape a hundred years ago, when professional "wreckers," or salvagers, plied their trade along these open shores, hauling up cargo from the shipwrecks that occurred here with such regularity before the Cape Cod Canal opened in 1914. The old wreckers used teams of horses, hawsers, and simple pulley systems instead of today's diesel horsepower and mechanized cranes, and the wreckage, in the case of the Murphy cottage, came from the opposite direction, from the land itself rather than the ocean. But in the end the basic process was the same: men making money from hauling away what the ocean had caused to be deposited on the beach.

January 2011

TEN YEARS AFTER

This morning I went out to Cahoon Hollow a little before seven. The air was crystal clear, calm, in the low sixties. The surf was milling, muscular, menacing. From the parking lot the slanted path to the beach held a river of human footprints, spilling and spreading out onto the beach like a sea of little sandy waves. Already the waves themselves had scaled the summer's beaches and reached the base of the cliffs, wiping out large sections of the season's footprints from sight and memory.

As I walked the beach I found myself distracted from my surroundings. It occurred to me that I had been walking the Outer Beach, more or less regularly, for more than four decades, in all weathers and all seasons. How much distance had I covered in that time? Say a mile every two weeks? Say twenty-five miles a year for—oh, forty years. Say roughly a thousand miles, then. A thousand miles—an almost biblical figure. And yet somehow meaningless in a place like this. You can walk for hours, days, years, even, and have no sense of having made progress. You merely plod along in shifting, unchanging sands as the beach curves and constantly recedes in front of you.

And how much time have I spent out here? It might be a moment, or a million years. Time on the beach does not signify progress or duration, but only repetition. It does not define or control events but merely marks them. It does not even set the pace. "Time and tide wait for no man," we say, but on the Outer Beach, it is time that waits on the tide, for the tide and storms and currents can freeze time, hasten it, make it run and jump, or crawl. Though nothing ultimately escapes time, here it is the pawn, the fool, the toy of the earth's implacable and cyclical forces.

Sun and shade race over the outer cliffs' ancient, veined face with almost comical regularity. The invisible growth and life of the land behind the cliffs roll over and down the face of the scarp like succeeding generations, leaving little bright petals of green against its barren dry cheek for us to make of what we will. For that matter, even the notion of generations is ours, arbitrarily marking transitions in an undifferentiated community of human arrival and departure.

Nothing escapes time, though it can give the illusion of doing so. There are certain individuals who seem to defy aging and mock death—George Burns, or the Queen Mum, or Betty White. They are like those rocks that protrude and hang out over the beach cliffs for years, seeming to defy gravity and erosion—only to be found one morning prostrate on the sands of time.

So I trace emerging and disappearing forms here on the beach. I mark the passage and return of seasons and their passengers, catch its contours in the net of my own memory, and even project its future continuance. And yet in the end, it is all a going down and a refunding—and time, time itself is timeless.

September 11, 2011

THE QUIET TIME

Midweek, early September. These are the days we wait for. This is the time when, as year-round residents, we reclaim the beaches for our own. We share them, benevolently, with young families carrying preschool kids, scattered college students with late-starting semesters, and retired couples with smiles on their faces, as if they have some deep secret.

Yesterday at dusk I drove down to White Crest Beach in South Wellfleet. There were only two cars in the parking lot. White Crest lacks the sublime scale of Truro's Long Nook, but it shares that same expansive sense of bare space and pure sand, of the body of the Cape spilling itself out onto the apron of the sea.

I walked along the waves' edge, simply savoring the serenity of the day's end. The surf was insignificant—more like that of the bay than the ocean—a half foot at most—formal and regular. There was an object in the water about fifty feet offshore. In the dying light I first thought it was a lobster buoy, or even a plump shark fin. (We're allowed to think "shark" now on any of our beaches, since the arrival of great whites off our coast a few years ago in pursuit of the Outer Beach's exploding gray-seal population.) But it was a seal head—a gray seal—relaxing, its nose in the air, the back of its head resting on the surface of the swells as on a pillow. The seal remained in this position, unmoving, for at least five minutes, totally unaware of me, or of itself as shark bait.

I passed a young woman in her late teens—her blond hair tied back in a ponytail, her modest beach bag set neatly above the wrack line, her jeans rolled up. She toyed solemnly and barefooted with the low waves. To the north a young couple with an infant riding in her father's backpack also strolled barefoot in and out of the curling seethes of water and foam. So we play in the soft teeth of the ocean.

On the darkening bluff behind them, lights came on in several of the beach cottages. These soft lights, too, seemed to partake of the evening's calmness and the peaceful surf. Yet I could see these lights only because the cottages they belong to are now perched precariously near the cliff edge. Each year the number of these oceanfront cottages grows fewer. Last winter three more were claimed by the sea in our town; or rather, they were condemned and dismantled before the ocean took them. It seems to me curious that the owners of these modest, weathered structures command such a full view of the instrument of their imminent destruction. I wonder, Do they learn the skill of letting go more readily than the rest of us? Does the sea give them the gift of acceptance with grace in exchange for what it takes from them? From the public comments of those who have lost their sea perches, it seems that this may be so. And if so, what does it feel like to close the door and hear the click of the latch for the last time on a place still tangible, but already a memory?

September 2012

MILDLY LAWLESS

Beachcombing—or salvaging, or wrecking, whatever you want to call it—contains certain inherent ethical, if not legal, questions. No one would hesitate to pick up, and keep, a length of rope or a two-by-four found on the beach. On the other hand, if you come upon a lobster pot that would look great on your front lawn, but has the name and license number of the owner attached to it, you have a moral as well as a legal obligation to try to return it.

But there are many gray areas in beachcombing, where the questions are not so easily answered. When does something on the beach become officially abandoned? How long should one wait for an unidentified owner to return and claim it?

A little over a month ago I was walking the beach and there, just north of Cahoon Hollow, I came upon a beach-volleyball net, supported by two pressure-treated twelve-foot four-by-fours. Flung over the net was the bottom half of a flowered bikini. The net had probably been there all summer. It was now several weeks after Labor Day, most of the summer people were gone, and there was no sign that the net was still being used. I was tempted, but decided to wait a while to see if the owner or owners would come to reclaim it.

Last week I returned to the site to find the volleyball net still there, though the bikini bottom was gone. It seemed clear to me that the structure now qualified as "wreckage," so I decided to salvage it. First I spent ten minutes unraveling the Gordian knot of polyurethane string, plastic rope, and bungee cord that attached the net to the landward post. Then, using a short-handled, flat-bladed shovel, I dug out about two feet of sand around the post and easily lifted it out of the sand. It was heavy, but not too heavy. I carried it on my shoulder up the long, diagonal footpath in the bank to the parking lot. When I reached the top I was breathing heavily, but I loaded the post on top of the car and returned to the beach. (There's nothing like exertion to help create a sense of entitlement to something you're trying to lay claim to.) I decided not to take time to unravel the other end of the net, but simply rolled it around the post and carried it back up the sand path to join the first post.

When I arrived home I unloaded the posts and the net, feeling satisfied with my haul. Then I began thinking what I might do with it. I first considered using the posts to expand our fenced-in dog yard. On the other hand, I remembered my wife, Kathy, saying how much she liked playing badminton. Perhaps it would be appropriate to have it serve as a badminton court, a variation on its original use. In the end, though, utility won out, and I used the posts to construct a new compost bin for our garden, and mounted the net on some stakes to serve as a trellis for our climbing peas and beans.

So what once provided recreation on a summer's beach now holds last summer's garden herbage and this fall's kitchen garbage. Over the winter it will perform its composting alchemy to grow next spring's fruits and vegetables, some of which will have support provided by the mounted volleyball net. Truly the beach is, if nothing else, a place of transformation.

October 2012

10

....

Newcomb Hollow

THE SECOND HAND OF TIME

Most of us who live near the Outer Beach are aware that its gla-cial bluffs are gradually eroding, We may even be aware of the average rate of erosion that's usually given—about three and a half feet a year—though this rate, like the "average American," exists in no particular place and in any case appears to be increasing with accelerating sea-level rise. Summer visitors, lounging on a wide sum-mer beach, with the surf lapping peacefully, safely, at their bare feet, may wonder how this happens. Those of us who stay and witness a fall northeaster, think we know.

Two weekends ago the parking lots at Coast Guard and Nauset Light Beaches were crowded with cars. It was a weather day: The rain had paused, the gale winds and tumultuous seas still raged, and Cape residents had come out, one was tempted to say, to peer over the edges of their land and check its foundations. But most, in fact, stayed in the shelter of their cars to watch the show, and those who had climbed out and breasted the wind to the edge of the bluffs wore curious, embarrassed smiles. There was almost a festive air, a sense of sharing a ritual that lifted us out of our daily trivialities, as though for once we had found something better and more genuine than matinees and ball games to turn to on a rainy weekend afternoon.

Standing in such places, with the sand and surf stinging our faces, watching the storm surf nibble and chomp at the cliffs' underpinnings, erosion is obvious. Nevertheless, the actual *recession* of the cliff face goes largely unobserved. We know it is happening, from measurements and photographs, but for the most part it is too slow to see, like the movement of the hour hand of a clock. Or else, like the minute hand on one of those old industrial clocks that jumps from mark to mark, the cliff face may fall back in sudden, dramatic collapses of entire sections. But again, unless we happen to be in the right place at the right moment, even these dramatic examples of punctuated equilibrium occur unwitnessed by human eyes.

The first, or gradual, type of erosion usually takes place where the cliff face is a mixture of fine to medium sandy till deposited by the Wisconsin Stage glaciers. The second, or catastrophic, form of erosion usually occurs where older clay deposits are undermined and give way suddenly. Such an event occurred at the Clay Pounds in North Truro in September 1972, when ten thousand cubic feet of cliff went in a single storm.

But there are other places, when conditions are just right, where (to continue the clock analogy) the sweep of the second hand of the erosion clock is clearly visible—that is, where the steady, moment-to-moment gradual recession of the glacial bluffs is in plain sight. This tends to occur where the bluff is composed of alternating layers, or steps, of clay and softer, sandy till.

There are many such places along the Outer Beach, and a few days after the last storm I visited one that lies about halfway between Newcomb Hollow Beach in Wellfleet and Ballston Beach in Truro. At this point the bluffs are about 150 feet high and seem to consist of alternating layers of blue clay several feet thick and seams of lighter, softer, sandier till. At the bottom of them the National Seashore has posted signs that read "KEEP BACK FROM SLIDING CLIFFS."

When I approached the bluff to look for evidence of sliding cliffs, I encountered instead a vast panorama of miniature "sand falls": cascades of fine sand pouring over the series of clay terraces, just as waterfalls pour over rock outcrops. But unlike most waterfalls, such sand falls do not flow all the time. Weather conditions have to be just right, as they were that day. The cliff sand, loosened by the recent storm, had had time to dry out, and now a steady northeast wind was blowing out over the lip of the bluff and down its face. For the most part the sand falls seem to consist of fine, uniform grains of quartz. Where the sand slid over the clay ledges it produced a fine tingling spray that felt like dry rain against my bare arm.

As they descended the slope, these dry cataracts of sand increased in volume until at the bottom, they spread out into wide deltas or fans of perfect sifted sand, ready for a mason. These sands were up to twelve feet high and twenty feet wide. Being finer and looser than the compacted cliff material, they lay at a flatter angle to the beach. Since it was virtually windless at the base of the sheltering cliffs, these formations lay in a delicate balance. By scooping out only a few handfuls at the base, I could cause the entire fan to slide down several feet.

These lovely ephemeral sand forms are fragility itself. Like the surf that sinks in seconds into the sand of the upper beach, they would in a matter of a few tides be largely removed from the bluff and reformed into new, smooth beach. Yet, like their liquid counterparts, the streams of flowing sand produced visible grooves and channels in the clay ledges as they cascaded over them. Here and there large chunks of dislodged clay lay upended on the beach, testimony to the erosive action of sand itself on these sea cliffs.

Erosion is not a simple result of ocean storms (though that is the impression we get from TV and newspaper accounts, or even from casual observations during northeasters), but a complex process involving surf, rain, wind, currents, ice, spray, beach pebbles, air pockets trapped in storm waves that "explode" against the cliffs, sand, and even salt. The complexity of erosive forces working against the cliffs of the Outer Beach reflects that of its own glacial origins, a tangled and still-unraveled series of ice advances and withdrawals, sea swal-lowings, sedimentation, ice upthrusts, overlayering, and peelings-off.

The landscape of the earth is a mutual product of its larger and smaller forces. The larger forces of Earth—its inner fires, climatic epochs, the collisions and subductions of the continental plates—tend to produce a rough and chaotic terrain upon which the more steady and humble forces—wind and rain, wave and sand, even life itself—conspire to smooth the roughness, sculpt the forms, and clothe Earth's nakedness in pleasing continuities.

Yet, oddly enough, it is here, in these modest, delicate sand falls, that the millennium-long process of erosion can appear most awe-some, most relentless. It is here that the very sands of Cape Cod can be seen running out upon themselves.

September 1976

NANCY

The Outer Beach makes discrete gestures, presents them to us for our regard, contemplation, consideration, or whimsy, and then, whether or not we have managed to extract some meaning or moral from them, withdraws and extinguishes them. They last for the duration of a tide, a moon cycle, a season, and, in rare instances, for a span of years.

Such was "Nancy," a tear-shaped sea stack, round on her seaward side, tapering toward the rear, that separated herself from the retreat-ing glacial scarp of the beach during the autumn storms of 2002 about a half mile north of Wellfleet's Newcomb Hollow Beach. I remember standing on the bluff during one of those northeasters, watching the waves slipping around her form, which was still tenuously attached to the base of the cliff like an umbilical cord, though the connection grew thinner and thinner with each surge. When it finally snapped, the stack stood some forty feet from the cliff.

Nancy was a discrete glacial wart, an unconsolidated conglomerate composed of yellow, beige, and blue clays, leached iron oxide, gravel, and sand. Because these materials are harder and more compacted than the surrounding glacial till and drift, the waves acted as a natural sculptor, slowly releasing the sea stack's form to stand as a distinct figure in the landscape for two and a half years.

At her birth, Nancy was some fifteen feet tall, with a flat, butte-like top, and some twenty-five feet long from front to back. Over her lifespan I and many other Wellfleetians made brief, regular pilgrimages to her, as we would to a wrecked hull or a stranded whale. We admired the stack's complex colors and textures, her ever-changing shape, her different aspects at different hours and in different seasons. Sometimes Nancy appeared as a shaggy mammoth, crawling out of the sea; at others, in the intense light of dawn, as a bit of red-rock canyon from Utah. In winter she occasionally appeared as a piece of snow-capped mountain ridge, or a prehistoric menhir. On other days and in other lights she assumed the shape of a benign saurian face, or that of an ancient hawk. She became a mutable but familiar visage, gradually diminishing in front of our eyes. We loved her stubbornness and futile resistance, her air of calm resignation in the face of her inevitable destruction; in that, perhaps, we saw what was most us, or at least what we hoped for when our time came.

One September evening, about a year after Nancy's birth, I paid a solitary visit to the sea stack. Though the light was long gone from the beach and floated serenely on the virgin blue waters far offshore, its slanted soft glow still bathed the upper slopes above the beach. The sea stack looked much smaller than I remembered, but when I finally came up to her, she was about the size she had been last June.

In the purple evening light, Nancy looked even more like a desert formation, a miniature Great Basin butte plucked up and set down here on the beach. She looked so dry, so finely wrinkled and parchment-like, the color almost totally bleached out of her, more worn, it seemed, by time, wind, and rain than by the sea, though it was the sea that birthed her and the sea that would take her back. A few patches of strong color, facets of what appeared to be bloodred vitreous stone, proved to be only the thinnest veneer of a polished iron leachate covering the uniformly green-tinted beige of the clay. Over the summer the stack had been worn mostly by human activity. Her sides, I noticed, had been hacked out in places, apparently to create footholds and handholds for intrepid beach climbers to ascend her mighty twelve-to-fifteen-foot-high summit, leaving a considerable amount of clay scree at the base.

Not far from the sea stack was a tall, bent, steel well pipe that once drew water for a vanished beach cottage that stood in the air above it several decades ago. Perhaps because of the increased beach traffic to this site during Nancy's existence, the pipe was transformed into one of those numerous improvised beach installations—sculptures, collages, mobiles, even rude shelters—that spontaneously appear on the Outer Beach each summer. Many hands decorated the well pipe with found beach materials: driftwood, plastic bottles and tubs, buoys and floats, pieces of fishnet and lobster pots, shells, seaweed, balls, and crabs, giving it a festive air. One of the floats was a bright red-orange piece of Styrofoam with "NANCY" engraved on it, which gave the stack its local name.

Seen from a certain angle, the decorated well pipe appeared to bend over the sea stack in a protective, almost maternal way. Each winter the storms would come, and these beach baubles grew ragged and heavy, bending the pipe farther over and giving it a defeated or mourning look. Gradually Nancy's bulk was worn away by the relentless battering of storm waves, until at last, by early 2005, the pipe stood alone, naked on the beach, looking somehow bereft.

One does not have to give in to sentimental anthropomorphism to feel the sense of a bond between two such inanimate objects, or the suggestion of some elemental, universal drama in which we all share. Here once stood this stubborn, discrete shape—a disappearing sea stack we called Nancy—a momentary, changing, yet recognizable form amid the chaos and mutability of the Outer Beach. How can we not see our own condition in such a phenomenon? We marked her gestation, her birth, her emergence, her vicissitudes, her diminishment, and the extinction of her brief existence. We gave her a name. She became a familiar presence, and, in spite of ourselves, we could not withhold feeling some affection, and empathy, for this insentient, beautiful, passing form.

December 2002–February 2005

THE ADVENT WHALE

On December 16 a humpback whale washed up just south of Newcomb Hollow Beach in Wellfleet. She was a six-year-old forty-foot female named Beacon. We knew this because she had been named and followed for years by the Provincetown Center for Coastal Studies. Because she came ashore in the weeks before Christmas, some of the locals dubbed her the "Christmas Whale," or the "Advent Whale."

I first saw the body three days after it beached. By that time the weekend crowds had dispersed, and there were only a few other curious onlookers. The whale lay near the base of the cliffs, draped over the break in the beach and oriented seaward, its massive fins splayed out on the sands. On its left side the carcass had been cut or ripped open, and all the guts had spilled out. Nearly all the blubber on that side had been flensed, or stripped off the torso. Things were pretty ripe downwind.

At first I didn't understand why the torso had been so thoroughly flensed, but I later learned that the Seashore would not allow the Marine Mammal Stranding Network to remove the carcass whole. They felt it was too environmentally risky to allow trucks or front-end loaders on the narrow, steep winter beach. So perhaps the flensing was a way of removing what they could to hasten decomposition.

I went out again the next morning in the midst of a driving northeast snow squall. This time I had the whale to myself. The wind was herding crashing green breakers onto the beach, and white snakes of snow dust hissed and sizzled around my ankles. When I came to the whale the snow had cast a thin white veil over its windward side, as if trying to provide its violated body some shreds of dignity. A small flock of gulls stood patiently on the beach a little to the south. I went around to the leeward side of the body, where its immense bulk provided a windbreak. The frozen air had stifled the stench as well. Sand had already begun to pile up on this side too, covering one of the flippers. Perhaps, I thought, the beach would accomplish its own burial.

Far to the south, obscured in the flying snow, I saw a four-footed figure skulking along the base of the cliffs. When I lifted my binoculars to my eyes, it had disappeared. A coyote? A fox? A feral dog? We were not the only ones with an interest in this event, or, for that matter, not even the ones with the most compelling interest. After all, it was just a whale to us, not a matter of life and death.

The day after Christmas the whale was gone. A howling gale the night before seemed to have done the trick. I spoke to a man who had been on the beach during the storm. He said he watched the shelf on which the whale lay being undercut by the surf, until suddenly the decomposing carcass rolled down the beach into the foaming surf and was gone. Just like that. The ocean had solved the cetacean disposal problem on its own. It made the whale's appearance seem more like an apparition than an advent. There was no sign of it left on the beach, or any sign that it had ever been there. Had it actually been there? The beach has a way of making even the most solid and permanent objects seem like illusions.

December 2004

A MYSTERY WRAPPED
IN A CONUNDRUM

I often wonder what it is that compels us to find such curiosity in things washed up on the beach. From clamshells to pieces of glass, from pieces of driftwood to fragments of fishing nets, from beached whales to beached shipwrecks, they draw us to the beach like bees to honey. Couch potatoes who wouldn't walk ten feet to crack a cold beer will slog half a mile over wet sand to view the stranded and stinking carcass of a dead whale. Stay-at-homes who wouldn't consider driving five miles to visit a sick aunt will drive across three states to snap photos of the waterlogged hulk of an old schooner.

Of all the things that draw us to such beach wrack and wreckage, first and foremost is the mystery of what they are and where they came from. Our imaginations seek a story for such beach finds, and if the facts are not known, we will make them up. Over the years I have heard people tell the wildest and most improbable stories about objects found on the Outer Beach, with the passionate conviction of personal knowledge.

The other thing that draws us to objects on the beach is simply the fact that they come from the sea. Whether they are natural or human-made, there is something inherently mysterious about anything that is offered up or given back by the sea. Even if the object is familiar or known, it has suffered "a sea change" by being submerged in an element that, despite the findings of contemporary oceanography, remains largely mysterious.

For the past month the residents of Wellfleet—and hundreds, prob-ably thousands, of out-of-town visitors—have made a pilgrimage to the latest mystery thrown up by the sea. On the night of January 28, 2008, during a fierce northeaster, the sea lifted up the hull of an old wooden schooner and, with incomprehensible force, depos-ited it intact on the upper beach about a thousand feet south of the Newcomb Hollow parking lot. The wreck is an imposing and impres-sive sight. About sixty feet long, it is composed of a series of mas-sive, curved six-by-ten-inch oak ribs with three-inch-thick planking attached by wooden pegs and iron spikes. Although the hulk must have lain on the sea bottom for close to a hundred years, the wood appears to be in a perfectly preserved state.

All shipwrecks attract crowds, but one of the things that has added to the lure of this particular wreck is the mystery of its identity. Despite its massive size and well-preserved state, there seem to be no distinctive clues. Experts who have looked at it have offered dates of its age that range from the early eighteenth to the late nineteenth century. With more than three thousand wrecks along this coast over the centuries, there are plenty of candidates for the name of this one, and several have been suggested, but none with any conviction. No one can say when or how the ship was wrecked, or how long it had reposed under the sea. In fact, there is not even any agreement as to whether, at the time of its sinking, it was an active fishing vessel, or whether it was a cut-down version, transformed into a barge after its life as a schooner was over.

But beyond the mystery of the ship's origin and identity, the whole scene has been wrapped in additional conundrums about human behavior itself. The other day, when I visited the wreck again, there were several dozen people there, including a young boy who stared at the ship in wide-eyed wonder, then asked his father, "Do you think it's a Viking ship, Dad?" The grown-ups around him smiled and chuckled in condescending appreciation of the boy's imaginative naïveté, but I thought, Do we really know any more about the ship's identity than the boy does? Doesn't what we think we know really come from what we have read or what somebody else has told us? In other words, could any of us really say how we knew it *wasn't* a Viking ship? For that matter, how many of us could *prove* that the sun doesn't revolve around the earth? So much of what we regard as personal knowledge is literally *received* wisdom.

Another conundrum has to do with our attitude toward the ship and its legal status. Stuck in the sand surrounding the wreck are several small official signs on fragile little sticks warning visitors that, because it beached on land administered by the National Park Service, the wreck is a "protected cultural resource" under federal law and that it is therefore illegal "to excavate, remove, disturb, deface or destroy" any part of it, and that violators will face "severe penalties." Fair enough, if the National Seashore actually planned to preserve the wreck for study or to make an exhibit of it. But they don't. The signs themselves admit that the wreck will, in time, be reclaimed by the sea, "to be buried again until the next time the sea uncovers it."

Such abstract prohibitions test human nature. Just a couple of generations ago, any shipwreck on the beach was fair game for local residents, and many old houses on the Cape are partially framed, sheathed, or decorated with material from such wrecks. I was pleased to observe signs that the old instinct is still alive. Despite the warnings, several chunks of the ship's ribs have already been sawed or chipped away. Moreover, I could see the old Cape Codders' covetousness still alive in the eyes of the law-abiding visitors. I even heard one mutter, "I wish there weren't so many people around—that peg there looks pretty loose."

And why not? If the wreck is going to be reclaimed by the sea anyway, why not let us grab some piece of it before it goes, something that will give us some tactile connection, if only in our imaginations, with a more adventurous and earnest past, a time when, in Cape author Joseph Lincoln's words, "Men must die so men can live"? In our increasingly digital and virtual world, we seem to crave, more than ever, some contact with something so solid, something fashioned by hand from oak beams and iron spikes, something that could last so long at the bottom of the sea, and be thrown up, as if in rebuke, to our wondering eyes.

January 2008

BEACH BALL

Over the years I've picked up and carried home from the beach any number of objects—beach stones, shells, lobster buoys, driftwood, odd lengths of rope, unidentifiable bits of flotsam and wreckage, and once, a dead dovekie (the smallest of our pelagic seabirds). Most of these items have lingered on my porch, or in my study, or in my freezer, until I finally discarded them.

But I didn't fully realize the depth and power of the beachcombing urge until one day last month when I arrived at the ocean. I was the only one on the beach. The tide was still low, but coming in. A hundred yards from the parking lot and halfway down the foreslope of the beach sat a large, round dark object. When I got to it, it proved to be a steel or iron ball. It was about twenty inches in diameter, with a three-inch opening running through the middle of it. It must have weighed at least seventy or eighty pounds. It was obviously hollow, however, and airtight, or it would never have floated up on the beach. I assumed it was some kind of float, perhaps a stabilizer for a light buoy. Whatever it was, it had *substance*, and I knew immediately that I had to have it, or would at least give every effort, short of a heart attack, to possess it.

I set my shoulder against the ball and began rolling it up the soft wet beach. Getting it up to the high-tide line wasn't easy, but it was doable. At that point it occurred to me that I could leave the ball there and go for assistance, or even come back the next day. After all, did I really think that someone else would be crazy enough to try to move this useless, heavy object up the beach in my absence? Well, *yes*.

So I put my shoulder to the ball again and rolled it across the wide flat expanse of upper beach to the base of the slope leading up to the parking lot. Here there was a fairly steep rise of some ten to twelve feet. I started pushing the ball up the sand path that slanted obliquely down to the beach, but I was able to move it only a few feet at a time before having to stop for breath. At this point I realized I was on the brink of reenacting the Greek myth of Sisyphus, who was condemned to roll a rock up a steep hill, only to see it roll back down every day. If my object rolled back down the beach, I knew I wouldn't have the strength or the resolve to try it again.

Eventually, however, I managed to roll the ball up the slope and onto the asphalt. I had just enough strength left to hoist it up into the back of my van, packing and padding it with blankets and cardboard boxes. I drove the ball to my friend Ralph, who can identify anything. Sure enough, he identified it as a "bottom roller," part of a fishing trawler's rig that attaches to the bottom of the net to help it roll smoothly across the ocean floor. This would explain both its heaviness and its buoyancy: heavy enough to keep the lower edge of the net on the bottom, light enough to be retrieved easily at the end of a trawl.

I knew there were many environmental objections to bottom-trawling, but this bit of fishing debris seemed relatively benign, and it would make a fine addition to my collection of what I refer to as "conversational landscape objects."

I took the ball home and unloaded it in my driveway. The next day, after it dried out, it gained an unexpectedly lovely patina of golden rust that stretched like water shadows over its surface. It was one of the very few objects I have collected that actually became more beautiful after I brought it home from the sea. But then, I knew it wasn't really "home"; it had only been loaned to me from the sea for a little while—oh, say, a few thousand years.

February 2008

SEA DAWN

Whenever we give visitors directions to our house, we usually say, "You can't miss it. It's the one with the large upside-down boat in the drive." The boat in question—and it is hard to miss—is the thirty-five-foot wooden hull of *Sea Dawn*, a Sam Crocker–design racing schooner built in 1929. Nor was *Sea Dawn* just any racing schooner. It came to us with an aura of world history about it.

Its original owner, we were told, was an Englishman, and at the beginning of World War II it participated in the evacuation at

Dunkirk, the heroic rescue of more than three hundred thousand besieged Allied troops on the coast of Normandy in the spring of 1940 by hundreds of English vessels, private and military, large and small. After the war, in honor of its participation in this historic event, the *Sea Dawn*'s owner renamed it *Wooden World II*, a fact attested to by a rotting life buoy bearing that name that hangs from one of its beams. Subsequently it was sold to someone in Bellport, New York, who had a quarter board with the boat's rechristened name affixed to its stern.

Eventually the schooner made its way to Wellfleet, and in the late 1980s it was acquired by Kim and Philippe Villard, the people who built our house. They were building a sailboat of their own in the driveway and acquired *Sea Dawn* for parts. After they'd stripped it, they managed to turn the hull over and set it up on wood pilings to serve as a rather unconventional carport.

In the years since we have lived here, the large upside-down hull of *Wooden World II*, née *Sea Dawn*, has provided a landmark for visitors and UPS trucks, a durably interesting anecdote to tell friends, and a magnet for our neighbor's young children, Clemmie and Lyle, who think it would make a great clubhouse.

But two weeks ago the boat became part of a tragic local story that has left a hole in this community. On the morning of April 1, Jan Potter, a longtime resident, master builder, and well-known figure in Wellfleet, walked out to Newcomb Hollow Beach and shot himself in the head. I don't intend to dwell on the incident or to speculate on the reasons that Jan took his life. I simply want to speak of my connection to him, which was not unusual or notable except in one regard.

I knew Jan for many years, though we were not close friends. On the other hand, he was something more than an acquaintance. I frequently saw him at the local coffee shop, where he always had a friendly and slightly ironic greeting. We spent several late evenings in the local bar watching Red Sox playoff games together. Ours was at most a casual friendship, the kind that local gathering places foster without imposing any of the responsibilities or obligations of close friends. But it was real nonetheless, one of those informal but reliable relationships that make you feel you belong to a true community. Last summer, when Jan's oldest son, Caleb, suffered life-threatening injuries in a skateboarding accident, my wife, Kathy, and I, along with the rest of the town, rallied around Jan and his family as best we could, because that is what a community does.

The boat, however, gives me a tangible connection to Jan that I value even more now. For you see, one summer in the late 1980s, Jan and his young family lived on *Sea Dawn* in Wellfleet Harbor, and it was from Jan that Kim and Philippe acquired it. Last fall I put a long-contemplated plan into effect and closed in the space beneath the hull to make a workshop out of it. It was something I thought Jan would approve of. In fact, when I rather proudly told him about it, he did seem pleased. I said he should stop by and see it sometime. He said he would, and seemed to mean it. He never did.

But there was another, even more remarkable connection. Our neighbor, Galen Malicoat, the mother of little Clemmie and Lyle, who have so frequently visited that boat, passed Jan walking toward the beach that fateful April morning as she drove the kids to school. She said she was late or she would have stopped to greet him. Two days later Galen gave birth to a new son, Ryland James. It was a home birth, with the aid of her husband, Beau Valtz, and two midwives. It was an easy delivery, and mother and son are doing very well.

Now, as a confirmed rationalist, I don't believe in cosmic alignment. But the juxtaposition of these two events, one so dark, the other full of light, seems to stretch the bounds of coincidence. As I contemplate the nexus of death and birth that somehow gathered around *Sea Dawn*, there come unbidden into my mind the words of Laura Nyro's great anthem from the late 1960s: "And when I die, and when I'm gone / There'll be one child born and a world to carry on, to carry on."

April 2008

SHELTER ON THE BEACH

Wednesday afternoon was one of those bright, sparkling, September days that we live for and just want to walk through all day long. It was a day that confirmed F. Scott Fitzgerald's assertion that life seems to begin anew when the air first turns crisp in the fall. Kathy and I, with our dog, Putt, went to the beach, following a path from one of the ponds through a cut in a small dune that had been worn by the innumerable feet of summer.

Just north of the cut was one of those improvised beach shacks that seem to spring up over the summer, made of driftwood and other available flotsam washed up on the beach. These impromptu shelters seem to have no more functional purpose than sand castles, but, like them, seem to spring from some atavistic architectural urge to create some structure at the edge of the land, to leave our signature on the beach.

This one was tucked into the base of the sand cliff. It was in the shape of a trestle, with two short posts connected by driftwood cross-ties, sloping back into the cliff and creating a shallow lean-to shelter about ten feet wide, eight feet deep, and three and a half feet high at the opening.

The roof was boarded over with driftwood two-by-fours, providing nearly solid shade but hardly waterproof. The lintel post had been painted black, and on it "WELCOME" was printed in white letters. Flanking this word were several child-size white handprints that reminded me of those I have seen in Neolithic caves in France and Spain.

Despite its primitive structure, the bones of the shelter were highly furnished and decorated. The sides were covered in white canvas sheets, in which small holes were charred around the edges. A lobster pot was placed at the back of the space, providing a low table or a shelf to lean against. There were two broken aluminum-frame folding chairs inside. But the most impressive addition was a series of hangings nailed over the opening, most of them onion bags containing beach pebbles, shells, beach glass, and gull feathers. There was a lobster buoy, and a rather large stone hanging from a rope, to which a green toothbrush had been attached. It seemed to have all the amenities.

We went inside the shelter and sat on the sand, and I was struck by how instantly this simple structure framed the ocean, as if we were watching it on a screen inside a derelict movie theater. Putt placed herself in a Sphinx-like position, crossing her front legs, directly in front of us, just beyond the nonexistent threshold. There was an unexpected but powerful sense of peace embodied in her look of utter animal contentment and belonging. It was as if we were some kind of primeval family looking out of our cave, as if we had always been here and always would be. It was as close as I have ever come to a racial memory.

Because of its placement at the upper edge of the beach, I thought the shelter would last at least through the winter. But when I went out looking for it one day later in the month, it had utterly vanished. Many pieces of driftwood and plastic debris lay strewn about the site, but it was impossible to say which pieces might have been part of the vanished shelter and which were random beach flotsam. There was no verifiable sign that it had ever been, and I even had doubts that this was the specific site where it had stood. So utterly had it disappeared that I had to wonder if, in fact, it had ever actually existed, or if I had imagined it. Once again, the beach seems to say, it all comes to nothing.

Speak to her, cherish your children, do good work, dance while the music plays, for the night cometh when no man dances.

September 2008

CLAY

September 24, 1976. Just south of Newcomb Hollow in Wellfleet is a large clay outcropping, some thirty to forty feet high and about 150 feet long, protruding like some massive dark rounded brow from the surrounding cliffs. Most of it is composed of Gardiners clay, or, as it is more commonly known, blue clay. Blue clay, the geologists say, was laid down as lake-bottom deposits during one of the interglacial periods, when the sea levels rose, covering all but the highest hills of the Cape and Islands. Minute particles of blue clay were sorted out and deposited in thick and almost pure layers in several places on the Outer Cape, and the outcrops at Newcomb Hollow are some of the largest and most dramatic. Unlike clay deposits on other parts of the shoreline, these are not stratified but rather a jumbled mixture of the hard blue Gardiners clay and a lighter tan outwash till. The clay projects several feet beyond the softer, more easily eroded till on either side of it, and its face is scored and veined with a complex pattern of rain channels. Where the unconsolidated sand cliffs all have a slope, or "angle of repose," of about thirty-seven degrees, the clay formations are tilted seventy, eighty, in places ninety degrees and even more—unscalable cliffs, even more so than the mountainous precipices they mimic, for picks and ropes and crampons would find no hold in these solid-seeming walls.

January 29, 1987. Blue clay, when wet, is soft and highly malleable, like modeling clay. The other day, out at the Newcomb Hollow outcrop, I carved out a chunk of the clay, molded it into a sphere about two and a half inches in diameter, and brought it home. I put it in a small bowl on my desk, and left it. It was so gumbolike and squelchy in consistency that I expected it would simply melt into the contours of the bowl, but two days later, to my surprise, it had not only kept its spherical shape but had become bone dry and so hard that I could not dent it with my fingernail. It had also recovered its lighter blue-gray color and glinted with thousands of tiny shards of light, micro particles of quartz that covered its surface. It looked like a miniature moon of a miniature planet.

I held the hardened globe in my hand, contemplating it, and found that the glinting needles of quartz transferred to my skin. It seemed to be saying, I can be near-liquid or dry and hard as a bone, all at the same temperature, with just the addition or subtraction of moisture. There was, in fact, something organic about it, as if it were not just an inanimate, inert substance, but something shifting and transforming, like one of those microscopic tardigrades, or water bears, that can in the absence of water become dry and nearly permanently dormant, all of its organic processes suspended indefinitely, its state not contingent upon any internal processes but a change in external conditions, a change for which it might wait for with illimitable patience.

This comparison of blue clay with life-forms, it turns out, is not mere fancy. I shaved off some of the sphere's surface onto a slide, put the clay dust under a high-power dissecting scope, and was surprised to see that it was full of tiny, intricate, crystal-like needles. Curious about what they were, I turned to Barbara Blau Chamberlain's *These Fragile Outposts: A Geological Look at Cape Cod, Martha's Vineyard, and Nantucket*. Though published in 1964, it is still one of the most informative—and lyrically written—books about the Cape's geology. Chamberlain describes these outcrops of blue clay as "slices of an exhumed the sea bottom, dried and alien in today's bright sun." She identifies the crystal needles I saw as "many tiny siliceous sponge particles, or hard parts of the sponge animal" that were laid down with clay particles in the rising sea level. In other words, what I was looking at were the fossils of ancient sponges.

Under a higher-power lens, I could also make out the fossils of diatoms, or microscopic one-celled plants, as well as an infinite number of pollen grains—pollen from long-disappeared boreal forests that flourished here before the first invasions of the ice. Of these most tiny pollen nanofossils Chamberlain comments, "So great is nature's regenerative drive that these vital kernels of plant propagation were shaped and armored for a seemingly indefinite survival—and have survived for some fifteen thousand years."

February 18, 1995. On Thursday Kathy and I took a short excursion to Newcomb Hollow. I don't know if it was because I had been away from the beach for so long, but I saw it as if for the first time, a glorious and fascinating place. The surf was moderately high, multi-colored and smelling strongly of seaweed. The surface of the swells looked especially glossy and flecked with froth, as if glass had been melted and allowed to congeal roughly in the shape of waves. We walked down the beach into the sun, past shelflike outcrops of blue and yellowish clay. I picked up a handful of the former and kneaded it into softness as we walked, surprised at how much cold it contained. Portions of the lower bank collapsed gently in places, and little balls of frozen sand ran out onto the beach like scurrying mice. In other places there were veins of a very white, very fine sand, approaching the consistency of talc. Near the top of the cliff, ten to twelve feet below the crest, there ran a ragged horizontal line of dark blue-black material, a foot or more thick, likely a portion of the old soil line that had been covered by sand blown up from the beach.

The beach seemed wonderfully varied, and when we turned back, with the sun at our backs, the whole line of back-tilted cliffs and clay ledges had the aspect of a Southwestern landscape, with all its variety and promise of discovery. I felt exhilarated, and as we passed the first clay bank, threw a hand-softened clump of clay back into the mass, where it stuck like an eye.

April 23, 1996. Yesterday an atypically nice spring morning, too nice not to go out to the beach. There was one other vehicle in the parking lot, and on the beach a young woman and two little girls with a pile of gaudy plastic beach toys, rushing the season a little.

I walked south toward the eroding clay bluffs. They had clearly changed since last I was here. The warm dry weather of the past week has dried them out, draining them of color and giving them a parched, desertlike look. Chunks of light dark-blue clay lay strewn across the lower beach. At least a hundred yards beyond the bluffs a new wall of solid clay had been exposed, perhaps six feet tall and twenty-five feet long, flatly curved, divided by shallow vertical grooves that seemed to be made of iron-oxide encrustations. This newly exposed wall of clay had the look of ancient tablets waiting to be inscribed. In fact the only inscription on it was a crudely scratched game of tic-tac-toe, reminding me of Emerson's observation on the disproportion between natural forces and the uses to which we put them (when he saw the mighty paddlewheel of a river steamboat being harnessed to flush the toilets and clean the asses of its passengers).

I placed my palm, fingers spread out, on the face of the clay wall and immediately felt minute grains of fine sand falling in a light rain from the sandy slope above. It fell in a steady drizzle, pleasant to the skin, with occasional larger pebbles softly striking the back of my hand like gentle hailstones. Within half a minute the sand had filled and obscured the valleys between my fingers, the folds of my knuckles, the mole tunnels of my veins. At the base of the wall the falling sand had already built up a wedge-shaped pile two feet wide and more than a foot tall. The flowing sand fell on it, too, like rain—that is, it made the same pelting marks as rain falling onto dry dirt—but it also fell like snow, visibly building up the wedge as I watched. It occurred to me that if I were to lie down at the base of these gentle sand falls, I would, within a half hour, have been completely buried by this arenaceous precipitation.

Coming back, I noticed, perched on a clay shelf near the top of the scarp, a large glacial erratic, or boulder, some seven feet long, cantilevered several feet out into the air. I made my way up to it, wondering what I would do if it began to tumble, but catastrophe, it appears, takes its time here.

February 11, 1998. Rain, heavy this morning, winds gusty from the southwest. Rain coming down in sleeves off the roof, rattling down the dry throats of the downspouts. Quite dark at 9:00 a.m. The chickadees eat at the feeders like there's no tomorrow. The chickadees always eat like there's no tomorrow. There is no tomorrow

Last Friday morning we went to the beach with Ollie after the storm. The air was shattered and misted in light, intensifying lines and colors of near objects, diffusing the background into luminous shades. The wind was from the north, ripping shreds of foam from the edge of the sliding breakers and sending them scudding like shorebird flocks, or pucks on ice, down the beach, Ollie ran joyfully after them, barking and biting into their insubstantiality with a hunger he neither understands nor can assuage. Otherwise the beach was remarkably wide and clean. The storm had crated some fantastic carvings along the blue clay outcrops, including a cavelike cavity, some twelve feet high and six to eight feet deep, of blue and iron clay, looking like one of those "blowholes" on the rocky coast of Maine—though this one, I know, is a feature of very temporary duration.

February 27, 1998. Clearing yesterday, with a stiff northerly wind, temps in the low forties. I went out to Newcomb Hollow, where the tumultuous surf was a mixture of pure, wind-driven foam and muddy volutes. Heavy erosion continues. The clay cave to the south has collapsed. The storm washed over the line of low dunes to the north and left a large pond of salt water behind them. The wind blew low sand along the beach, getting into Ollie's eyes. At one point a large block of Styrofoam came tumbling down the beach at him. He was startled, then aggressive—taking it personally.

November 12, 1998. The storm cleared out by late afternoon. At midday there was a lull, and Ollie and I went out to the beach, where the waves were large and gray-green but regular and ruly in their coming.

This stretch of cliff, with its massive and various deposits of blue and brown clay, iron deposits, and some large erratics, mimics a rockier coast like Maine's, creating ephemeral, sheer, and even recurved walls, caves, rock slides, and avalanches. Near the top of the bluff the large, protruding glacial boulder that I first observed two and a half years ago has become even more exposed. It looks as if I could dislodge it with a shovel, but it hangs on, like a loose tooth that refuses to fall out.

December 1, 1998. This was the day winter should have begun but didn't. It stayed above fifty degrees overnight, and now at 9:45 a.m.

a light but cold steady rain has begun to fall on the deer hunters out this week. I got in the car and drove out to Newcomb Hollow, where a gusty breeze blew out of the southwest. The sea surged in in strong but stately swells, each foamy one forming a thin, delicate but distinct ridge of sand about a half inch wide and an eighth inch high on the smooth upper beach. In such small, measured, modest increments is nature content to work its most dramatic effects. So the Grand Canyon and the Rocky Mountains were formed, drop by drop, grit by grit—so millimeter by millimeter were Europe, America, and Africa split asunder.

I walked south, into the eye-hurting sun, past the clay outcrops. A new wide parabolic slump of iron conglomerate has spilled out and over the cone of smooth material below it onto the beach, like an opened fish net. In other places, thick rivers of sand have flowed out and around rugged outcrops, some new slumps of yellow clay have created several shallow caves, and in one place a sheer wall of yellowish-brown clay some twelve feet high looks as if it has been clawed vertically by a giant bear. It looked like a recent excavation site, and it was—one older and more continuously worked than the ancient marble quarries of Carrara.

The seven-foot boulder near the cliff top still hangs, a geological tease.

As I turned to go back, the procession of variously colored clay outcrops—yellow-white, blue, gray, orange-yellow—receded up the beach in what seemed to be a "Western" light—that is, slightly hazy and dispersed, at once softening and luminous, that lent scale and dimension to the formations. Once again I literally saw them in a new light. The nearest and largest outcrop, with its stark yellow-white color and sharp convex ridges, seemed particularly ancient, as a dried cod head can look like a paleontological artifact. Not only shape and scale but time is highly mutable on the beach

February 26, 1999. The previous night's high tide had apparently licked six to eight feet up the beach, but also appeared to have *lifted*

the beach, giving it a higher tilt than is usual this time of year. The rest of the bank was plastered in wet, white snow, so that especially along the outcrops of blue clay, the cliffs resembled the snow-covered upper slopes of the High Sierra.

Offshore the wild surf was breaking in six or seven ranks, as far out as a thousand feet or more, and actively, forcefully plunging as it fell, in striped ranks of green falling water, tinged with the beige of sand sucked up into its rolling fall. They reminded me of those old cinematic images of printing presses with their great, roaring rolls of paper striped with the blur of newsprint, bringing us the news of the world.

November 4, 1999. It blew hard Tuesday night and then rained steadily into Wednesday morning. There's been recent extensive erosion of the clay bluffs, forming new and fascinating formations, including a semicircle that looks like a giant Egyptian necklace of blue-gray clay decorated with rusty laminations of ferric oxide. There's been a slump of several feet in front of the protruding erratic that stops just short of it. The whole situation looks very unstable, and I will be surprised if the rock doesn't go this winter.

January 21, 2000. A little after noon yesterday I drove out through the ponds, all now frozen and snow covered, to Newcomb Hollow to look at the beach before the storm. It was about two hours after high tide, and the beach had that strangely bare-washed look adjacent to the snow-covered slopes. The air was calm, but the tide had obviously reached the cliff base. On the sandy slopes frozen salt ice armored the lower two to three feet, and at the vertical clay cliffs, the ice had reached twelve feet in places, conjuring the dramatic sight of waves crashing against the frozen bulwarks, as if against stone cliffs, only hours before.

This stretch of cliff seems to have reached a dramatic peak. There are sheer promontories of yellow and blue clay twenty feet tall, caves of iron conglomerate hollowed out, with trails of stones and chunks of clay running out of their mouths down the snow like animal tracks. There is a solid seam of pure blue clay three to four feet high running along the base of the cliffs here for several hundred feet. The ocean has been washing and carving this wall the past few days, giving it the look of cave drapery, dark Swiss cheese, and volcanic lava.

About halfway to Cahoon Hollow, shortly beyond the cut into the small pond behind the dunes, I came upon a remarkable formation: a shelf of frozen sand about twenty to twenty-five feet above the beach that had been undercut by the looser sand beneath it running out, creating a frozen sand sculpture of a breaking wave, its crest about a foot thick and more than four feet deep. Bits of loose sand were still running off its underside, and I knew such a formation would not last long. Wanting to get a closer look, I started to climb up the slope, a mixture of loose and frozen chunks of sand. The slight shifting I made by climbing proved critical, for all at once I saw that the whole formation was collapsing. I turned and headed straight down to the beach, but the slide overtook me just at the base, and I sprawled forward on my stomach. I was simultaneously shocked and amused when I realized I could not move my legs. A chunk of frozen sand some three and a half feet long had landed directly on my lower body, pinning my left leg tightly. It took me only three or four minutes to wriggle and pull myself free. As it was I suffered only a bruised calf and a slightly abraded ego. But I came closer than I ever have to becoming a part of what it is I observe.

January 24, 2000. The clay formations at Newcomb have, if possible, become even more dramatic, especially at the base of the blue clay layer. Here it was as if the ocean, tired of waiting for potters to come and use the material, had decided to take matters into its own hands, fashioning minisculptures and hangings right on the clay walls, small animal sculptures that protruded out of the clay, Miró-like installations of small stones set in carved round holes and large moons of yellow-brown clay set in the blue. At one point there was a rounded alcove of reddish-yellow sandy clay interrupting the blue, and on its back wall some inspired winter beachcomber had scratched recognizable imitations of the Lascaux Cave paintings: an antelope, a bull, and, to give it a local touch, a fish.

February 10, 2000. The clay bluffs are bathed in warm, soft morning light (despite a cold wind that chills my gloveless hands), deepening the red-orange, blue, brown, and yellow-beige colors of the clay. This remarkable stretch of cliffs, no more than two hundred yards in length, gives me all the drama of the entirety of Big Sur, though it is only one-thirtieth of the latter's height and a considerably smaller fraction than that of its length. It is as rife with ongoing form and ongoing change as a living garden, and blossoms anew for me every time I visit it. And just as its scale is condensed, so is its pace of change. Each time I go out there major changes are taking place in its face: sudden slumps and striated new bowls, large exposed concentric chunks of blue and yellow clay, sharp ridges, and miniature pinnacles of dry, flaky blue clay.

The cantilevered boulder glows in the young light like a bluish-white egg, the egg of some giant roc perched on an unanchored cliff nest. Below it and to each side the twenty-five-foot-high cliffs of blue clay have become uniformly sheer and streaked with vertical gouges from, I presume, the groundwater leaking out over their edges. The rock must go soon, I think.

February 17, 2000. Erosion at Newcomb continues, though slowed by lesser tides of late. The lower layer of blue clay appears to have collapsed, like shattered blue plaster, and lies in jagged heaps at the base of the cliffs. There is a new deposit at the north end, some thick, dark-red iron oxide that appears to have been dissolved by recent rains and flowed down the bluff face out onto the beach, where it congealed into a stiff, boardlike layer of fluid forms about one inch thick. The thin wrack of the last high-tide line was fringed with a broken lacing of bright-green sea lettuce, or Irish dulse. Three or four crows stood on the beach just in front of the first shelf of blue clay. When I got up to it, I found a piece of coconut shell, its white meat still intact, resting on top of the shelf—perhaps floated up from some Caribbean island on the Gulf Stream.

March 29, 2000. Newcomb was fresh washed and shining this morning after two days of rain and wind, stirring up rough-bearded surf in a spring sea that has suddenly recovered its deep-blue color.

The clay walls only get more and more dramatic and make me want to paint, or at least to sketch. Now some of the blue clay walls stand at eighty degrees or steeper, and some of the caves are sprouting small gray stones, a foot or more across, out of their arches. The blue clay protuberances look more and more like the prows of ships emerging from the cliff, framed by dark-red cirques of iron oxide.

The boulder still stands, shining, seemingly impervious and impregnable on its blue-gray pedestal, casting a shadow now beneath its seaward-facing shelf. Even at midmorning, the clay wall supporting it, while steep, is only seventy degrees or so, suggesting that it could erode several feet more before collapsing. But with the summer berm starting to form in front of it, it could easily last the summer without further erosion.

April 20, 2000. How the beach changes from visit to visit! It is like visiting a new country each time, even without the overlay of light and weather that is always different. I should've been documenting this stretch of cliff with a camera. I was struck this time in particular by the finely carved parallel sets of rain streaks down the face of the tall, steep clay banks, pooling in solid little puddles on the sand below. They were all about a half inch wide and a quarter inch deep, markedly parallel, like the strings of a harp, and they seem to weep silently for something. Then there are also dozens of remarkable clay "blossoms": roughly round and petal-like discs of reddish clay up to a foot in diameter that seem to bloom in the side of the blue clay face—like found abstractions.

As Ollie and I sauntered south along the beach there were other signs of recent erosion. Where the deposits were mixed till and sand, the whole face of the cliff, which had formed a thin skin of wet, wind-blown sand, had cracked and slumped, breaking into numerous sand floes separated by shallow fissures, giving the impression of a sloping earthquake, which in fact it was. On these little floes rode both the new plants of the season—mostly bright new spears of beach grass—as well as vegetation fallen from the cliff edge, from small shrubs to beach-plum trees eight feet high. These were mostly blackened and dead, though some had thick tufts of bright-green turf grass still growing around their bases. One curious bush had canted over nearly horizontal. Its branches were bare, but all around its base were doz-ens of long white vegetable fingers nearly a foot long, the kind you get when you try to grow shoots in a dark room, suggesting that, whatever this plant was, it had been buried in sand until recently. So the slow river of descending plants calves off from the great turf cap above, like the great river of icebergs carried down from Greenland by the Labrador Current. And like them, these traveling plants take several years to complete their journey before melting and disappear-ing into the warm sands of the beach.

June 20, 2000. A sunny, hot, dry presummer day. I began photo-graphing the clay cliffs at Newcomb Hollow this morning, shooting about half of the five-hundred-foot stretch of clay outcroppings. There are some interesting new formations: sand-and-clay pillars a foot or two high, like miniature Utah Needles. Several glistening bank swal-lows were gliding in front of the clay banks, darting in and out of the freshly dug nesting holes these birds excavate just below the grassy lip of the cliffs. A salient feature of this landscape is its Heisenbergian character: One often changes the lay of it significantly in the act of observing or photographing it.

June 17, 2002. The clay formations grow more and more fanciful, arabesque even Moorish, eroding into ever-more-convex sculpted shelves lined with fantastic patterns of sand, iron leachate, blue and yellow clay. It must be reaching some kind of elongation limit, some kind of aesthetic peak, after which it will begin to collapse into more prosaic repose once again. I begin to think this really is some once-in-a-lifetime flowering, which I can write about as something that will be gone before my news is published.

November 3, 2000. On Monday afternoon Ollie and I went out to the beach, where a cut five to six feet high ran almost up to the base of the clay banks. An enormous amount of sand had been removed from the beach by the new-moon tides and easterly winds in the past couple of days, revealing a horizontal floor of blue clay along the base of the cliffs, continuing down the beach for least 200 feet in a band 20 to 30 feet wide. These ledges were a mixture of solid blue and the yellow reddish clay mixed with iron oxide, the latter feathered with those thin exfoliations one finds on the vertical cliffs. The impression was of walking over a slick and fragile tessellated marble floor. Never have I seen this particular formation on the Outer Beach, a result, no doubt, of the swiftness with which the covering layer of sand was removed. At first I was sure the big boulder must have dropped, for I spotted a large round stone among these horizontal ledges, but I was wrong. This stone, nearly five feet long, of pure uniform granite, must have been there on the beach all along, with the clay ledges, and like them had simply been rapidly exposed. In the meantime, the Hanging Boulder, as I have come to think of it, remains in its Damoclean perch, the ocean not having quite reached its base.

Ollie and I were the only ones on the beach that afternoon and possibly the first since these ledges had been exposed. The cut in the berm was so high and sheer that I had to jump and flop myself over the edge to get back up on the upper beach, like a seal hauling itself up on a sandbar, while Ollie casually leaped from the upper to lower beach and back again as if to ask, What's the problem?

November 9, 2000. I had planned to go out the next morning to photograph more of the cliffs, but the next four days were full of wind and rain, with strong winds from the northeast and east. I finally got out yesterday afternoon at three thirty, just a little past high tide. The cut in the beach has softened and sloped considerably with subsequent overwashes, but to the south was a scene more reminiscent of the Oregon coast than Cape Cod. Through a mist of shattering wave, a furious surf was flinging itself head-on, as if with self-destructive intent, full force against the lower third of the clay banks, bursting in tremendous crashes and flinging spray twelve to fifteen feet into the air. There was no way to approach the cliffs by way of the beach. It would've been suicide to try it. Beyond this fury, several hundred yards to the south, there was exposed beach again, and lying upon it, like stranded sea beasts, the wrecks of several trees, their size impossible to gauge but, as with all objects on the beach, looking quite large.

This morning the weather cleared, and I went out to Newcomb Hollow again at about eight thirty, an hour and a half or so before low tide. The wind, though still out of the northeast, had lessened, and with it the fury of yesterday's surf, but not its agitation. The breaking swell slid up from the depths of the lower beach in great rolling slathers of foam. Everything seemed to have happened at once. The exposed layers of clay and the granite stone on the beach were still there, but at least a foot of sand had been redeposited over them. The clay banks themselves had been actively and substantially eroded; great squarish chunks of pure blue clay were scattered onto the beach like giants' blocks. The large reddish cirque at the near northern end had been further scooped out; only now a clear and distinct run of yellowish-green clay had emerged like a thin distinct rim of a goblet, sitting atop the foundation of blue clay, and containing a wine of loose reddish sand.* Up above the clay deposits, a nearly continuous array of sand falls, blown back by the dry onshore wind, created a veil of white mist-smoke that swirled and rippled away south in the morning wind.

---

*   I have decided to call this cirque of iron oxide "Red Gulf," knowing that the designation will be as temporary and fleeting as the formation it designates. But on the beach each man is his own Adam.

It was one of these days when one expects extravagance, and the beach did not disappoint. A ten-foot-high scrub oak, on its way to becoming one of the stranded, blackened skeletons strung with seaweed that littered the beach beyond it, still stood halfway down the slope, its yellow-brown leaves fluttering as if celebrating its own death.

At one point, as I stood looking up at the cliffs, a twelve-foot-wide section of blue clay slightly to my right detached itself and fell over with an enormous *thump!* at my feet. Farther to the right and near the top of the cliff a miniature avalanche of darker sand, at least six feet wide, streamed down the slope. It seemed that for once, the scarp of the Outer Beach, not content with merely mimicking the ocean in its frozen form, was actively trying to rival its motion in real time. It was like watching something frozen and rusted come alive, with stiff but powerful movements of its limbs and torso, destroying itself in the effort. The beach and the cliff were once more on the move, in a symphony of form and motion.

January 2, 2001. Clearing and cold this morning, in the low twenties. I went with Ollie to Newcomb Hollow this morning about seven thirty, wishing to see what effects the weekend northeaster might have had on the beach. There were a pair of men's briefs and a few paper cartridges of spent fireworks on the upper beach, but below the high-tide line, everything was clean and smooth. There appeared to be no major new erosion, though a considerable wall of reversed-slope clay eight to ten feet high has developed just north of the Hanging Boulder, and the large blackened skeleton of a cliff bush has been thrown up by the waves into the Red Gulf.

We walked the length of the clay bank, which was dry and brittle from the last two days of clear cold, but most of its pale-blue face was veiled with streams of yellow-brown clay from above that had run and hardened like dried glue. It put a kind of tattered scrim over its face, making it look even older, as if it had been left abandoned for ages, and had become covered with a ragged curtain or cobwebs.

The spot where two months ago I had walked and gazed at a shining layered bank of white sand, smoking and blazing with white fire in the wind and sun, is almost unidentifiable, as if burned out—which in a sense it has been: burned by the sun, wind, and waves. What is it that this endlessly suggestive beach does—bringing forth all these ephemeral forms: sad, heroic, stoic and elevating in their resigned dignity, making such a grand gesture as they go down to oblivion—but remind us of ourselves? What are these lively inanimate forms but our own lives writ large and accelerated? Why else do I spend so much more time looking at them than at the sea?

January 10, 2001. The tides have reached the base of the cliffs these past few days, and the undercut of the clay continues to reach farther south, almost to the Hanging Boulder. The rain of the previous night has caused the clay to run and pool at the base like frozen molten lava. But the striking aspect of the beach was the wide section above the wrack line just below the parking lot. Here the sand appeared spotted with streaks of white everywhere, like white spots on a tan leopard, hundreds and hundreds of them, and then I saw that each white spot was a length of snow that had lodged in the windward crease of a depression made by a human foot.

February 28, 2001. Windless, about forty degrees, slightly overcast. This stretch of clay cliffs, which I have observed and investigated for so many years now, seems to be entering a very precarious state, though no storm tides seem to have reached it lately. The whole bank seems to be contorting itself into a series of bulging overhangs composed of vertically compacted clay. In places great sheets of the clay two to four inches thick have separated and fallen to the sand, leaving the bank looking like outcrops of light blue-gray slate. In other places brown clay has leached out and covered strata of iron-oxide deposits with a veil of fine filigree work, like the most delicate and intricate of stalactite formations. In another spot a section of yellow and blue clay had removed itself from a deposit at eye level, leaving the perfect mold of an upper human torso, as if someone had made a clay angel without wings or limbs. I could come back and photograph it, but it would likely be gone by this afternoon.* There is at the moment the rather large blackened skeleton of a tree that has been deposited on the high beach just in front of the parking lot. From the south it appears to dominate the beach in the same way that, in Thoreau's description of discovering the remains of his friend Margaret Fuller on Fire Island, her drowned body "had taken possession of the shore, and reigned over it as no living one could."

March 8, 2001. A much-ballyhooed "monster storm," hyped as a worthy successor to the Great Blizzard of 1978, passed through here over the past three days, dropping only a little more than an inch of wet snow, causing no power outages, and in general pulling its punches. There were gale winds and heavy gusts, but most of the effect was felt on the Outer Beach.

On the beach there was a strong northeast wind, stiff as a board, with light rain. The sea was a majestic jumble for several hundred yards out. For the first time I felt fully the accuracy of Thoreau's description of the surf as "a thousand Niagaras," for everywhere I looked, a mighty jade breaker was heaving itself up and spilling over itself in a momentary cataract, spilling, it seemed, convexly, rather than concavely. Out in the white and gray-green chaos, the black hulls of small trees were being tossed about with a slow majesty that gave them the dignity of storm-tossed ships.

The surf was still washing against the base of the clay cliffs to the south, so I walked along the cliff top, brushing through the stiff low scrub oak, emerging at the edge just above and to the left of the Hanging Boulder, which still held. In fact, what must have been a hard and

---

* I was reminded of a Ray Bradbury short story I read in *Playboy* decades ago: The narrator was walking along a beach on the French Riviera when he saw, at some distance ahead of him, the figure of a short, round elderly man who appeared to be drawing figures in the sand with his cane. By the time he reached that spot the old man had vanished, but he saw that the drawings in the sand were unmistakably the work of Picasso—and that the tide was coming in.

prolonged pounding appeared to have made little inroads into the cliff. I turned back and saw the force of the wind in the misty sheets of rain and spray being slung landward across the parking lot. Inland, the pines around our house had barely swayed their tops, giving no hint of the wild fury out here, and I was reminded again of how protected this land has become with the regrowth of its trees.

I also rediscovered that aeolian phenomenon of the cliffs, whereby if one walks about five feet back from the edge in a strong easterly blow, the wind off the beach is whipped up the face of the cliff and over one's head, so that one walks in a bubble, a tunnel, a volute of calm, much as if one were riding the trough in the breaking curl of a wave.

March 10, 2001. One flails for metaphors or correspondences for this landscape that the glacier gestated and the sea has brought forth. Most immediately it suggests to me the lurid, surreal terrains of the EC ("Educational Comics") science-fiction I read as a boy that so affected my imagination, especially the lower clay formations with their distinct and flowing color layers and boundaries. There are several recently revealed formations that look like giant geodes, crenellated ridges of iron conglomerate within shells (Venus- or Madonna-like) of blue clay, but with a tissue-like complexity that makes them seem organic forms temporarily solidified—but only momentarily—moving or inclining to move even as I watch.

Yesterday the upper levels of the cliff face had the aspect of arid, desert cliffs of blown sand, in close, slanted strata, revealing here and there the chops and cheeks of new clay deposits, like ancient sculptures about to be revealed by what had buried them.

Other sections of the cliff presented a solid face of wholesale, fragmented slumps, like the wall of a building caught and frozen at the moment of implosion, its facade broken but not yet fallen. Though there was little actual movement of the cliff while I was there, nothing suggested rest or repose, but only momentarily arrested motion.

The few people on the beach seemed bent on disporting themselves in this new landscape, posing serenely in self-conscious meditation in one of the newly deepened hollows, picking among the new-fallen rubble or the wrack line, fingering hearts and names in affectingly ephemeral testimonials to romance on the smooth face of the clay.

March 12, 2001. There was a small,but sociable and familiar crowd on the beach today, including our town moderator/volunteer EMT Danny Silverman and his wife, Janice. We stood contemplating the Hanging Boulder, whose base has been increasingly undercut by successive storms this past month, but that nonetheless looks as permanent as ever.

Danny and Janice proposed that we should establish a local pool to bet on the day it would fall, "but," our always-prudent town moderator quickly added, "with half of it going to the Mustard Seed Food Kitchen so that we won't be shut down for violating state gambling laws."

As we stood there, tacitly calculating our own dates for when the boulder might fall, Danny got a call on his beeper. "Some 'investigation' being reported at Newcomb," he said, though we could see nothing happening on or off the beach. After another couple of minutes a town rescue vehicle pulled into the lot. Danny went over to talk to the driver and shortly returned, shaking his head: "I can't believe it. It seems someone called the Fire Department about a 'dangerous boulder that was about to fall'—probably some New Yorker who wants everything on the beach totally risk-free, but because they got a call, they have to respond. And since it's on National Seashore property he'll call them and then he'll have to sit there until they arrive. What's next—someone reporting heavy surf?"

May 8, 2001. Yesterday afternoon we went out to Newcomb Hollow for the first time in weeks. It was a bright, sunny, brilliant afternoon with a cool south wind blowing up the beach. A few wet-suited surfers bobbed in the waters offshore. The high late-spring sun gave an unwonted brilliance to the deserted beach and dark-blue waters. The ocean appears to have retreated for the year, and the shape of the beach was pretty much as we had left it.

The Hanging Boulder remains, though some large chunks of clay have detached from the base below it and its front face appears significantly undercut. Viewing it from above, I saw that the mass of the boulder narrows as it enters the cliff, and so perhaps extends farther into it than we thought, though it would be a very unusually shaped erratic if it did. I could not help but think that a little work with a shovel would dislodge it, but I refrained, in part because I had already picked a day in next November as my fall date in the local Hanging Boulder Pool.

May 29, 2001. The rock has fallen! We went out to the beach yesterday afternoon and found it lying on the beach about eight feet from the base of the cliffs. Behind it was a shallow crater perhaps eighteen inches deep, and the rock itself was sitting on a slightly elevated pedestal of sand. Apparently when it fell, it kicked up a mound of sand in front of it and then bounced or, more likely rolled, up onto it. I took out my tape and measured it. It was more than eight feet in length, five feet high, and about six and a half feet at its widest point. Not among the largest glacial erratics on Cape Cod, but impressive nonetheless, especially in Wellfleet, where boulders of any size are comparatively rare.

I don't know who, if anyone, won the betting pool, but the rock, it seems, is destined now to become part of the beach landscape, an object for kids to jump from, a windbreak on windy days, a place to pose for pictures. Few except those of us who had followed its progress would know of its history, its gradual exposure over the past several years, its bulk that seemed to defy gravity, only to be pulled, at last, to its final resting place.

July 18, 2001. A wide summer berm has built up in the last month here. Yesterday the surf was low and viscous with dark, thick reddish-brown seaweed locally called "mung." The lower beach was plastered with it, and at times the breaking waves looked more like mud splashing than water.

I noticed for the first time that when I stood about six feet from the clay wall, the sound of the surf bounced off them simultaneously with the surf itself so that it was like hearing the surf stereophonically. Not quite, though, for there was, if not a lag, a difference in the texture of the sound coming off the wall, so that it was more like hearing a ghost-sea breaking somewhere just behind it.

November 5, 2001. On the Outer Beach stories never end. We thought to have closed the chapter on the Hanging Boulder, but we now have the Mystery of the Disappearing Boulder. On Saturday KS, Ollie, and I went out to Newcomb Hollow for the first time since early last summer. The sea was in one of its calm moods, its surface nearly flat and lightly quilted, with only low waves curling tamely at its edge. An ordinary scene, but I felt there was something strange about it. Then with a shock I realized that there was no sign of the large boulder that had fallen from the clay cliffs last May.

I tried to account for its disappearance. It seemed unlikely that the National Seashore had removed it. What reason would they have? The obvious explanation was that the beach had covered it, but that, too, seemed unlikely. Over the summer the upper beach, or summer berm, does widen and build up somewhat. Still, it seemed improbable that, in the months I had been gone, the beach had built up over five feet. But what other explanation was there?

Just as strange as the boulder's disappearance were the answers I got when I questioned friends and acquaintances about it. Yes, they all remembered when the rock had fallen, but no one could recall just when and how it had disappeared. It was as if a gap in the communal memory had occurred.

The clay cliffs in general continue to lose color and soften their forms. Farther south, the new outcrops of blue clay that seemed to be emerging last spring now seemed less exposed, as if they were, in fact, retreating back into the cliff, or as if the cliff had changed its mind and were recovering them. Nothing, not even erosion, seems to be linear here.

November 22, 2002. Each season has its songs. There is something elegant and strong about the dark twisted shapes of blackened scrub oaks and beach-plum bushes clinging to the smooth, broad flanks of the bluffs. White finger sponges are cradled in the black wrecks of bayberry bushes half buried on the beach. These sponges are one of the great suggestors found in the wrack lines: Some with their perforated spiracles look like the plaster casts on broken fingers; others, of course, resemble spent condoms; and still others, the bi- and trifurcated forms of ginseng "men."

July 5, 2005. It is remarkable how little time people on the beach ever spend looking at the cliffs. They are all Frost's watchers, satisfied to "turn their back on the land" and "look at the sea all day," rather than turning and contemplating this weathered scarp, which is a book that displays our crumbling bulwarks, where our history and our future are exhumed for our examination.

Yesterday evening at six thirty I went out to the beach, where in place of the now-twice-destroyed steps to the beach, one of the town's bulldozers had pushed out a thick tongue of clay hardening onto the beach, providing a substantial if somewhat awkward access to the beach.

The clay cliffs continue to deconstruct and transform themselves. New outlying chunks of clay teeter and totter on the beach like the ruins of cliff dwellings. I gaze up at the deeply grooved, ancient-looking, sheer and reversed slope—mighty clay formations rising forty feet or more above me—and think that this would be considered one of the more dramatic and rugged coastlines anywhere, a natural attraction that would draw thousands to see it, if only it would hold its profile and countenance for more than a couple of years, or a few months, or even several weeks. It is too malleable and mutable to give us that sense of rugged resistance we seek in more rocky coastlines. Too much is constantly moving and changing for us to take in. Instead of the sublime we experience vertigo and nausea.

August 31, 2005. Yesterday the first rains in more than a month fell on our parched and porous land, pushed northward by the weakening wrath of Katrina. I went out to Newcomb Hollow, where perhaps a half dozen cars huddled at the eastern edge of the dampened, puddled parking lot. One black SUV was backed up right to the edge of the beach access, its rear hatch door raised. Inside a young couple lay prone on raised elbows, each holding a book—making the best of a bad situation.

August 20, 2008. As I walked the beach today, I noticed a scattering of beach plants—sea rocket, dusty miller, even a few tufts of beach grass—creeping out as they do every summer from the base of the cliffs to establish beach holds for a season. What blind optimism! The winter storms will come in as they always do, and root and scrape out these intrepid pioneers, but that will hardly discourage them from trying again next summer. Given global climate trends, a drop in sea level in the foreseeable future is not something anyone would prudently plan on, but if one should occur, these plants will be ready.

May 9, 2010. The winter storms have stripped layers off the clay bluffs, revealing a whole new layer of bright colors, much like the new plumage on the goldfinches at our feeder. They seemed like a transposed section of the Gay Head cliffs on the Vineyard, or, stretching the comparisons further, a short stretch of the Canyonlands, presenting only one side of the canyon. More than these, though, it suggests a concentrated collection of various landscapes, like the faux–New York skyline in Las Vegas, where various icons of the Big Apple—the Empire State Building, the Statue of Liberty, the Chrysler Building, and so on—are jumbled together. Here we have a bit of Katahdin's knife edge, sculpted in blue clay and rusty iron oxide; there a bit of the sandstone cliffs of Morocco or Afghanistan; here a bit of coral Utah rimrock; there beige clay that seeped out over the upper beach has hardened and cracked, presenting the aspect of a dry lake bed from Death Valley. At the top of the bluffs the new bright-green foli-

age of scrub oak, beach plum, and other shrubs droop over the crest
of the cliffs like hanging gardens, or slide imperceptibly down the cliff
face on islands of turf that have broken off the crest.

We think of ourselves as rushing through life, in the fullness of
health, toward the precipice of death, like leaves being carried with
increasing velocity toward the universal cataract, but this scene suggests the opposite: that we are the stationary figures, rooted in our
lives, cultivating the illusion of permanence, as our mortality rushes
toward us, a reverse cataract, rushing up out of the seabed, harvest-
ing the generations in front of us, undercutting our own foundations,
and taking us at last, like Everyman, unready and unawares.

September 8, 2010. The experience of the Outer Beach is divided:
On the one hand, the rapidity of change in its topographical and geological features can give one a sense of having observed it over long,
even geological periods of time, which in turn can give one the sense
of actually having lived for ages. On the other hand, that same rapidity and mutability, combined with the unending restlessness of the
sea itself, accelerates the sense of one's own transience, of one's own
presence disappearing. Even as you watch the land disappear, grain
by grain, or in races of sand, or great sliding shifts, you literally feel
your own foundation shift as a gentle swash swirls up and around and
over your naked feet, and the damp, saturated sand gives suddenly,
forcing you to regain your balance.

December 13, 2010. On Saturday I took little Sammy, our eight-
week-old standard poodle, to the beach for the first time. The clay
cliffs, though still massive and impressive, are probably at one of their
least colorful levels. In the middle of the clay bluffs, however, there
is then a recent large slump of yellow-gray clay, at least thirty feet
across, and pushing out into the beach for several yards. Entangled
in the collapsed material are not only a number of small scrub-oak
trees and bushes, but a number of sizable rocks, one to three feet in
diameter, with sharp edges, as if they had broken off larger boulders.

The clay formations are almost unrecognizable from a decade ago. Gone completely are the vivid cirques of iron-oxide and blue-clay deposits nearest the parking lot, leaving only a couple of large clumps of clay on the upper beach, rounded and gray-blue, like abstract sculptures of beached whales. The great clay cliffs to the south are dried out, almost pale fleshlike in color, bleeding in cracked scale-like sheets onto the beach. In one place at the very bottom of the cliff, a large clump of bright-green-and-yellow ragweed was in full bloom, just as if it were in the place it ought to be, instead of at the edge of destruction. The foam-edged overwashes crawled sluggishly along the troughs, reluctantly, as though they wished they could stay in bed. A windblown plastic milk carton provided animated distraction for Sam all the way back.

September 29, 2011. Yesterday was one of a series of warm, soft, gentle September days we have had over the past week. It was a weekday, and there were only about a dozen cars in the parking lot at Newcomb. These days the beach belongs to retirees, young couples without children, or children too young to be in school, the unemployed (presumably), and locals without "real jobs," like me. They were spread out with their blankets, chairs, umbrellas, and wind tents in a luxuriousness of space, a dozen small clusters spread out over a thousand feet of beach, perched at the edge of a three- to four-foot berm whose contour was rounded and benign. It was so quiet I was startled to hear a woman cough at a distance of a hundred yards.

January 16, 2012. A dry cold day in mid-January. Ten degrees at 11:00 a.m. The weather satellite photo shows a circular mass of frozen precipitation filling the bowl of Cape Cod Bay and spilling over its rim. All morning sea snow has been falling, blowing, and swirling over the cracked and warped surface of the deck outside my study. It looks like something organic, something alive—but not quite.

Later that afternoon, curious to see how this dry snow behaved on the beach, I bundled up and went for a walk at Newcomb Hollow. A dry river of light, sparkling snow swirled around me and rolled down the beach, driven by a fierce north wind. At times the swirls of snow surged up the cliff face, like protoplasmic extensions of gigantic waves, not quite reaching the top. They looked like a racing, transparent veil, a ghost river with no mass, just velocity.

Nothing inanimate—not rivers, not lava, not blown leaves, not even the crashing surf itself, seems as alive as these wraiths of dry snow blown by the wind. Watching this phenomenon, I think it must have been the inspiration for certain cinematic effects, such as the transparent, avenging spirits in *Raiders of the Lost Ark,* or the soul-sucking Dementors in the Harry Potter movies. Like them, these snow wraiths embody the notion of restless, damned souls racing to and fro, seeking something they know not what. They come, trace the contours of what they move over like demons in search of a home, and then move on, leaving no mark, only the memory of fragile, unearthly beauty.

April 13, 2013. This morning I went back to photograph the clay ledges above the beach. The tide was now fully out but still crashing powerfully on the inner bar. The shallow intertidal valley between the bar and the beach was filled with seaward-running lagoons of seep water, sparkling like a zillion razors in the morning sun. I stood facing the wall before one of the giant fans of sand as small flat stones steadily, but irregularly, detached themselves like falling leaves from the upper ledge and rolled on edge down the face of the fan with what seemed like animate glee. They averaged about one per minute, a rate comparable to the heaviest meteor showers, and like such showers, they seemed to fall from a particular limited area of the cliff, though each one's appearance and location was unpredictable—and like meteors, they, too, seemed to enjoy their brief but exuberant slide downward into the empty void.

I thought again of the multifarious ways that the cliff erodes: in discrete, visible ski rides of small stones like this; in equally visible and more dramatic sand falls (like waterfalls, eroding and retreating, breaking down its ledges), and even more dramatic sand devils, wind driven, flying upward toward the sky and over the lip of the bluff; and then the invisible forms, which we have to read backwards to see: these giant sand fans; the more organic sand pseudopods; great slabs of blue or brown clay, like fragments of fluted marble columns, shattered like Ozymandias; and the occasional glacial erratic, perched one day on an upper ledge, prostrate on the beach the next, like a furtive lithic suicide.

May 30, 2013. I went to the beach with Kathy and Sam yesterday afternoon. It was the first time I had been there in more than two weeks. We walked down the makeshift path from the parking lot to the beach, then turned right and headed toward the clay cliffs (the beach in the other direction having been posted for nesting plovers and least terns).

I find I am increasingly reluctant to gather any more material from this beach, but it keeps on giving, whether I will or no. The clay cliffs and the iron-oxide cirques just north of them continue to prove my mourning for their demise premature. Each week they continue to regain, and even outdo, their former glory. The colors of the clays and minerals grow more intense; thin tentacles of clay-mud crawl out over the dark-blue clay faces; small sea caves have been carved into the lower walls, just deep enough to let the imagination push them even deeper; other, sheer faces are stained with yellow and green washes, giving them the appearance of walled-up entrances to secret and sealed places. Rubble lies broken at their feet like rocks, only to melt and spread out in a sticky film over the sands.

A few hundred more feet to the south, another act is opening. Where, a year or so ago, there were small outcrops of blue clay and ridges of iron deposits, a major new outcropping of clay appears to be emerging. It is just as if a new play—nay, a new theater—were opening on the beach, even while the older one has just staged a smashing revival. Don't worry, the beach seems to say, as if I had asked: We

have enough tricks up our watery sleeves to amuse you for your lifetime—and beyond.

LOOKING AT THE SEA WITHOUT CURIOSITY OR AMBITION

I am sitting on the wooden bench at the end of the Newcomb Hollow parking lot, looking out to sea. Despite the beautiful clear evening light, there is only one other person there, a fisherman far up the
beach to my left.

The ocean spreads out before me in all of its vast blue splendor,
empty of boats, and, with the exception of a few cruising gulls, apparently empty of everything else as well. I am glad, since all I want is a
moment of peace, a moment of balance between sea, sand, wind, and
light. The waves break as they do—as all they will ever do.

In recent years I have spent my summers on rocky shores to the
north, and I often involuntarily compare the beaches here and there.
This evening I find myself indulging in musical analogies. On a
straight, sandy shore like this one, listening to the surf is like listening to an endless Vivaldi concerto, composed of clean, elegant, and
inventive variations on a limited set of themes. On rocky shores the
surf sounds more like a symphony by Beethoven or Mahler—more
complex, sensuous, conflicted, polyphonic, overreaching. At another
time I might explore the similes further, but this evening I'm content
to let them go and simply listen.

Out of habit I experience some slight urges to stand up and do
something: to go down to the edge of the surf, to converse with the
fisherman, to check out recent erosion of the clay cliffs to the south,
to explore the newly fenced-in plover-nesting area to the north—but
these fleeting moments of ambition and curiosity quickly fall from
me, like leaves from a rock: No, I am content just to sit, to let my
years of memory on this beach do the walking for me.

I do manage to lift my binoculars and focus them on the vast expanse of deepening water in front of me. When I do, I see a hitherto invisible city of lobster buoys in bright electric colors, bobbing across the surface just beyond the bars: hundreds of them, scattered across hundreds of acres of water surface. How empty the sea is! How busy it is! I start to wonder: How do lobstermen know where to place their traps? Do they have grants to specific areas of the ocean floor, as oystermen do on the tidal flats? But once again I let curiosity and ambition go, and simply watch.

This would be a perfect time and place to meditate, if I practiced meditation. But I don't want to empty my mind. Rather, I want to *fill* it more deeply with what is there. I don't wish to detach myself from this solid, perishable world, but to feel it even closer, to pay it the attention it deserves. The shadows of the low cliffs have already crept out over most of the beach, but the low sun still highlights the breaking brows of each long wave. Randomly choosing a natural clock, I decide to stay here until the breaking waves are no longer hit by the sun. And so I do, content merely to notice how slowly, steadily, and unhurriedly the sun sinks behind me, casting its ever-venturing light farther and farther out over the purple sea, until at last it blinks out and there is no holding back the night.

June 2014

11

....

Ballston Beach
to Higgins Hollow

ON THE SUMMIT

When I pulled into Newcomb Hollow, the beach was curiously empty. There were only three cars in the parking lot, and two of those left almost immediately. The waves were low and quiet, silently tossing massive logs and bright flags of sea lettuce about in the surf. A low fog was sitting on the beach like a cool shroud, though I could feel the hot sun, like a weight, beating down on it.

I walked north along the beach, my eyes smarting from a stiff, moist north wind. The first stretch of sand cliffs here is nearly completely barren of growth, partly from the constant foot traffic of the beach users. Farther on, the vegetation begins to reassert itself, climbing up the smooth slopes out of the wrack line. At the bottom were the stitched lines of beach grass, spreading by underground runners, and above them clumps of fleshy-leaved sea rocket, bristly sea burdock, seaside goldenrod, and tufts of dusty miller with its lobed, pale-green leaves and long stalks of yellow flower clusters.

Beach figures in the distance proved to be improvised stick structures, erected and left on a previous summer's day. And though the footprints and vehicle tracks in the sand were so numerous that the beach in places resembled a railroad yard, I neither met nor saw another soul from Newcomb Hollow to Brush Valley in Truro, nearly three miles away.

A dense fog continued to blow down the beach, shrouding visibility at both ends. The unexpected absence of people, and the desolate feeling of the fog, gave the impression of a mass exodus and brought to mind Thoreau's comment about this same beach, made more than a century ago, that "a thousand men could not have seriously interrupted it, but would have been lost in the vastness of the scenery as their footsteps in the sand." Even the Concord tourist's hyperbolic imagination, however, could not have envisioned the millions who would someday visit here, so that those same footsteps would actually threaten to alter the scenery; and yet, it seemed, a little moisture and sea breeze that day had blown them all away like sea foam and restored the beach to its ancient vastness and majesty.

As the cliffs began to rise above fifty feet in height, I left the beach, climbing up one of those human-made, improvised diagonal foot trails cut into the face of the scarp, which was comparatively firm after the recent rains. Reaching the top, I continued on the path that runs along the crest just back from the edge. This path is, like the beach, both permanent and ephemeral, and constantly forced to relocate as the cliffs recede from year to year.

The dips and rises of the crest, the fantastic topography, the occasional views of the receding beach, and the long, rolling vistas landward make this perhaps the most exhilarating stretch of bluffs to walk along the entire Outer Beach. Here is one place, at least, where the Cape's extremes are vertical as well as horizontal. The highest point of land on the Outer Cape is along this section, a summit marked on the U.S. Geological Survey maps as "Pamet," climbing a giddy 177 feet above the beach (though this figure likely changes from year to year).

Yet everything is on the Cape's characteristically diminutive scale, so that I felt like a giant striding with a few steps from summit to summit along a sandy mountain range, complete with miniature peaks, cirques, bowls and knife-edges. Where the crest trail swung out to the edge, I peered over and flushed a flock of gulls that were roosting on the slope, sending them out into the fog where they disappeared, reassembling farther north, where, later, I would start them again—a kind of larger version of the shepherding game one plays with flocks of shorebirds along the beach.

To the west I looked out over a vast and tilted plain of stunted vegetation. The drifting patches of fog both veiled its outlines and intensified a remarkable variety and succession of greens, starting at the cliff edge and moving inland: patches of poverty grass, carpets of bearberry, beach and upland grasses, thickets of beach rose, bayberry, and beach plum, bands of shiny scrub oak and dark pitch pine—surely one of the most distinctive and recognizable landscapes anywhere.

At intervals the crest trail swung inland and joined a wider and more substantial jeep trail. Along its soft surface were numerous fresh tracks of deer that had apparently been coming in my direction, had scented or heard my approach, and turned off the road. They were probably bedded down within yards of me somewhere in the low, dark-green blanket of scrub oak, but I knew I could wait there all day and never see or hear a sign of them.

I strode, with my folded umbrella set across my shoulders like a yoke, across an open field of bright, rounded tufts of beach heather surrounded by tall, waving beach grass, among hardy stands of gnarled and weathered chokecherry, through thickets of beach plum with their hard green fruits already as large as marbles in this year of excellent berry sets. Their stiff twigs were entwined with numerous vines of wild grapes, all sprouting clusters of lime-green fruit as yet no bigger than grape seeds, glowing beneath the broad, arched grape leaves. How lush and thick and heavy with promise these eroding fragments of beach bluff can appear!

Shortly beyond the Pamet summit I descended to the beach again, staying on it until I reached a break in the cliff face at Brush Valley, a short distance south of Ballston Beach. As I walked up the hard narrow path of this ancient glacial valley (one of the few on the Outer Beach whose gradient runs west to east), the uninterrupted hills of scrub oak rose sharp and huge into the fog. The screams of the invisible gulls loomed over me, dwarfing my presence. We need to be overwhelmed like this, on occasion, by some unpeopled expanse of the land where we live, even to fear it a little, that it goes on so long without us.

August 1976

RAVISHED

I walked up Higgins Hollow in North Truro this morning, a fine old crease of a road tucked away in a glacial valley between Green and Small hills. On my left I passed an old house where Edmund Wilson once came in 1920 to ask Edna St. Vincent Millay, whose family was summering there, to marry him. She didn't reject him outright but said she "would think about it."

A little farther on, where the pavement turns to dirt, I came upon a specimen of *Phallus impudicus,* or the penis mushroom, the fungus that provoked Thoreau to such a passion of attraction and revulsion in his journal.* And no wonder. It is a remarkable natural mimicry: a thick white firm stalk, more than one inch in diameter and about three inches long, with dark furry mycelia at the base and a rounded pinkish-orange conical head, creased at the top. Indeed, some days nature can seem peculiarly vulgar.

Eventually I turned right onto a paved driveway that climbed

---

* "Pray, what was nature thinking of when she made this? She almost puts herself on a level with those who draw in privies" (*Journal,* October 16, 1856).

a quarter mile or so up to the site of the old Ball mansion.* From here there is a fine view. This area, known as the Truro Highlands, is intensely cratered with dozens of small but steep kettle holes. The elevation rarely dips below fifty feet above sea level, however, so that even at the bottom of the steepest bowls there are no natural ponds.

To the south and north the beach headlands are steeply tilted to the west, their shaggy, sandy heads rising up like gigantic swells about to crash down on the beach 150 feet below. To the west one can see across the bay to the Manomet Hills in Plymouth. The ocean was calm and overcast, like a vast lake, with few walkers on the beach and only one jeep visible, but the sands were crossed and recrossed with vehicle tracks like a switchyard.

Working my way down to the beach, I met two women in jeans, smoking cigarettes and wading in the low surf. They had collected a dozen or two surf clams with kelp holdfasts attached, that had been thrown up by the waves. They gave me one, which I later ate—good, but not as tasty as quahogs.

I climbed back up to the crest at Long Nook and walked north. Most of the cliff face in this stretch is uniform and sandy, with only a few clay "steps" near the top. Purple asters showed everywhere through the fruiting bearberry. Halfway between Long Nook and the North Truro Air Force Base I came upon a deep bowl filled almost entirely with a pure stand of the finest beach plums I have ever encountered. All the bushes were thickly hung with bright, ripe mul-ticolored berries, asking to be picked, waiting so for hands. I fell on them, picking over two quarts in less than twenty minutes, grabbing

---

* This building, torn down in 1986, was part of a thousand-acre private ocean-front estate owned by New York businessman Sheldon W. Ball in the late nine-teenth century. It included the "Balls' Town Bungalows Colony," a resort complex at the present site of the Ballston Town Beach that contained at least a dozen buildings. These included a clubhouse, a dining hall, a bowling alley, a number of so-called primitive cottages, and a nine-hole golf course known as the Pamet River Golf Club, which stretched along both sides of the river. Nothing of the resort remains.

them wantonly by the handfuls, ripping them off the twigs, crushing
some in my haste, spurting the red juice over my hands, my feet, now
and then stuffing an entire particularly ripe bunch into my mouth.
Like the berries, this land conforms to the contours of my imagination; it holds the lineaments of my desires.

September 1977

DEAD DEER ON THE BEACH

O n the last day of the year I came upon a tableau, the final scene
in a natural drama whose arc I could only guess at, but which
nonetheless required me to surmise. I was walking the beach north of
Higgins Hollow when, several hundred feet ahead of me, I saw a fairly
large object lying on the upper beach, which I took at first to be a log of
some sort. But as I got closer it appeared to be furry—a seal, perhaps.

When I came to it, though, it was a deer—a good-size animal
stretched out on a thick wrack of kelp as if resting. It lay on its side with
its right hind leg extended gracefully behind, as though in the act of
running. But its head was bent backward 180 degrees, and in its mouth
was a sprig of rockweed. The eyes were intact, but the gulls had been
at its torso (their drawn-crossbow tracks patterned the sand around
it), exposing the rib cage, through which I saw a dark-green mass of
entrails. The genital area was eaten away beyond identification, and the
exposed muscles of the flanks were striated a cold, marbled gray-blue
and ivory. There were no other marks on it. It appeared to have been
thrown up by the last tide, and its limbs were not yet stiff.

It may have been chased into the surf by dogs and drowned. Deer
seem to flee into the ocean to escape predators the way that whales
seek the beach when injured or ill to avoid drowning, preferring a
larger, more abstract danger to a smaller, more immediate one. Whatever had brought it there, it was a vivid reminder of the implacable

terms of existence, what it means to accept the reality of the physical world in which to live, where there is no escape, only a choice of fates.

December 1990

ERECTIONS ON THE BEACH

Driftwood being free, like sand and sun, the temptation to play with it is strong. As with sand castles, it seems to bring out an aboriginal architectural urge in people, as well as a need to leave behind a signature on the beach, however ephemeral.

—ROGER DEAKIN, *WILDWOOD*

People seem to have an irrepressible desire to build, shape, or decorate on the beach, and the variety of human constructs found on the Outer Beach is often astonishing. Over the years these constructs, in my mind, have sorted themselves into three categories: beach sculptures, beach erections, and beach shelters.

The first of these comprise representational or abstract forms shaped from natural or human-made materials found on the beach. Sand castles and other sand sculptures are the most common and familiar of these forms. Others are no more than cairns, or piles of stones and pebbles, gathered from the lower levels of the beach and placed in simple patterns or designs. Still others are substantial, elaborate installations that may use large pieces of driftwood, logs, or old shipwrecks, bent well pipes from long-vanished cottages, or a blackened scrub oak that has slid down the slope of the cliffs above the beach as bases. These templates then become adorned over the summer months with fantastic and motley accumulations of natural and artificial objects: seaweed, polypropylene rope, starfish, plastic sleeves, small bits of driftwood, netting, broken moon-snail shells, plastic milk bottles, lobster buoys, plastic oil bottles, sneakers, beach thongs, tampon applicators, large pieces of Styrofoam, bottle caps, and so on.

I've noticed that these beach sculptures are often begun shortly after easterly storms, probably because of the abundance of material thrown up by the sea then. Over the course of a summer some of these spontaneous beach sculptures rise notably above the ordinary in their complexity and imagination. Some have the whimsical aspect of a Miró painting or the kinetic quality of a Calder stabile. Others take the strange attenuated shapes of the surrealistic structures in Dalí's desert landscapes. Some use flattened beach stones stacked to create miniature versions of *inuksuk,* those human-shaped stone sculptures traditionally made by Inuit and other peoples of the Arctic.

Once, below a particularly colorful and elaborate beach sculpture, I found a bouquet of still-inflated blue balloons that had washed up in the surf. On each one was printed the message: "DUNLAP INSURANCE—Call for Information," with a 603 New Hampshire number. No insurance for sea turtles, I thought. I picked up the balloons and tied them on to the sculpture. I was, of course, violating environmental protocol that would require me to remove all nonorganic debris from the beach in the name of strangled gulls, intestinally distressed sea turtles, and other victims of the immense amounts of synthetic trash that washes up on our beaches at all times of the year. But I confess I find it difficult not to participate in such a seemingly innocent and communal form of human creativity.

The second of my categories of beach structures is beach erections. These are generally monoliths, usually wooden pilings or tree trunks that have been thrown up by storm waves and subsequently raised and set upright into the sand. Compared to the whimsy and complexity found in the more elaborate beach sculptures, beach erections tend to be simple, unadorned, even stark, yet impressive in their own way. They are, of course, obviously phallic and strike me as authentic contemporary versions of the prehistoric stone menhirs one finds all over the landscape of Great Britain. Like them, they seem to represent both a challenge and a celebration.

One of the most impressive of these beach erections stood recently on the beach below the tall, soft slope of White Crest Beach in South Wellfleet. It was a single, large, vertical, sea-silvered tree trunk, likely that of a pine or spruce carried down from Maine. The exposed portion was about twenty-five feet tall, some sixteen inches thick at the base, tapering gradually to about seven inches where it forked at the top. From this fork dangled a long piece of rope.

I don't know when it was raised, or by whom, but I could reconstruct in my mind the probable process of its erection. It had withstood at least two winters of storm tides on the beach, indicating that it was firmly rooted, perhaps eight to ten feet deep, in the sand. I suspect that a group of young men (in my experience it has always been young men hoisting these driftwood monoliths) dug a hole in the sand and attached a rope to the narrow end of the tree trunk. Then some of them took the loose end of the rope and climbed up the slope, pulling on the rope while others maneuvered the base of the trunk down into the hole.

However it was done, it would have been an impressive process to behold, and it was another indication that the beach seems to be a place where elaborate, ingenious, labor- and time-consuming efforts are made for no other reason than to see if it can be done. In this sense, one could say, it was an enterprise not entirely unlike our going to the moon.

Two elements seem to be common to both beach sculptures and beach erections. The first is that there is obviously no expectation of permanence. Creativity, not endurance, seems to be the aim. Many, no doubt, are created by visitors who are here for a day, a week, a month, and who in any case will never see their creations again, nor do they expect them to last beyond the next tide, or at most the next season.

The other—and to my mind the more significant—shared characteristic is that these beach structures, especially the larger ones, tend to be communal. Some, such as large beach erections, are necessarily so, requiring several bodies and an organized effort to lift them into place. But others, especially the larger sculptures, tend to be serially communal. That is, they may be started by one person, but over the summer numerous anonymous hands tend to add bits of colorful or unusual items to the original structure, so that the initial creator might not even recognize his or her handiwork by the end of the season. In this sense it may be the purest form of communal art we have here.

The third category of beach structures is what I call beach shelters. Compared with the beach sculptures, they are usually not as elaborately decorated but are more substantially constructed; and though they are not as impressive in size as beach erections, they tend to be much more complex in design. I call them shelters, not so much because they actually serve as protections against the sun, wind and weather, but because they *suggest* shelters, often in remarkably economical ways.

On a beach walk one early October day, one such shelter caught my eye. It consisted of three boards set on three beach stones, creating three sides at right angles to one another, the open side facing the sea, and each side no more than eight feet long. With the stones they were no more than sixteen inches high, yet they suggested walls. I entered the space and sat down, and though the structure could not have been more open, I somehow felt I was sitting in a *room*. I felt enclosed, protected, and suddenly missed the presence of another for conversation—of Gaston Bachelard,* perhaps.

Unlike the more communal efforts of beach sculptures and beach erections, beach shelters are commonly the work of one individual— or at most two or three. On a warm afternoon in mid-October, about halfway between Long Nook and Ballston Beach in Truro, I came upon a man in bathing trunks who had built a rather massive and complex windbreak, incorporating an eleven-foot-high wooden pole that rose out of the sand, three creosote ties that he had lugged by himself several hundred feet down the beach, and several other posts and boards that he had set up around a hollow scraped in the sand, in the middle of which he had set his beach chair. Two fishing poles

---

*   French philosopher (1888–1962), author of *The Poetics of Space* (1958), a meditation on how we experience intimate spaces.

stood in their black plastic sleeves on the lower beach. The man was about thirty-five, with flaming red-gold hair and mustache. When I asked him why he had gone to such an extraordinary effort, he chuckled, "Sun's out—nothin' else to do, heh-heh-heh. Waitin' for the fish."

Then, pointing to the wooden pole, he said, "I'm goin'to hang my telephone there—heh-heh-heh. My girlfriend will be able to see me whichever way she comes onto the beach. She'll appreciate this, a lot more than the wife did—heh-heh-heh."

Finally, there are some beach structures that combine elements of both shelter and sculpture. On a day in early September I came upon an elaborate example of this about a quarter mile north of Ballston Beach. It appeared to be a life-size abstract sculpture of a whale, some thirty-five feet long, set up against the base of the cliffs and facing the ocean. Its creator (or creators) had ingeniously used two curved pieces of driftwood, each at least fifteen feet long and hung with dried seaweed, to suggest the jaw and baleen, several sea-weathered boards and beams to trace the torso, and two pieces of cut and staked canvas at the rear to serve as flukes. Inside the space were two broken aluminum folding beach chairs, and couple of blankets, and two or three chipped cups—a shelter fit for a Jonah, a mock whale for a mythical prophet.

September 2003

AN OLD GOD

This afternoon I decided to walk along the cliff trail south of Ballston Beach in Truro, in part to see how much of it has been lost to recent erosion. It was, perhaps, the loveliest day of the month, more like the beginning than the end of September. I parked the car along the road that leads down to the public parking lot, and took the unmarked footpath that led southeast through Brush Valley to the beach. The valley passes through thick, shady pinewoods, then through open, low, back-dune vegetation to a low cut onto the beach. As I walked through it I heard the roar of the surf unexpectedly loud, as if the tunnel-like valley itself were acting as a megaphone.

I had been surprised at the number of cars parked at the entrance to the valley this time of year, particularly when the parking lot itself was mostly empty. But once I gained the beach I realized that this was the preferred entrance for September nude sunbathers taking advantage of this month's warm, soft weather, as well as the lack of voyeuristic crowds and Seashore rangers handing out citations.

I recalled a summer's day nearly a quarter century ago when our family took a walk down Higgins Hollow up to the site of the old Ball estate, about a mile north of Ballston Beach. At that time the beach below the estate was an unofficial nude beach. Even then nude sunbathing was against Seashore regulations, but since this area was a good half mile from the nearest public beach, it had been tacitly ignored by Park officials. And so it might have remained, but the voices of decorum clamored so loudly that a few years later the Seashore was forced to take action. Citations were given out, fines levied, and the sunbathers eventually dispersed, at least during the high season. It always struck me as disingenuous that the Seashore based its actions not on "moral" but "environmental" grounds, claiming that people who came to see the sunbathers were "trampling fragile vegetation." To my mind this was like banning public hangings because the crowds that gathered for them increased the spread of infectious diseases.

At that time the beach at Higgins Hollow was still marginally accessible from above. We made our way down through thick scrub oak, unaware of the nude sunbathers below. My daughter, Katy, and her friend Colleen, both about eight years old, led the way; then they both came running back, red-faced and grinning, and Colleen shouted in a hoarse whisper, "They're *naked*!"

It was too far to turn around and go back, however, and we eventually emerged, fully clothed, onto a plain of dozens of bare bodies, some of whom gave us dirty looks as they snatched up towels and bits of clothing, while others simply ignored us. But what I remember most strongly is that it was we, the clothed intruders, who felt exposed, embarrassed, uncomfortable, and ashamed.

This time, however, I was alone and felt neither shame nor much curiosity, hardly tempted to look at the sunbathers. Perhaps I have become jaded by the prevalence of nudity in our contemporary culture. Or perhaps I sympathized with Henry Beston, who, in *The Outermost House,* describes a naked young swimmer in the surf. The sight evokes in him a complex reaction about public nudity:

> Watching this picture of a fine human being free for the moment of everything save his own humanity and framed in a scene of nature, I could not help musing on the mystery of the human body and of how nothing can equal its rich and rhythmic beauty when it is beautiful or approach its forlorn and pathetic ugliness when beauty has not been mingled in or has withdrawn. Poor body, time and the long years were the first tailors to teach you the merciful use of clothes!

Whatever the source of my indifference, I shortly left the beach again and began to climb the trail that leads up to the top of the bluff. As I ascended I passed two extensive swatches of pure poverty grass of a robust, almost iron-gray-green color, with no hint yet of its raggedy floor-mop gray appearance in winter. In fact, though summer had passed, everything seemed somehow at the height of its health: the bright yellow tongues of ragweed, the colorful shiny leaves of poison ivy, the hidden clumps of wild grapes, glistening cowlicks of beach grass, and bright blue-gray clusters of bayberry.

I reached the crest and looked down, thinking how thin and vulnerable the beach appears from this perspective, though it must have been at least fifty to sixty feet wide. When you're actually down on the beach itself, especially at low tide, its breadth seems commensurate with that of the sea. Even though you see water out to the horizon, the ocean appears foreshortened and limited in scope. But from the high crest, the beach below seemed a fragile ephemeral strip of earth, a pale thin line merely marking a momentary edge of the vast, incomparable, and all-encompassing sea.

The trail encountered increasingly dense thickets of scrub oak that would have required serious bushwhacking for me proceed any farther, so I stopped and sat in the shade of a ledge below the lip to have lunch. As I did, I noticed a single sunbather on the beach far below me, a man in his late fifties or early sixties, with short, thick steel-gray hair. He was lying facedown on a towel, but after a while he got up and sauntered unhurriedly down to the edge of the waves. He had a large paunch, but his body was still muscular and strong, and his pink skin heavily tanned. He might've been a magazine ad for business executives "getting away from it all."

At first glance it seemed that the figure of this middle-aged, large-bellied man on the beach below me confirmed Beston's cautionary words about older naked bodies. The man was certainly no longer young, and his body was well past its prime. But as he stood there, at the edge of the surf, his thick arms folded, looking out at the sea where a single white-and-blue sloop skipped over the waves, he seemed to give the lie to Beston's pronouncement. He seemed somehow not just unashamed, but a proud figure—alone, unself-conscious, dignified, contemplative—an old god, perhaps, surveying his domain.

September 2005

SHUT OUT

Over the years one of my favorite beach walks has actually been not on the beach at all, but along the crest of the eroding cliffs above it. The most dramatic stretch of this crest trail has been a roughly two-and-a-half-mile section running from just south of Ballston Beach in Truro to Newcomb Hollow in Wellfleet. The highest point of land above the Outer Beach is along this stretch, climbing to nearly 180 feet above sea level. The dips and rises of the crest, the fantastic topography, the occasional views of the beach far below, and the long rolling vista landward have always made this the most exhilarating hike along the Outer Cape.

Of course, like the eroding cliffs themselves, the crest trail has always been changing, moving back with the retreating edge. Still, it seemed to have a dynamic stability, changing but enduring, like the beach itself. I'm not the only one who saw it this way. In 1997 my friend Adam Gamble published a book titled *In the Footsteps of Thoreau*, in which he gave detailed directions to walking this crest trail. It seemed to give it a kind of official status, though there have never been any signs pointing out its route.

It had been several years since I had walked this stretch of the cliff path, so it was with a sense of anticipatory familiarity that I recently set out from its north end, at the end of Brush Valley in Truro. I began climbing the established diagonal trail up from the beach and got about halfway up when I came to a spot where the thick growth of scrub oak had closed over the path, making further passage difficult. After a while the path opened up again, but then it veered toward the lip of the crest and completely disappeared over the edge. I stood there, mystified and stymied, and eventually had to give it up as impassable.

A week or so later I tried accessing the crest trail from the south end. I reached the cliff edge easily enough, but as I tried to progress north, this trail also disappeared over the edge, like a sudden loss of memory, and another impenetrable thicket of scrub oak and beach plum forced me to give it up.

When I got home I pulled out a USGS topo map, on which I had recorded a walk along this stretch only seven years earlier. I had marked significant features on it, like "Great Beach Plums!" "Old Concrete Block Foundation!" and "Wild Grapes!"—all of which, it seemed, were now as vanished or as inaccessible as ancient Mayan temples swallowed up by the jungle. In less than a decade this crest trail, which I had walked for forty years, and which had seemed for all that time a permanent feature of the landscape, has been lost to me.

I take the closing of this cliff path personally. It is as if whole sections of my own past have disappeared or been blocked off as well, like returning to one's hometown after a number of years and finding it not just unrecognizable but literally obliterated. It was not a human decision that effected this change. It was not National Seashore officials who had closed off the path to prevent erosion, though it was unlikely they would take any steps to reestablish the trail, or to allow others to do so. Rather, the path has been obliterated by two seemingly opposite forces: erosion and plant succession. The waves have claimed more and more of the cliffs themselves, while impenetrable growth has increasingly occupied the terrain above it, to human exclusion. I feel squeezed out on both sides.

September 2011

HOW MANY COUPLES HAVE COUPLED ON THIS BEACH?

How many couples have coupled on this beach? Hundreds at least, maybe thousands. Did it ever live up to their expectations? I for one have never made love on the Outer Beach, though the rhythm of the pounding surf and the mingling of the overlapping waves are blatantly erotic. The setting provides an almost too literal—or littoral—counterpart to the act of love: a gathering impulse, swelling and quickening until the height of the wave can no longer sustain itself, trips on the bottom, collapses, crashes noisily onto the sloping beach, then, after the climax, extends itself in entropical seething to its farthermost point of impulse, then shrinks backward, sinking into saturated sands. Our human couplings are at best mere awkward mimickings of this magisterial and unrelenting intercourse of sea and land.

January 2012

12

·····························

Long Nook to Head
of the Meadow

COLD WAR FEARS AND
WARM CONJUGAL LUST

In my adolescence I was an avid science-fiction reader, and one of
my favorite books was Ray Bradbury's iconic collection of stories,
The Martian Chronicles, published in the 1950s at the beginning of the
Cold War and the nuclear arms race. One of the most poignant and
quietly chilling of Bradbury's tales is called "And There Will Come
Soft Rains." It is essentially a description of the slow process of the
decay of a house, full of high-tech automated systems, that continues
to function long after its inhabitants have been vaporized by a distant
nuclear blast, until the house, too, inevitably begins breaking down.

I think of this story every time I walk through the landscape of
the now-defunct North Truro Air Force Base, just south of Highland
Light, for I know of no better representation of what an American
suburb might have looked like ten or twenty years after a thermo-
nuclear blast or neutron bomb had killed off all its inhabitants but

left the buildings standing. As one walks along its cracked and grass-invaded asphalt streets, one passes a row of cheap wood-shingled and asphalt-roofed ranch houses, one-story buildings with low hip roofs, still with unplugged appliances inside them and decals that mark a child's bedroom in case of a fire plastered on the windows. The windows are curtained; the roof shingles worn or missing; the uncut grass rolls up over the front concrete stoops, and the trees and shrubs, some planted, some volunteer—salt-burned junipers, wildly tentacled Russian olive, metallic-looking stiff-armed oaks—all grow untamed and aggressive, lurching drunkenly against walls, scraping roofs, smothering windows. Overgrown ball fields and cracked-asphalt basketball courts stand in deserted silence. Wooden telephone poles and rust-stained street lamps still line the streets, but the wires dangle and loop slackly between the poles like tangled sleeves of black yarn, and the lamp bulbs are shattered. It all has the eerie look of an abandoned suburb, but it seems less an abandonment and more an affront or a rebellion, the repudiation by nature of all that the suburban aesthetic stood and strove for—order, control, security, separation, conformity—once its meek masters had left.

Of course these were never suburban houses except in appearance but, rather, cheaply built housing for military families who lived on the base, which in a way makes the imagined war scenario even more appropriate. Despite its official name, however, the North Truro Air Force Base, located on relatively flat and open grassland on the Highland Plains, was never an actual air force base. That is, it never had planes or runways. It began life as a rather primitive antiaircraft station during World War II, firing practice shells out into the ocean and using volunteer civilian spotters.[*] In 1951 it became part of the DEW Line system, one of twenty-three Distant Early Warning radar stations established by the Department of Defense at the beginning of the Cold War. At its peak, the North Truro base had five hundred

---

[*] A fascinating account of civilian plane spotters on the Cape during World War II can be found in Robert Nathan's 1943 memoir, *Journal for Josephine*.

residents (including family members of married servicemen). Some of these were engaged in maintenance and support for the original four radar domes (radomes, or "ray-domes") located on the base, but most were there to provide service and support to one of the so-called Texas Tower radar stations constructed on Georges Bank, 110 miles offshore. In the southeast corner of the base is a large square of cracked asphalt that served as a heliport to ferry supplies out to the towers.

The towers were part of the "first line of defense" for the North American continent against possible Soviet nuclear attacks. As one former base commander put it, the Texas Towers, or TT2s as they were called, were a critical defense "against a country that would not hesitate to use nuclear weapons in an atomic war," and he credited them with providing us with "thirty extra minutes to prepare for an atomic war." When I read this, I thought, Thirty minutes? For what? To pile more cans of Campbell's soup into the backyard bomb shelter? To have one last quickie with your spouse or girlfriend? To listen to Mozart's *Serenade for Violin and Viola*? It brought back all the literal madness of the Cold War.* When another TT2 located eighty-four miles off New York City was destroyed in a storm in 1961 with the loss of all hands, the other towers were dismantled and abandoned, and, presumably, we lost our thirty-minute edge to oblivion.

The NTAFB was located at the very eastern edge of the Highland Plains, and thus afforded a spectacular ocean view to its inhabitants. A double cyclone fence topped with barbed wire surrounded the base: an outer one around the perimeter of the base, including the cliff edge, and an inner one protecting the military compound and command center. The outer perimeter was patrolled by personnel at all seasons and in all weathers, though what they were looking for I cannot imagine (Soviet spies surreptitiously landing on the Outer Beach and scaling the cliffs?), and perhaps neither could they, for, according to one of the plaques installed on the grounds, "The

---

* The official U.S. nuclear warfare policy at the time was impeccably known as MAD, for "mutual assured destruction."

men complained about going out on winter nights, or in blizzards."
In a superficial sense these patrols echoed those of the Life-Saving
Service crews who also patrolled the length of the Outer Beach in all
hours and weathers a century before, looking for wrecks, but those
men at least knew what they were looking for, and actually saved lives.

The base was officially decommissioned in 1985, and subsequently
the property, along with all of its buildings, was turned over to the Cape
Cod National Seashore and renamed the Highland Center. Since then
the Seashore has attempted to beat this Cold War sword into a peace-
time plowshare. Specifically, it has sought private nonprofit "partners" to
help "foster the unique cultural and natural heritage of Cape Cod by
facilitating scientific research, the arts tradition, and educational pro-
grams atop the dramatic sea cliffs overlooking the Atlantic Ocean."

So far the results have been disappointing. A summer music-tent-
theater now stands on the site of the former chapel; a small scientific
lab inhabits one of the old military buildings; local high schools have
painted ecological murals on some of the masonry building walls; a few
abstract wind sculptures have been commissioned and placed in various locations around the property; and signage and guided walks have
been initiated by the Seashore to inform the public of the base's history. But the overall impression is still that of an ugly, empty, and deteriorating military compound. The reasons are many: The Seashore has
no funding to reimburse potential "partners" for necessary renovations
and, ironically, because it is National Seashore property, no new buildings can be built. There have been proposals to renovate and convert
the old dormitories and houses to AmeriCorps and low-income housing, but these are stalled also, due to lack of funding, the expense of
removing asbestos, and the specter of past toxic dumping on the base.

In other words, the basic aspect of the old air force base remains
essentially unchanged, and walking through it, it is easy to imagine
the lost life here, when the air force personnel and their families lived
in the houses, mowed lawns, celebrated birthdays, cooked barbecues,
watched TV, played baseball games, went bowling, prayed at services,
or had a drink at the NCO club. . . .

But it is here that history catches up with me, or I with history; for a half century ago I lived on the Cape just a few miles from the base when it was active, and though I never actually saw it then, I encountered several of its residents. In the fall of 1962, when I was nineteen, I worked in Provincetown as a reporter for the *New Beacon,* a small local weekly newspaper. The air force base became a vaguely unsettling presence in my mind when the Cuban missile crisis raised its apocalyptic head in late October. There were rumors that, because it was part of the DEW Line system, the Soviets had designated the base a "Primary Nuclear Target," though presumably such information would have been classified. In any case, nuclear fears grew to such heights during those twelve fraught October days that most towns and cities across the country held civil defense meetings. I was assigned to cover Provincetown's, which was called by the town selectmen to discuss what to do in the event that "one of those Commie missiles went off-course and landed in Provincetown." The specific concern (I am not making this up) was that if a nuclear missile hit the town hall, the records in the town vault would be destroyed. One of the selectmen moved that, "For the duration of the crisis, the town records should be removed to the safe in the Community Center"—two blocks away. The motion failed to get a second.

At that time Provincetown was a virtual ghost town in the off-season. I was lonely and carless and took to hitchhiking on weekends to visit friends in Orleans. There were many fewer cars on Route 6 in the off-season than there are now, but I knew that if I could make it as far as the North Truro exit, I could always catch a ride with one of the enlisted men from the air force base on weekend leave, cheerful and expectant, heading up Cape to the world of light and music and women—or men—in Hyannis or beyond. (In those days no one, gay or straight, went to Provincetown in the winter—there was nothing there.) On the other hand I tried to avoid getting a ride back from Orleans with one of these servicemen at the end of the weekend, when they were sad and spent. They had usually been drinking and many of them, I am sure, would not have passed a sobriety test had they been stopped, had there been any police cruisers on the roads in those days to stop them. But every now and then, desperate for a ride, I would accept a lift from one of them back to the base. On one occasion the driver must have noticed my hand's white-knuckled grip on the armrest as he wove his way along ice-slicked roads at ten on a moonless night.

"Don't worry, kid," he said (he must have been all of twenty-two or twenty-three). "We'll get you back in one piece. You know why?"

I mumbled something unintelligible between clenched teeth while thinking, *Because you want to protect your country from godless Communists . . . ?*

"Because when I get back to the base I'm going to fuck my wife!"

Well, okay, I thought, there are worse motivations for vehicular survival—and sure enough, he dropped me safely off at the North Truro exit with a new appreciation of the steadying power of conjugal lust.

October 1962

DANCING WITH LIGHTS

Earlier this spring I spent several days and nights in one of the dune shacks deep in the Provincelands. At night I would go outside and look to the southeast, where, because of the shack's position in a hollow between the two outermost ridges of dunes, the only earthly lights visible were the stately, measured, double flashes of Highland Light some three miles to the southeast and, on clear nights, the fainter flash of Nauset Light some fifteen miles farther down the coast. Looking at them, I thought, Two giant steps backward for Cape Cod lighthouses, two small but significant steps forward for our human connections with this landscape.

Now, in October 1996, both lights are temporarily extinguished during a massive relocation project to save these historic structures from the relentless encroachment of the ocean on the Cape's Atlantic shore. For a while it seemed as if the sea might win the race, especially for Nauset Light, which has only thirty feet of glacial bluff left between it and oblivion. But this summer, years of technical planning, political maneuvering, public fund-raising campaigns, complex cooperative efforts between private preservation groups and the Cape Cod National Seashore, and the engineering wizardry of the International Chimney Corporation (the firm moving both lights) finally coalesced to preserve these buildings for posterity—or at least for the next several generations. Groundbreaking for the moving of Highland Light, the larger and older of the two, began last May, and Nauset Light is expected to reach its new site by mid-November.

It has been strange not to see their comforting beacons on the dark eastern edge of the Cape. But Highland Light has already reached its new location six hundred feet back from the edge; if all goes well, in a few weeks its thousand-watt beams will be revolving again, and a small but historic hiatus in the rhythms of our night sky will be over.

Lighthouses, like certain other human features of the Cape Cod landscape—ancient cemeteries, old houses, harbors, church steeples, cranberry bogs—have existed for so long that they seem a part of the natural landscape around them. But lighthouses also assert their presence in mysteriously compelling ways, so that we who live on this constantly assaulted land often forge strong, if unconscious, connections with these illuminated towers. The connections are probably stronger now for those of us who live on land than for those at sea, since for navigational purposes lighthouses have for many years now been supplanted by onboard electronic positioning systems. Nonetheless, standing as they do in harm's way, on the brink of destruction, they emanate a human meaning that few other structures do.

Like most of us who live on Cape Cod, I have taken the presence of these lighthouses for granted—like the sunrise, or the annual return of songbirds. It has been only during the past few years, when the fate of these two particular structures seemed literally to hang in the balance, that they began to compel my active attention in ways they had not done before.

One moist evening last April, as I was driving past Pilgrim Lake on my way home from Provincetown, I became unusually aware of the great flashes of Highland Light, moving in quick spaced arcs from east to west. Its glow was intensified, magnified, by the haze in the air. It rose and set, rose and set, over and over, like a fugitive sun, like the wink of God, like the shadow of the bright hand of God over the face of the night. It seemed to say its own name—Highland Light, Highland Light—again and again to a night sky that remained unconvinced.

I found myself strangely drawn to it, perhaps because I knew that its light would shortly be extinguished, never again to shine from the spot where it had shone for nearly 150 years. Like a moth drawn to a lightbulb, I turned off Route 6 at the North Truro exit and followed the dark road eastward as the flashes expanded and began to tower over me. I drove past the Truro Historical Society's museum, past the clubhouse of the Highland Links golf course that flanks the lighthouse, past the ranks of beige golf carts lined up beside it, and finally out to the empty parking lot. I was surprised that I could actually do this. I expected someone to stop me or check me. And then there I was, standing beside, beneath, this incredible radiance.

The white-brick tower looked somehow larger at night, its dimensions expanded by the beams emanating from it. Two gauzy cones of light, directly opposite each other, wheeled in stately symmetry from the glassed tower, washing the hills, the trees, the fairways, the museum, the clubhouse, and other structures at its perimeter. It was clear, from this perspective, that the beams were not horizontal, but slanted downward, pointing, it seemed, directly at the horizon. The lights moved in magisterial isolation and dignity, and I was filled with a sense of its magnanimity and beneficence as it dispensed its largesse of light across land and sea alike.

I had been out to this light at night many times before, but strangely I could not remember any of them. It was as if I were seeing it for the first time—or rather, as if the presence of the light tonight had

washed away all previous memories of it, as a new and glowing love
for someone can wash away all memory of former meetings.

The light tower and the attached keeper's house were fenced off,
but I could walk around them out onto the bluff. I made my way
haltingly, the way one goes through a dark room during a thunderstorm by flashes of lightning. My way was lit by the slow-motion
strobe effect of the rotating beams—image and afterimage—so that
I advanced and stepped to the beat of the light and its intervening
shadow, in what I gauged as five-second cycles. It was a curious, formal movement, as if I were engaged in some stately gavotte—step,
step, halt—step, step, halt.

As I walked west along the dark edge of the cliff, a series of small
raw ravines gave evidence of recent storm erosion. There still remained
the broken arcs of an old walled road that once circled in front of the
light. From the edge of the bluff the light lit up the surf below, illuminating furious overlapping skirts of dead-white lace pounding against
the dark base of the cliffs. It also lit up the clouds overhead, revealing
with each sweep sudden panoramas of silvered cumulus formations
far offshore.

To the west, out of the dark wetlands behind the Clay Pounds,
came the anomalous singing of spring peepers against the ocean roar.
Their singing had a chanting pulse to it, as if these amphibious tin-
tinnabulations were also linked to the whorls of light sweeping over
them, as if the great revolving spokes of light were, in fact, a kind of
cosmic metronome, setting a beat that drew all of us—waves, frogs,
and me—into a hypnotic dance of light.

Back in the parking lot a yellow flag on the seventh green whipped
wildly in a south-southeast wind. I stood again beside my car, watching the long shafts of light turning slowly, smoothly, powerfully, like
a giant incandescent helicopter that had landed and might lift off
at any second. It struck me as a beautiful thing, a source of wonder, something otherworldly and monstrously delicate, balanced for a
moment on the edge of our world. It embodied the human spirit and
the human condition in so many contrasting ways; but most of all,

that night, I liked thinking that it must retreat to survive, and that, knowing this, we have chosen to have it retreat.

October 1996

LONG NOOK

I would give up much to live near Long Nook, perhaps the loveliest of Cape Cod's ocean "hollows"—those dozen or so long, truncated, glacial valleys that perpendicularly intersect the Cape's Atlantic cliffs from Head of the Meadow Beach in North Truro to LeCount Hollow in South Wellfleet.

Long Nook, in Truro, is one of the highest and steepest of these Outer Beach accesses. Set between high, camel-hump dunes and ridges, it drops vertically some sixty feet down an unvegetated sand slope to the beach. There are no permanent steps or trails. Instead, diagonal footpaths are made and remade throughout the year as the cliff face itself is constantly reshaped by storms.

One April morning, following an easterly blow, Kathy and I arrived at the small parking lot about nine thirty. The air was sunny, calm, and full of water vapor and negative ions. We felt exhilarated even before we saw the water, which gradually appears between the steep slopes forming the sides of the hollow, as if filling up a giant, V-shaped vase. The ocean was astonishingly glorious, as it often is the day following a storm. What struck us first, even before we could see the surf, were the colors on the sea's surface: Contrasting shades of opalescent greens and pale moiré blues spread out over the ocean's vast surface like some fabulous Asian bazaar of silks blowing in the wind. The blues were of the exact hue and texture of the vapor-softened sky, so that sky and sea blended indistinguishably at the horizon, and from there to shore islands of blue sky floated on a jade sea.

Then the surf came into view—a magnificent milky aftermath of yesterday's blow—a quarter mile of range after range of foamy, plunging breakers, blanketing the shore with a continuous, thick roar. It was nearly low tide when we arrived, so that the beach was a good seventy-five yards wide, leaving a hard, nearly flat sandy highway for walking. We headed south and at first were aware only of the surf to our left. Its impending power translated irresistibly into images of assault: enormous breakers pounding ashore like waves of amphibious panzers. The lines of swells were perfectly parallel to the shore and, crashing far out in the calm air, they exploded like watery mortar bursts, sending up choreographed geysers of spray into the air. By the time the fury of the breakers reached the beach, it had been rendered into viscous sheets and probing fingers of foam, like scouting parties, advancing up the shallow incline twenty, thirty, fifty feet, then retreating with whatever information they had gleaned. It was D-Day on the beach that morning, but a benign invasion, a symphonic version of destruction, heavenly warfare.

At first it seemed as if the night's high-ranging tide had swept the beach clean in a shallow arc that flattened near the water. Ours were the first footprints of the morning. But a closer look revealed signatures of the deep reach and throw of yesterday's storm. It had scattered dozens of sea clams along the beach, including two that were still whole and alive, which we retrieved to sweeten the previous evening's oyster stew. It had torn several brightly colored lobster buoys from their moorings and tossed them along the very uppermost part of the beach, where they lay like a string of party lights. During the night the retreating tide had left a series of light, overlapping arcs of rockweed down the face of the beach.

Close to the surf we came upon the washed-up, wave-battered form of a common murre, a penguin-like pelagic bird, the size of a small duck, that breeds on the rocky cliffs of Newfoundland and Labrador. Its black-and-white plumage was matted; its breast had been cleanly plucked by something in the ocean; but its light-blue eyes were still intact, and the serrated lining of its long, thin, black beak was as yellow as a child's raincoat.

We continued on to the first break in the cliff, about a mile from the parking lot. From there we gained the crest and headed back along the cliff-edge trail. The landscape of the crest still had a solidly wintry look: bare, blue-gray jungles of scrub oak branches with a few dangling dead brown leaves; wind-burned tufts of creeping pitch pine; bleached-straw waves of beach grass on the dune slopes, and gray rags of poverty grass lining the trail.

But as we rose and dropped across its contours, this drained and unresurgent terrain gradually gave hints of a new season already in progress. Here, small, efflorescent, pale-green rosettes of dusty miller protruded from the sand; there, sharp-pointed bright-green spears of new beach-grass blades rose out of last year's dead collars, like souls half emerged from their bodies. Mats of bearberry were beginning to undergo their mysterious transformation from dark-wine to dark-green hues; and from the thickets of bare oak branches came the clear, territorial song of the song sparrow.

At such moments we are filled with a profound satisfaction with life and with our bodies' own motion, with the health of the landscape before us and its life independent of us—the wide expanse of sea and sun-washed beach. Whatever personal avulsions we carry with us, whatever nagging mental knowledge of the earth's worsening wounds dogs our heels, stay gratefully at the edge of consciousness, and for the stretch of a morning we assent to Thoreau's triumphant assertion that "surely joy is the condition of life"—in all its amoral, physical totality. The flattened blossom of gray feathers I find on the path, sign of a violent and fatal encounter, are as beautiful and healthy as the forced narcissuses on the breakfast table. The strong scent of skunk that filters through my nostrils is as sweet and bracing as the flowers' perfume, or the smell of a newborn's head. How lucky are we who live in proximity to a landscape that has such easy powers to lift us out of our narrow lives and self-made blinders, and so seduce us into seeing who we really are.

The fresh-washed nature of the morning seemed to transform everything into a benign version of itself, even reminders of the human urge to self-destruction. As we descended the final hill to the parking lot and our car, the two white radar domes of the North Truro Air Force Station were visible a mile to the north. Once a primary target for the defunct Soviet Union's ICBMs, they now appeared like twin full moons rising against the sun-washed camel's hump of Long Nook's dunes—as if earth, sea, and sky, and all their inhabitants, were twice blessed.

April 1998

THE SWEDISH NIGHTINGALE AND THE GEODESIC RADAR DOME

One of the oddest architectural juxtapositions on Cape Cod can be found at the boundary of the old North Truro Air Force Base and the Highland Links Golf Course immediately to its north. Some years after the base was officially closed in 1985, the original three radar domes were dismantled and replaced by a single, larger, white geodesic dome. The stated purpose of the new dome is considerably more benign than the earlier ones. It's under the authority of the Federal Aviation Administration and is used to monitor commercial flights. Up close it looks like a giant soccer ball, or a vanilla ice-cream cone on steel girders. If one walks east across the golf course early in the evening toward the break in the ocean cliffs, the dome appears to move across the tops of the intervening swath of woods like a pale, nearly full moon rising just after sunset, or like a benign spaceship sailing across the sky in grand, slow majesty.

Less than a hundred yards from this high-tech, space-age radar dome, and in striking architectural contrast to it, is a tall, medieval-looking stone structure known as the Jenny Lind Tower. It's a crenel-lated rook of a tower built of massive cut-granite blocks and is about seventy feet high and fifteen feet across at the base. Though quite visible from the golf course, its fairy-tale appearance is intensified by its difficulty of access. Thick stands of nearly impenetrable scrub oak surround it like the thicket of briars that protected Sleeping Beauty's castle.

Like all good fairy tales, the story of the Jenny Lind Tower has numerous variants. One version goes like this: In 1850 the famous European soprano Jenny Lind, known as the "Swedish Nightingale," gave a concert in Framingham, Massachusetts. The concert was sold out, and several hundred disappointed fans lingered outside the concert hall, hoping to catch a phrase or two of the Nightingale's song. Not wanting to disappoint her admirers, Jenny Lind gave a free concert the following evening from the battlements of a decorative stone tower attached to the Framingham railroad station. Nearly eighty years later, when the station and its tower were slated for demolition, a local businessman named Henry Aldrich bought the tower, had it transported to the then-barren plains of North Truro, and reconstructed it on its present site.

Why did he do it? If the story is accurate, Aldrich wasn't even born when Jenny Lind gave her memorable outdoor concert. Was he so taken with the story of her generous gesture that he felt the tower should be preserved? But, if so, why move it to North Truro? No one seems to know, and there is little hard evidence to support any part of the story. But the tower itself is undeniably real. It sits, visible but inaccessible, walled off by its protective forest, waiting for its next nightingale. And I cannot help but think what a splendid and appropriate gesture it would be if the National Seashore were to commemorate Jenny Lind's legendary performance from the tower's battlements by inviting some present-day diva—Renée Fleming, perhaps, or Beyoncé—to sing to contemporary masses gathered on the fairways below it.

May 2010

13

....

The Provincelands

NIGHT IN A DUNE SHACK

Others than myself should be writing this. I have been at best an infrequent visitor to the dune country, or what used to be called the "outback" of the Provincelands. I no longer even live in Provincetown. It would be better done, I suspect, by one of the "shack people"—those enviable individuals who live among the dunes summer after summer, and even year-round, in those marvelous barnacle boxes still perched here and there along the outermost line of dunes from Race Point to High Head. Many of them have been writers themselves, ever since Eugene O'Neill worked on his early plays out there in the old Peaked Hills Bar Life-Saving Station. It is they who best know that country, those several square miles of sea-spawned, wind-shaped sand hills and valleys, domes and bowls, that sprawl between Route 6 and the Atlantic Ocean at the very tip of Cape Cod—a region once described by the Provincetown author Mary Heaton Vorse as "a little wild animal that crouches under the hand of man but is never tamed."

And yet I was once touched directly by the dunes in a way that connects me not only to them but to still another writer who lived there. So I want to begin with a personal anecdote, not just as a way of getting into a rather complex subject, but because such stories are important. Behind every passionate interest there is almost always some such story to be found.

Eighteen years ago Provincetown in the winter was a very different place for a young man out of sorts with the world. I had taken a year off from college and worked on the reporting staff of a now-defunct weekly newspaper. In fact I *was* the entire reporting staff, covering the obituaries, whist-party winners, Portuguese-American League dinners, high school basketball scores, and civil defense meetings that made up the meat of the off-season news in those days.

At that time everyone who graduated from the local high school seemed to be in a hurry to leave or get married. After the summer crowds left, there were few unattached people in the town between eighteen and thirty. It was three months before I got to know another person my own age. On weekends I used to hitch rides up-Cape to see friends in Orleans, and between work and these weekly escapes I had had little chance to explore the dunes in back of the town.

One day shortly after Christmas, however, when the paper had shut down for a week, I packed a lunch and walked out of town along Howland Street, across the old railroad bed (railless for years even then, but still paved with ties), across the state highway, up into the oak-covered hills east of Grassy Pond, and finally into the dunes themselves.

I was totally ignorant of their geography then, and went mapless into that country with all the careless assurance of youth, though I was aware of the tall granite tower of the Pilgrim Monument that loomed over my shoulder as a constant landmark, should I need it. I had heard of, and had in part set out to find, Mount Gilboa and Mount Ararat, two of the largest of the dunes. I was actually more than a mile west of those sandy summits, but I had no way of knowing that. Nevertheless, the impression of the dune landscape was immediately biblical, reminiscent of those valleys and desert wildernesses I had always imagined the tribes of Israel wandering through. There is something fundamentally allegorical about the dune country: Each feature—every bush, bog, ridge, and buried tree trunk—stands out from its background with a kind of concentrated suggestiveness. The scale is small and uncluttered, an Expressionist landscape that seems created for parables and myths.

I remember it was a sunny day, for I watched my shadow elongate as I gained each ridge, shoot out across the wide, hollow sand bowls as I chased it down the slopes, then shorten again and slow as I climbed the flank of the next hill. Even then I had a sense of undulation, of the dunes as a series of waves, though I had no notion of their origin or their behavior other than that they seemed very unthreatening and accessible, even on a cold winter's day, to human probing.

Stretched along the outermost ridge were the dune shacks, more numerous than they are now. I spent an hour or more poking around them in idle curiosity, working my way gradually west, where I had some vague idea Race Point Beach lay.

At one point I came upon a shack, smaller than the rest, perched in a little hollow just behind the foredune of the beach. The day had clouded over and was beginning to get chilly. I thought that if the shack was open, I might borrow its hospitality long enough to eat lunch and warm up a bit before heading back to town.

The shack had apparently not been used recently. The door was banked with at least a foot of sand but was unpadlocked. I scooped the sand away, pulled the door open, and entered. This was no ordinary dwelling, even among a community of eccentric structures. Against one wall were two bunk beds, each covered with real bearskin blankets. On another wall a series of rough bookshelves supported an extensive and remarkably eclectic library. There were esoteric works by Swedenborg and Kierkegaard, a volume of Beethoven piano sonatas, a large poetry collection (including first editions of Sandburg and Frost), a novel done completely in woodcuts, and cheap nineteenth-century editions of Hawthorne and Dickens. But there were also dozens of paperback science-fiction novels and Westerns, many of which I remembered reading in high school.

On the floor were scattered piles of oversize 78 rpm records, mostly classical and operatic selections on old and obscure labels. I picked one up, an original Caruso recording dated 1916, that was completely blank and smooth on the opposite side. The cabin, it seemed, had been abandoned for some time. Sand had seeped in through the cracks in the windows and walls and had formed a thin layer over everything on the floor, including the records. I gathered these up and carefully blew off the sand, wrapped the discs in a towel, and placed them on the top bunk.

I stayed beyond lunch, fascinated by this solitary and quirky outpost of learning, until I realized that it was beginning to grow dark. It struck me that I might spend the night here; there was no reason to be back the next day, I would not be missed by anyone, and no one was likely to come by at night this time of the year. The bearskin blankets looked warm and tempting, and there was a kerosene lamp and even a woodstove that looked in working order.

I decided to stay, and went outside to gather some driftwood to burn. By the time I returned with an armload of wood it was nearly dark. I could still make out the dim looming head of the monument far to the south, blinking its red aircraft-warning lights as though in a final call. But I had resolved to spend the night outside the town. If I should change my mind later in the evening, the tower would always serve as a beacon by which I could steer home any time I chose. I bent my head and entered the dark shack with the wood.

I set about building a fire in the small stove that stood against the west wall. I filled it up with the pieces of driftwood I had gathered, and then noticed that where the stovepipe went through the low roof, the metal collar had rusted out, leaving a gap of an inch or two all around the flue through which sand, wind, and rain had poured, badly rusting the top of the stove. I stuffed some rags around the opening and lit the stove. In those days I was innocent not only of natural history but of woodstoves as well.

The wood caught fast enough, but a few minutes later I noticed that the rags I had stuffed around the chimney were beginning to smolder. Quickly I reached for a stick and began to try to dislodge them, but the metal stovepipe, either rusted out or flimsily put together to begin with, came loose from my jabbing and quickly fell apart, collapsing in several sections at my feet.

Within seconds the entire shack was filled with black smoke belching from the top of the chimneyless stove, and I was forced out into the night, stumbling, choking, and blind, up onto the dune beside it. I stood there in helpless panic and painful self-recrimination, certain that at any moment the smoldering rags would ignite the floor, or that the stove itself would burn out, causing the shack to go up in a fiery reprimand to my inept trespassing, a beacon that would bring swift and humiliating retribution from the town. I had a strong impulse to run as fast as I could back to town, but I was held, as though mesmerized, by what I had started, by the plume of smoke issuing from the hole in the roof, to see what would happen.

Nothing happened. The rags apparently did not catch fire, and the kindling burned itself out without mishap. It was fully dark now, and I was cold and hungry in the damp wind, but it took several long minutes before the smoke dispersed enough for me to reenter the shack. When I did, I saw there was no hope of rebuilding the chimney that night. I suddenly felt very tired and drained, more from panic than exertion. I managed to cart the pipe sections and the charred rags outside, stuffed the roof opening with more rags, and set a heavy frying pan on top of the stove hole. Then, resolving that I would leave first thing in the morning before any passing beach buggy or the absent owner should discover me and my folly, I crawled into the lower bunk under the heavy bearskin blanket and sank into sleep like a stone.

When I woke up in the morning, I looked out the window and saw nothing, or nothing I recognized. Thinking it was the smoke that had sooted up the glass, I rubbed it with my sleeve and peered out again. I still saw nothing, but more clearly now, and with a sense of unpleasant surprise. A world of white in motion swirled about the shack. An ocean snowstorm had apparently crept up the coast during the night (I was innocent of weather reports in those days, too) and had reduced visibility to nearly zero.

I was cold and stiff, and thirsty as well, but I stepped outside into a brisk northeast gale that was racing along the beach toward Race Point. The storm had already laid down some three to four inches of snow, which was blowing and drifting furiously about the shack. I could see maybe twenty yards, and there was no sign of the monument in that dimensionless sky.

With more surprise than anxiety, I found myself somewhat marooned. I had brought no compass, and though I guessed that the storm came from the east, the wind swung about from minute to minute and was probably even more capricious inland. If I were to try heading back to town, I might wander among the featureless dunes for hours. I could have walked west along the beach until I reached the Race Point Coast Guard Station, but I had no idea then how far away it was, a half mile or five miles. I was trapped more by my ignorance than by the elements.

I decided to make the best of it until the storm stopped, or at least let up. Laboriously I brought the pipe sections back inside and reassembled the chimney up through the roof. This time I stuffed the opening with a roll of aluminum foil I found in a cabinet, and managed to start the stove again without further trouble.

My supply of wood, however, was not large and not easily replenishable, so I decided the best course was to keep the fire going as slowly as possible and to stay under the blankets to conserve heat. In this manner I managed to spend a not-too-uncomfortable morning, perusing several volumes of my unknown host's eclectic library and getting up now and then to tend the fire.

By noon, however, hunger began to gnaw at me, and I rummaged through the rough cupboards and drawers near the stove for food. Here I encountered an eccentricity even greater than the library. The only edible items I could find were half a dozen cans of anchovies. I have never liked anchovies, even at parties. Here they seemed like a bad joke, and I put them back, half disgusted and half amused, and crawled back into the bunk bed. But in a short while I retrieved one of them, grateful that it had a self-opening key on it. I don't really remember what they tasted like, except that they made me powerfully thirsty, so that I made several trips outside for mouthfuls of snow.

The storm was still going strong at noon, and showed no signs of abating through the afternoon. Several times I considered trying to make it back to town, but decided against it. By dusk, however, I began to get worried. The snow had now piled up to nearly a foot on the beach, and drifted constantly against the east-facing door so that periodically I had to clear it away to keep from being trapped inside. If the blizzard kept up all night, the dunes might well be impassable by morning, or at least very tough going. My wood supply was just about gone, and my clothes were still damp. What if I should come down with chills and fever during the night, and grow delirious?

To keep my strength up I forced down another can of anchovies (and nearly lost it again in doing so), after which I resolved that if, by some cruel fate, I were to die in this crummy place, I would do so on an empty stomach. I dared not waste my flashlight, so I sat there in the bed for several hours in the dark and cold, all charm or interest in the shack long fled, contemptuous and alarmed at the situation I had so innocently fallen into. It seemed now a too-real metaphor of the state of my life at the time, and I wished earnestly only to escape back to what I had been escaping from.

When I finally fell asleep I don't know, but I remember waking joyously in the middle of the night to the unexpected sound of hard rain on the roof. It was my first experience with the capriciousness of the Cape's winter storms, but I seemed to know what it meant, and went back to sleep with a pervading sense of release. In the morning I woke again to see a soggy, ruined, steamy but suddenly revealed landscape. The snow was almost entirely gone, like a bad dream, and the monument once again crested the dunes. I followed it back to town like a prodigal son.

Much later I found out that the shack in which I had spent two nights had belonged to Harry Kemp, Provincetown's famous ex-pugilist and self-styled "Poet of the Dunes," who had lived alone there during the last years of his long life. He had died the spring prior to my stay at the age of seventy-seven. Not long after I left, the shack fell into the sea—not, I hope, before someone saved the poet's remarkable library, or at least the Caruso recordings.

Last summer I saw an advertisement for Provincetown's new Heritage Museum that referred to an exhibit of "Harry Kemp's Dune Shack." Intrigued, I paid a visit to the museum. The exhibit proved to be a "replica" of the shack, built from boards and other lumber salvaged when the little house tumbled into the ocean. It was a curiously compressed, sort of bas-relief affair, built out from the wall less than four feet into the room, purporting to reproduce the interior of the poet's dwelling as it was. But it was not Harry's shack. Everything was too spare and tidy. There were no bunk beds or bearskins, no stove, no records. The only books in sight were a few of Harry's own volumes arranged neatly on a small, plain, wooden desk, as though the only thing writers ever read were their own works.

And there were no anchovies.

December 1962

ACCIDENTAL

For generations Provincetowners have referred to the Provincelands—that great expanse of wooded hills, swampy ponds, dunes, sand valleys, and remote beaches that stretches behind the town from Pilgrim Lake to Race Point—as the "back country" or the "outback." The local phrases have a wary feeling to them, a sense of the townspeople looking back over their shoulders at something that they have coexisted uneasily with over the centuries and that they are still not sure of. The feeling has some justification to it. Like all Cape Codders, Provincetowners had an early predilection for clear-cutting their forests and grazing their cattle on the open land; only here the consequences were more serious. Once loosed from their prison of roots and runners, the great dunes threatened for decades to roll in like breakers and inundate the town.

Unlike the rest of the Cape's Outer Beach, the unprotected back side of Provincetown has no formidable glacial cliffs to confront and absorb the shock of high surf and ocean storms. Twice the town has built large dikes—first at East Harbor (now Pilgrim Lake) and then across Provincetown Harbor to Wood End—to protect its harbor from ocean breakthroughs, and extensive beach-grass-planting projects have been carried out to keep the moving dunes from burying the town. Though somewhat tamed now, the sand hills of the Provincelands, formed by wind and wave, present only the gentlest of barriers to the sea and remain one of our wildest and most exposed of shores.

Farthest out of these outback shores is Race Point, the knuckle of Provincetown's fist, wearing its homely little nineteenth-century lighthouse like an illuminated diamond ring. Race Point gets its name from the deep channel that runs just offshore, causing the ocean currents to "race" around the point. Look at a nautical map, and you will see how the depth contours press in toward shore at this point, so that there is over a hundred feet of water less than two hundred yards out. Look at a shipwreck map of the Cape's Outer Beach, and you will see that the vessel grave markers cluster around Race Point like a swarm of bees, equaled in density only by those spread out on the treacherous shoals and rips of Monomoy, thirty miles to the south.

But its name also seems appropriate in a larger sense, for all the elements, animate and inanimate, seem to race around it. Here the winds blow hardest, the currents run strongest, and the surf breaks highest. Here can be seen in spring the great humpback and finback whales swimming just offshore on their migrations north, the fall flights of scoters as they round the Cape tip on their journeys south, and the herds of harbor seals that sometimes congregate in large numbers, as they did this winter, in Hatches Harbor, formed by the hook of the point. And at all times of the year, several times a day, small commercial airplanes take off from and land at the Provincetown Municipal Airport, located just behind Race Point Beach.

It was to Hatches Harbor to see the seals that I set off in my car one morning a couple of weeks ago. According to a Boston radio station it was "sixty-three and sunny" there, but a thick cold fog blanketed the Lower Cape, getting thicker as I drove to Provincetown, and a strong southwest wind pushed the mist in sheets across my windshield, obscuring both highway and landscape.

I set off on foot from the Herring Cove parking lot about a mile due southeast of the harbor, wrapped in sweaters and rain gear. The sand road was low and boggy and in many places carpeted with wild cranberry vines, with new runners snaking out across the sand and a scattering of last year's fruit, still tart and tasty after a winter's drying, on the wine-colored vines. At times the road became a watery channel, lined with phragmites stands on either side. On one dune slope a patch of Hudsonia plants had been undercut by the wind so that they stood on exposed crooked little stems four to five inches long, like bonsai trees. Like the beach grass, poverty grass seems able to withstand burying better than excavation.

Visibility was already less than a hundred yards, and I began to think I should have brought a compass with me. Even in the best of weather the dune country offers tricks of direction and perspective, and this was like walking into a cloudy sea. But ahead of me I heard the low, constant, double moans of the foghorn at Race Point Light, as if deliberately providing me with an aural beacon to follow, though the light itself was invisible.

I knew, of course, that I would be unlikely to actually see any seals at the harbor even if there were any, but I pressed on nonetheless, drawn more and more by the sound of the foghorn itself, low and whale-like in its breathy bellowing. By all the rules, it should not have been a good day to see birds either—cold, damp, foggy, windy weather being the worst time to go birding. And yet it was birds that I saw.

I trekked on toward Race Point, following blindly the sound of the fog-horn. Soon I passed through an area of small, convoluted dunes known as the Snake Hills. I have not been able to track down the origin of this name, but "Snake Hills" is oddly appropriate as, compared with the sweeping ridges and broad valleys of most of the Provincelands, these hills seem like a tightly coiled, slithering mound of sand reptiles.

As I passed through them, the back country of the dunes began to weave its spell, to take on an unfixed, fluid quality, where the elements seem to merge and transform into one another, so that I could not even be sure of the ground under my feet.

The fog stayed thick, and the driving southeast wind threw it in thick curtains across the landscape ahead of me. From time to time the sand hills on either side would emerge briefly like mirages, then disappear into the mist again. Only the booming foghorn at Race Point remained constant and fixed.

Then, unexpectedly, from high in the branches of a scrubby oak, I heard a trio of rusty blackbirds, small slender-billed birds with bright yellow-white eyes. Rusties are never a common sight here and are particularly unusual this time of year. Had they been blown off the mainland while migrating north and been caught by this hook of land? If so, how many more had not been caught and had gone sailing out over the ocean with petrels, shearwaters, and puffins toward Greenland? The life of birds is such a tightrope act. The gift of flight gives them great range and flexibility, but it also makes them vulnerable to sudden deviations, to being flung unawares into alien landscapes. These three birds, however, seemed to accept where they found themselves. Hunched into the wet wind, they piped out their high squeaky songs, a pale version of the redwing's more familiar liquid-throated call.

Farther on, out in the sand hills, a male marsh hawk suddenly hovered over me, appearing like a gray ghost out of the fog, and then veered off quickly into obscurity. A few minutes later, as I crossed the earthen dike that spans the harbor, I saw the larger female harrier flapping and sailing low over the brackish swamp on the right.

It seemed amazing that hawks could be out hunting mice and other small prey in such weather, when I had trouble keeping my bearings even to rough landmarks.

Halfway across the harbor dike I found a clump of gaily colored balloons lodged against its lee side. Attached to it was a plastic bag with a postcard in it from "Mrs. Cannell's class—Roosevelt School—Krugman Avenue—Ossining, NY 10562." I pricked the balloons with my marlin spike, stuffed them in my back bag, and, seeing no seals, pressed on past Hatches Harbor, across the tidal valleys now empty between the dunes, and out the sand road towards Race Point Light itself. The Fresnel lens beam of the light did not begin to appear until I was within a few hundred yards of it, and the small lighthouse, built a century and a quarter ago, looked frail and ineffectual in such a whirling, smothered scene.

But as I drew up to it, the sound of the foghorn attached to its side expanded into a mighty presence, felt rather than heard. I tried to sit in the lee of the boarded-up lighthouse keeper's house to eat a dough-nut, but the low throbbing bleats shook the concrete steps beneath me and tickled my throat, and the drainpipe thrummed in the wind like a giant guitar string. Race Point, like all the Cape's lighthouses, has long been automated, but I tried to imagine what it would have been like living out here in the lighthouse keeper's house, trying to sleep or eat breakfast or plan the day with such a sound rattling your foundations! I got up and made my way out to the southwest-facing beach, fronting directly on a surf and a wind that must have been approaching gale force.

Here, at the western tip of Race Point, the hook of Cape Cod has turned in on itself nearly 225 degrees, so that one actually faces *south-west* to look into the face of the open Atlantic. Here the land seems to breast itself out into the ocean—and in a sense it does just that. Though most of the beach from High Head to Monomoy is gradu-ally eroding, Race Point is apparently still building up. Longshore currents continue to bring a steady supply up from the south, ripped from the high sand cliffs of Truro and Wellfleet. Over the centuries the wind has formed this sand into three distinct ridges of dunes, spreading north and west across the Provincelands into the domain of the sea. Race Point represents the current western extreme of this postglacial sea-made land, and the deep channel of the offshore race is an obstacle to further expansion, but it continues to raise its head, in the shape of some ancient sea creature, or a newborn seedling, shouldering the earth before it.

And so I watched this paradox, a land growing and expanding in the face of its own destruction, while the green breakers roared in. Like most natural processes, the growth of the Provincetown Hook is not always direct, but frictional, to-and-fro, with a little net gain each year or decade or century. In places on the beach I found that the dune wall had been eaten away over the winter. Planks and boards buried six feet deep in grass-covered sand now lay exposed and protruding like spears or stakes set into a bulwark.

I noticed with some surprise the absence of herring gulls in this surf. I have long admired the gulls' casual ability to ride out even the heaviest of storms with apparent nonchalance. But now as I approached the very tip of the point I saw a flock of gulls gathered on the flats inside the protection of the harbor. They stood very quiet and subdued, chukking softly to one another and preening their feathers in a nervous way, as if to say, This we don't need.

There was visible justification for their attitude. Between the harbor and the long spit of the point was a little wash valley, flooded occasionally on storm tides with marsh grass and other debris. Here, after the last tide, the record of violence was formidable. There was wreckage, human and natural, strewn up and down its length. Mixed in with the sandals, bottles, headless dolls, beer cans, tampon applicators, and car mufflers were the wrecked carcasses of many gulls, both herring and black-backed. These were not merely contorted and thrown down in their usual way, but crushed and torn, literally torn apart and mashed down into these sands by some immense, withdrawn force.

Farther up the little tidal valley I found the still forms of two razor-

billed auks. These seabirds, relatives of the extinct great auk, winter
far out at sea and usually come ashore only to breed. Penguin-like
and smaller than gulls, they have a curious, vertically flattened bill
with a white stripe dividing it in two. They are rarely seen on the
Cape except when seeking shelter in the Bay after severe northeast
storms. As I turned the carcasses over I saw that their snowy-white
breasts were stained with thick black oil. Here, in this oceanic junkyard, nature's mindless violence meets ours, and they seem to prey
upon each other.

It was a scene somehow cruel beyond interest, and a little unnerv-
ing. Fog and wind played bleakly over a sad graveyard of human and
natural artifacts, speaking of some vast cosmic indifference that the
beach expresses more powerfully than any other place I know. Right
then, not having seen a human face all day, I found it almost malevolent, warning me not to linger. It was not only the gulls, huddling in
the harbor, who felt out of their depth here.

I came off the beach and started walking back along the sand service road that runs inland behind the dunes, lined with thin utility
poles and power lines to the light. Then I noticed a feathered lump
at the base of one of the poles. I almost passed it without stopping,
taking it for yet another herring-gull carcass. But it didn't quite look
like a gull; something about the shape of the beak was odd. I went
over to where it lay and saw that it was the body of a freshly dead fulmar, with its left wing missing. This was a mystery on several levels.
Fulmars are among the most common of North Atlantic seabirds.
Looking like small herring gulls in their general shape and coloration,
they are almost entirely pelagic. They soar tirelessly over the gray
Atlantic swells, feeding on small fish, crustaceans, and cephalopods.
Frequently they swarm by the hundreds around deep-sea trawlers,
following close in their wake to feed on the gurry thrown overboard.
They will fight and push for a piece of fish gut with every bit of the
pugnacity, clamor, and gluttony of gulls tug-of-warring over garbage
scraps at a dump or a McDonald's. Like gulls, also, they are aggressive
scavengers and will frequently steal food from other birds in flight.

Fulmars are part of the "tubenose" family of oceangoing birds known as *Procelleriidae*, which also includes shearwaters and petrels. They have a curious, distinctive hooked beak made up of several bony plates with the nostrils placed in twin tubelike structures on top. Ornithologists are still not certain of the tubes' function, but fulmars are masterful gliders, and the tubes may serve as a navigation aid, allowing the birds to detect subtle changes in external air pressure, enabling them to exploit the varying wind currents in which they glide.

Though fulmars are found by the tens of thousands on Georges Bank in winter, they are only rarely spotted ashore on the Cape. The first recorded sighting on land, in fact, did not occur until 1961. If they are blown inland during storms, they have trouble getting airborne again. Several years ago a fulmar was found wandering around in the Wellfleet woods by local police. It was brought to the Audubon sanctuary, where it was force-fed and then released back into the ocean.

But the dead fulmar I had come upon presented another mystery. It had not been washed ashore, but had fallen somehow, in the fog and wind, several hundred feet inland. It was only recently dead, for blood was still oozing from its left side, where the missing wing had been torn or chewed off. Had it been blown down into the dunes and, unable to regain the air, fallen prey to a fox or coyote? Why, then, would the predator have only taken a wing?

But there were no signs of a struggle, no tracks of any kind in the sand around the bird. Moreover, the wound was clean, as though the wing had been cut or sheared off rather than bitten. Except for the missing wing it also appeared to have been in a healthy state, judging from its large, firm flight muscles under the incredibly soft and thick feathers of its white breast.

Then I became aware of the thin sound of the electric wires singing in the wind and fog above me, and I realized that the most likely, if somewhat bizarre, explanation of the bird's fate lay there. It was at least possible that the fulmar, soaring swiftly across this narrow spit of land in thick fog and hard winds, had struck one of the invisible, vibrating wires with such force that one of its wings was sheared off cleanly. I could see no trace of feathers or wing on the lines overhead, but that proved nothing. So finely structured for wind are these birds that the wing, disembodied, might have continued on its own, sailing across the dunes and back out to sea. Stranger things have happened on the Outer Beach.

I lifted the fulmar and carried it with me back to the car. When I got home I looked up its status on Cape Cod. It was listed as an "accidental."

March 1976

CENSUSING THE TERNS

I first observed a tern mating ritual on a mid-June day in the late 1970s. I was with my friend, Dennis Minsky, who was then the tern warden for the Cape Cod National Seashore Park. Like many young people in wildlife management at that time, Dennis was a self-recruit from the humanities; that is, he was a former English major turned naturalist. This was a trend that seemed to me to indicate a shift in humanistic values, a recognition that it was not now so much human values that were endangered or needed to be studied, but rather the natural environment, which is the only context in which the humanities can flourish for any length of time.

We had been out all day, censusing nesting least and common terns in several colonies from Wood End in Provincetown to High Head in North Truro. After lunch we drove up to the High Head parking lot in a Park vehicle, let some air out of the tires to increase traction on the sand, and started out the jeep trail to the beach. It was a brilliant, windy, cool day—with wide dune bowls on both sides of us. The vegetation was almost pure beach grass, waving in the wind. The jeep trail wound through the dunes like an old wagon road through short green prairies. The arching purple-and-white blossoms of the beach peas were like brilliant prairie flowers. Even the small dune shacks behind the beach reminded me of prairie sod houses, dug in against the blowing wind. That seems to be the nature of the dunes; they always remind you of somewhere else.

We gained access through a long steep cut in the beach that brought us out right next to the High Head colony, which had been posted and marked off with string. Least terns nest somewhat later than commons and roseates, and that year Dennis said they were later than usual in what he called "getting down to business." Now, however, new nests were appearing every day. In the main High Head colony alone, we counted twenty-four active nests, a net increase of ten from the previous day.

We drove slowly along outside the perimeter of the colony, stopping to mark the new nests on a gridded map Dennis had devised. The terns are much less disturbed by vehicles than they are by pedestrians; apparently they don't recognize the shape of a truck as a threat. It took us about two hours to census the one colony, a meticulous and mentally exhausting task. Although he understands that censusing the birds and the nests is essential to effective management, Dennis confessed that all the abstract tallying and locating nests on grids can make him feel very removed from the birds themselves. There are whole days when he is so focused on recording nests on gridded plots that, as he put it, "We don't even see birds." What he really wants is more time for nest watching, one-on-one, which he believes is the only way to tell anything about bird behavior. He wants to get to know the birds as individuals, to wonder, without preconceptions, just what they are up to. Just an hour of watching the birds, he said, can redeem an entire day of abstract statistics.

As if to prove his point, Dennis suddenly trained his binoculars on a pair of terns standing roughly in the middle of the colony. "Look at that," he said, his voice growing suddenly excited. I looked. The male tern was standing behind the female with a small fish in his beak, wagging his head sharply from side to side. Dennis said that the fish is generally fed to the female during or immediately following copulation, a kind of carrot on a stick. "Now watch what happens next."

The female seemed to get gradually excited by the male's display, flattening her body out, looking expectantly back over her shoulder at the fish, and shivering visibly with increasing agitation. Things seemed about to happen. But the process of mating, it turns out, is not that simple or direct. The pair seemed mutually turned on, and on the brink of doing something about it; then suddenly they would break off and seem almost indifferent to each other. In the midst of their desire they seemed diffident, even hostile. Dennis said the birds had "good reasons to be wary of one another now"—that this was "probably the most vulnerable time of their adult lives."

We watched this on-again, off-again foreplay for at least ten minutes. A few times the female turned her head and tried to snatch the fish, but the male drew back, raising his wings and crying out as if saying, "No fuck, no fish." The other terns, some standing only a few feet away from the pair, appeared oblivious to their passion.

Eventually, though, the female began to wag her beak in synchronization with the male's, a sign that the copulation was imminent. He got closer, and finally mounted her. I was astonished to see him whacking her over the head with the fish in his beak, but she seemed oblivious to this amorous brutality. Then he cupped and spread his tail feathers down around her open cloaca, flapping his wings to keep his balance. As she twisted her head around to him, he finally fed her the fish. The actual act lasted just a few seconds, and when he dismounted, both birds stood about with a distracted air, as if at a loss for what to do next. Dennis vocalized for them: "*This* is what I came three thousand miles for?"

It was a fascinating and intricate ritual to watch, but in its fixed mechanical nature it had an odd abstractness to it, an impersonality, like two machines meshing gears. A little farther along the beach, we saw an even more graphic and startling example of this programmed behavior. Another male stood on the sand, apparently offering another fish to a nonresponsive female. But when we looked through our glasses, we saw that he was offering the fish not to a bird but to the broken shell of a sea clam, whose wind-smoothed edges did, I suppose, bear a resemblance to the swept-back, sculptured look of tern wings. He stood there, futilely wagging his beak at the dead molluscan exoskeleton, with all the apparent ardor and patience of a suitor smitten with a statuesque, if cold beauty.

At such moments a tern's world can seem to be as fixed and mechanical as an insect's, programmed to react to physical stimuli. A tern chick, for example, removed six inches outside the nest, will be ignored by its mother. At times like this they do seem to belong on a gridded census map, for all their grace and beauty in flight and courage in breeding. Birds may have gestalt perception, shape recognition, but they seem to lack—how shall I put it?—*passionate curiosity* about one another.

And yet, as we study animal behavior more and more, the mechanisms of ritual, courtship, attachment, can grow so complex and intricate that they eventually dissolve into that comprehensive identity we call personality. Moreover, we cannot judge those birds or their perceptions too strictly, or we will find our own end of the sliding scale in jeopardy.

At any rate, these terns are, like John McPhee's Alaskan grizzlies, one of those species that "imply a landscape," in their case miles of unspoiled beaches, schools of small fish beneath the sparkling waves, soft dunes in which they can scrape their minimalist nests, an untrammeled process of replenishment, and an entire world beyond them. Finally, perhaps, one cannot expect concentrated identity, let alone curiosity, in creatures that register and encounter so much in their little lives, like feathers blown about the globe.

June 1979

GHOST MUSIC ON THE DUNES

These are the wine days, the high autumn days on the Cape, and there is no better place to spend them than in the dunes.

Thanks to the generosity of our friends Gary Isaacson and Laurie Schecter, Kathy and I are spending a few days at Peg's, one of eighteen remaining dune shacks spread thinly across the broad, sandy expanse of the Provincelands.

Peg's is named after its former owner, Peg Watson, who was a social worker in New York City. About a mile east of Peg's was the shack of Charlie Schmid, the legendary "Bird Man" of the dunes who lived there year-round for twenty-three years, during which time he kept copious notes on the dunes' flocks of tree swallows. Charlie and Peg were said to have been close friends, lovers actually. Over the years Peg spent as much time as she could at her shack until her arthritis became too bad and she went to Boston for knee surgery.

After the operation Peg returned to the dunes to see Charlie, though friends said she really wasn't fit to come. The story is that, on the day of her death, she drove over the sand road in her jeep to Charlie's. When she left in the evening, Charlie watched her go until she disappeared in a dip, and then he went inside. What happened next is conjecture, but apparently the jeep either stalled or got stuck in the sand, and Peg, using her walker, tried to get to the nearest shack, Zara's, for help. There were two women staying at Zara's, and one of them had a dream that night in which she seemed to hear someone crying for help. The next day they found Peg's body in one of the wild cranberry bogs, a place still marked with a cairn of stones.

Charlie inherited Peg's shack. After his death in the early 1980s, it was acquired by the Cape Cod National Seashore and gradually fell into disrepair. By the time Gary and Laurie leased it from the Seashore, the porch was gone, the floorboards were rotted out, and the roof was about to fall in. Today Peg's has been restored to its original soundness with loving care and attention to detail.

In the mornings we awake to unexpectedly inland sounds: the calls of towhees and bluejays poking and flitting among the thick scrub oak and beach-plum shrubs that surround the shack. A song sparrow peeks up out of the brush to the top of a bayberry twig to see what is going on, chirping loudly. Hundreds of tree swallows buzz low over the shack, all heading west toward Race Point, skimming within a few feet of my head, as if they were flying bombing patterns. Dragonflies—hero darners the size of small helicopters—chop through the soft air, thick with memory.

To the south, heavy rains have flooded the cranberry bogs across the jeep trail, turning them all into miniature, deep-blue lakes. Beyond them, along the crest of the High Dunes, the sky-blue water tower and the top of Provincetown's Pilgrim Monument loom like the bordering skyscrapers over Central Park, but in reverse scale and situation. Here it is the park, or the seashore, which surrounds and contains the metropolis.

We are lazy and grateful, basking in the clear, lucent light under high, arching autumn skies. All day the old yellow sightseeing plane drones overhead along the dune ridges. Our friend Ralph, visiting us, remarks that the same plane has been flying across the same route every summer since he was a boy here forty years ago, "and probably long before that. I bet it's been flying since the 1930s, maybe the 1920s. It's that vintage. Heck, it's been flying so long it's worn a groove in the air. They don't even have to steer it anymore, just give it a kick to get it going."

By late afternoon deep shadows begin to curl into the north-facing hollows of the dunes. We see deer tracks, and large pairs of pawprints that might be coyotes'. In one place the seed stem of a beach-grass plant has been carried along the smooth flank of a dune, making a jagged lightning-bolt track in its flank.

Kathy says that the air surrounding these shacks is "old," by which I take it she means that it is full of memory. Peg's, like many of the shacks, has a log in which visitors are encouraged to write. In addition to the numerous expressions of gratitude for the gifts of solitude and beauty, there is a wealth of small, careful observations of weather, wildlife, and the shack itself that gradually forms a collective memory of this place. On one wall is a sketch by Bill Evaul, the Truro artist, of the view out the shack's eastern window. In it he has carefully indicated, against the silhouette of the dunes, the former and present positions of the tower of Highland Light, several miles to the south-east, that was moved back from the edge of the sea cliffs this past summer. An event that was publicly reported and celebrated is here recorded as a small but significant milestone in the history of this shack: a fixture in the landscape, already old at the shack's birth, has shifted slightly, but momentously.

Shortly before sunset, I come in off the porch into the shack and am immediately aware of faint, but unmistakable music. Kathy has fallen asleep on the bed, and I think perhaps she has left the portable radio on, but no, it is turned off. There is, nonetheless, unmistakable music in the air, just above the auditory threshold. It sounds vaguely Middle Eastern: a low flute, or wordless voice, with soft percussion. Perhaps someone in one of the shacks to the west is playing music that is drifting down on the wind. I go outside again but hear nothing except crickets and surf.

Doubting my ears, I wake Kathy, and she confirms what I hear: low, serpentine melodies with a steady, muffled beat underneath. We begin to search the shack from one end to the other, trying to discover its source, lying down on the floor, then standing up on the bed; but it seems to grow no louder or softer no matter where we listen from. Ghost music, it seems—like the crying of babies said to be heard at the sites of certain massacres of Indian villages in the West.

Then the music stops. The indistinguishable words of a woman's voice follow. I turn on the portable radio, twist the dial, and eventu-ally find WOMR, the local community radio station. Yes, it is their broadcast, but that only displaces the mystery: Where is it coming from? We are very close to its transmitter here in the dunes, so close that the station comes in on eight different frequencies across the dial. Could it be that the whole shack—its metal screens and spoons, its iron and pumps and aluminum pots, its metal pots and steel refrig-erator and stove—is acting like some kind of enormous antenna, the way that metal fillings in a mouth are sometimes said to do? It's a far-fetched idea, but there seems no other explanation.

Gradually we become more and more obsessed with finding the source, realizing we will not sleep unless we do. We open drawers, haul out boxes and duffel bags from under the bed, scour the shelves, dig through piles of blankets and clothes. Eventually we unearth an answer: At the bottom of one of the storage boxes Kathy finds an all-band portable radio. The radio is in fact tuned to WOMR and presumably was accidentally left programmed to turn on at a certain time.

There is relief, of course, in solving the mystery but, as with all mysteries revealed, a certain disappointment as well. Even as I sink into surf-smothered sleep, I continue to hear a faint, disembodied, plaintive voice, singing somewhere out among the dark dunes and memory-flooded bogs.

September 1996

TREE SWALLOWS IN THE DUNES

One day last week I took a walk in the Provincelands dunes. I started from the parking area at High Head and walked west through the area known as the Parabolic Dunes. These are wind-shaped formations with distinct contours: wide, smooth, low valleys surrounded by ridges of sand in a bent-bow or parabolic shape. These formations have been shaped by the prevailing northwest winds, and they slowly move southeast, burying everything in front of them.

After a half hour or so I stopped and had lunch at one of the east-ernmost of the remaining dune shacks in the Provincelands. This shack, a two-story structure with a wraparound deck, is actually built on the second dune ridge back from the beach, so that one looks out onto a swelling crest of waving beach grass, higher than the shack itself. I wondered if the ridge fronting the beach had actually formed since the shack was built, thus blocking its original ocean view.

As I sat there speculating on the geological past of these dunes, I became witness to one of the great autumn spectacles of the dunes: the migration of tree swallows along the Cape's outer shores. In mid-September they pour down from the north in vast, dense flocks, following their insect food supply south for the winter. Now a tremendous storm cloud of several thousand birds seemed to materialize in the air, an electric horde of small, iridescent birds swirling and shifting around the shack. Their blue-green heads and backs shone in the sun in various stages of molt, sending a fractured glare of color back to the eye.

After a few minutes several hundred birds landed in the bayberry shrubbery on the south side of the shack. Of course, to say they "landed" is a misnomer—rather, the vortex of swallows lowered and touched down, like a feathered tornado—shifting, changing places, chittering like static electricity. They seemed to have that unconscious introspection of colonial masses, aware only of one another and the intense conversation and interaction between them, so that when I got up and moved toward the landed swallows to get a better view, I found I could get within seven or eight feet of the closest birds without starting the flock.

As I continued west and eventually came to the high dune overlooking Pilgrim Lake, two more large flocks, of perhaps a thousand or more swallows each, soared back and forth over the valley to the north. They intersected, then parted, then intersected again. I wondered, Do the separate flocks actually exchange members during these momentary joinings?

Seen from a distance, these swallow flocks seemed more meteorological than organic. With grackles, and even starlings, one gets the sense that their flocks are always moving from one place to another, even if the purpose is not clear. There's a deliberateness in their movements, whereas swallow flocks seem much more passive, much more cloudlike to watch. They seem to expand or contract like smoke or leaves blown in the wind. Scarves of a hundred or so birds would spin off and then be lifted several hundred feet up into the sky, in a whirling spiral, only to descend again back into the mass. It was like watching a storm of birds, moved by an unseen engine of energy, under a hot, clear late-summer sky. It had that coordinated chaos of storm clouds, or surf on a rocky shore, so that each part of it seemed both independently passive and yet connected by some larger, invisible force.

September 1996

WITH ART COSTA TO EUPHORIA

Each of the dune shacks in the Provincelands has its own unique character, but the one called Euphoria seems to have a special place in the memories of those who have stayed there, particularly writers. Euphoria is modest in size, even for a dune shack, about twelve by ten feet, with a low-pitched roof sloping to the south, and matchboard interior walls and ceiling. It seems a shack made for writing, with double windows on the east side facing the sea and the dunes, a large wooden table under the north windows, and two smaller ones on the east and west walls.

The first time Kathy and I spent some time in Euphoria, we hired the legendary Art Costa to take us and our supplies out to the dunes in his van. Art has been taking people out to the dunes for more than fifty years. His business, Art's Dune Tours, is a Provincetown institution. Art is a large man with a big head, kind eyes, and red-dyed hair that makes him look younger than his nearly eighty years. He is hard of hearing, and didn't always respond to our questions. Instead, as we drove out the sand road, he launched into an automatic but still enthusiastic spiel that he had been giving, elaborating, and refining for five decades. Art's stories followed a groove as well-worn, and occasionally shifting, as the sand road we traveled over. He talked about the old dune dwellers that he had known, most of them now dead: Peg Watson, Charlie Schmid, Jan Gelb and Boris Margo, Ray and Nicky Wells, and Hazel Hawthorne, who bought Euphoria just before World War II.

Art told us that the Peaked Hills Coast Guard Station used to stand just above the beach, but it was moved back several hundred yards and new concrete walls poured on three sides. He had a book that contained photos of all the vehicles he had taken out on the dunes over the years. His first dune buggy was a 1934 Ford Road-ster, and he told us proudly that he was "the first one to make it up the steep sand hill leading up to Boris's shack." He asked if we knew Lillian Fowler, a woman now in her eighties, and described her as "a babe in that black bathing suit." Once, he said, Rear Adm. Donald McMillan, the famous Arctic explorer and long-time Prov-incetown resident, commandeered him to take McMillan (who was married) and "a friend" out to the Wells shack. McMillan gave Art instructions to pick them up in two hours, which, he said with a wink, "I did."

We arrived at Euphoria just at sunset. All the way out the light grew more and more intense, igniting the dune crests. A slightly gibbous moon hung in the southeastern sky. The wind was still out of the north-west and growing stiffer. Art helped us carry our bags to the shack, speaking very deferentially and gentlemanly to Kathy, repeatedly offer-ing to come out and bring us back in for no additional charge.

As far as his stories go, I can't vouch for all his facts, and Kathy noted that some of his tales have gotten somewhat "elaborated" on over the years, but it doesn't really matter. What matters is the vitality of his long history that Art carries in his own person, the vividness and specificity of his memories, so that he seems to be seeing all the old shack people as if it were yesterday

"Oh yes," he said. "Frenchy, Dune Charlie, Phil Malicoat, Peg Wat-son. I know them all."

October 1996

DUNE DWELLERS

We are spending Memorial Day weekend at Peg's shack in the dunes. Kathy and Ollie, our miniature poodle, walked out earlier and met me at about two o'clock at the sloping crest of Big Dune.

"Here at last," I said.

"Not yet you're not," she countered.

By virtue of her long history as a shack resident, Kathy dismisses the common belief that one is "in" the dunes when one has crested the saddle of Big Dune. She maintains that one reaches the "real dunes" only after crossing the jeep trail that parallels the outer shore less than a quarter mile from the beach and begins to enter the area of the dune shacks themselves.

I don't quibble. I'm just happy to be out here. The wild cranberry bogs, almost bone dry last fall, are now long, low, intensely blue lakes brimming with the abundance of last winter's rains. Newly bloomed, the diminutive bright-yellow flowers of the poverty grass glow among the plants' dark foliage. The beach rose is fully leaved out and showing the first of its big, blowsy, fuchsia blossoms. On the beach-plum bushes hundreds of small, half-inch-long bagworms are dropping out of their tents onto the sand, squirming there, silently bawling.

Wherever the "real dunes" begin, one of their more striking aspects is their ability to create a remarkably varied patchwork of separate regions and distinct spaces that makes the whole area seem much larger and more remote than its four-plus square miles. This is as true of the mounded and chaotic hillocks and depressions of the Snake Hills to the west as of the broad majestic bowls of the Parabolic Dunes to the east. But it seems most striking here in the "core," or middle area, between Race Point and Pilgrim Lake, with its distinctive ridge-and-valley topography. Every dune valley here has its own character and charms, and each one contains a number of miniworlds or microhabitats: bogs, sand bowls, and the miniature forests of pitch pine and scrub oak.

When we reach the shack, we mount the water reservoir and hot-shower tank on the roof, pump it full with the big red cast-iron hand pump, start up the gas refrigerator, and admire the newly installed, old-fashioned nickel-plate-trimmed Glenwood gas stove. Then we eat lunch and take a nap. As Joyce Johnson, a sculptor and longtime shack dweller, put it, "When you first get here you fall asleep until you're not tired anymore. The environment both saps and renews you."

This evening a fog has begun to come in. When Ollie and I go outside to pee, I can see the veiled lights of several beach buggies to the west gathering for night fishing. Suddenly Ollie begins to jump about in the beach grass, lunging and nipping at something. In the dying light I see that the grass is full of June bugs rising everywhere with soft insistent dronings, like overloaded miniature brown helicopters. Also called May beetles or dor-bugs, *Phyllophaga* ("leaf eater") *fusca* lives as a grub underground for two or three years eating grass roots, pupates in the fall, and emerges en masse the following spring—probably as a strategy evolved to avoid heavy predation.

June bugs are one of those ubiquitous if narrowly seasonal insects familiar to almost every urban, suburban, and rural household. They have always seemed to me rather clumsy, bumbling creatures, constantly bumping into things as if too heavy and large for the world they inhabit. Now, though, they exhibit a passion I have never seen before, rising and falling in a kind of wild Dionysian nocturnal dance, tumbling off the long tapered grass blades as if drunk.

The fog socks in for the night, and there are pleasant periods of rain audible on the roof as we sleep. In the morning, in the spaces between the grass stalks, I find the bodies of several hundred of the June bugs lying inert, seemingly dead, on the cold sand, as if victims of some hangover they have not recovered from.

By 11:30 a.m. the fog has cleared. We pack a lunch and set off on the beach for the last cluster of shacks some two and a half miles to the west. It's warm walking on the beach, and we encounter a few fishermen engaged in the less-than-strenuous activity of bass fishing. At one point a man in a blue Speedo steps out of his Land Rover, recasts his line, sets the pole back in its plastic sleeve in the sand, and returns to his vehicle to listen to a ball game. A woman sits next to the jeep, her back to the sea, facing a polka-dotted windscreen and reading a book.

We eat lunch on the deck of one of the empty shacks and then walk back through the Great Swale: a marvelous, long, wide, shallow basin set between the rounded ridges of the beach dunes and the higher rough dunes of the inner ridge. It is especially here, on the floor of such a dune valley, that one feels enclosed in a separate world, out of sight of sea or town. Even weather and light modify and multiply these dune worlds. The swale today, for instance, with late afternoon sunlight casting intense fire on its slopes and hollows, is a completely different place than it was yesterday, with its overcast flat light. Some of the larger dunes, if approached from the west, are rough, shaggy, torn prominences gouged by the prevailing northwest winter winds; whereas the same dunes, approached from the east, present gentle, grassy, smoothly sculptured slopes.

At one point the jeep trail descends steeply into a sunken oak-and-pine ravine no more than 150 yards long, and yet the experience of walking through it is that of entering a rich inland woods where deer, rabbits, snake, mice, owl, towhees, catbirds, pine warblers, and other forest denizens roam, where the needle-laden ground is sprinkled with hundreds of tiny single-spaced starflowers and even an occasional pink lady's-slipper.

At the very bottom of the forest we encounter a large box turtle in the grass, the first one I have ever seen in the dunes. Its fiery red eyes glow, and it seems unintimidated by us. It does not, as these turtles are wont to do, shrink up into the sides of its shell at our approach. Ollie, in fact, seems much more intimidated by it. He barks furiously and crouches a safe distance away, adopting his ambivalent "aggressive-avoidance" posture, in which he plants his rear feet firmly in the ground behind him while simultaneously advancing with his forelegs and barking fiercely,

stretching himself out like some cartoon dog, until he finally falls flat
on his belly.

How circumscribed this woodland turtle's world is here, yet how
complete and sufficient. There is thick cover, plentiful fresh water in
the bogs, and numerous insects and mushrooms to eat. The dunes are
perhaps only a hissing rumor in its cold brain, a bringer of dry rain
on windy days, as this reptile moves and shifts its shell slowly through
the dark quiet woods and goes silently about the work of its world.

For a few minutes I feel not only in another world but in another
time, so that I half expect to meet one of the old Cape Cod horse-
drawn, wide-wheeled, sky-blue carriages carrying men in bowlers and
checked suits and women in veiled, wide-brimmed hats, smooth long
skirts, and leg-of-mutton sleeves. Instead, coming out of the ravine,
we meet the first of four dune tours we will encounter that day, and
give thanks that our shack is off the sightseeing route. The tour buggy
stops on a sandy knoll just opposite Euphoria, one of the most visu-
ally prominent dune shacks. The passengers get out, point to exposed
shack occupants sitting outside, take out their cameras, and shout,
"Hey, look—Dune Dwellers!"

May 1997

A GILDED CAGE

In the past few years, around the first of May, the Outer Beach
has begun to sprout strange new structures. These are wire "exclosure" fences, each about four feet square, with black nylon webbing
stretched over their tops. The exclosures, set out by the National Seashore, are designed to protect the nests of piping plovers from predators. Previous to the exclosures, plover nesting sites were marked off
by running twine between a series of wooden stakes along several
hundred yards of beach. The staked twine managed to protect the

nesting sites from most human intrusion by pedestrians and vehicles, but the nests were still being destroyed by local wildlife and domestic pets. The exclosures have a mesh large enough to let the plovers in and out, but small enough to protect the eggs from owls, skunks, foxes, dogs, and cats. On the whole, these nesting exclosures have proved effective in keeping out predators, but they've also fundamentally changed my experience of the beach.

I still remember the first time I came upon one of them on the beach, out near the Peaked Hills Bar at the eastern end of the Provincelands. I could see it a quarter mile away. The stretch of beach from Race Point to High Head is heavily used by beach vehicles during the plover's nesting season, and patterns of beach-buggy tracks braided the sands. Nonetheless, the plover nesting boundaries appeared to have been respected, for the most part.

As I approached the enclosure, the plover was already out of it, away from the nest. It peeped with that wan, plaintive, flutelike note that seems such a fitting complement to its fugitive, ghostlike appearance, blending in with the foggy beach and the soft sound of the surf. Standing outside the string boundary and using my binoculars, I managed to spot the scrape of the nest within the wire enclosure. Four tiny, gray, speckled eggs lay in its slight concavity.

Farther on I spotted another exclosure. This time the bird was on its nest, like a little monarch in its throne room, fluffing out its feathers, its orange-and-black-tipped bill clearly visible. *Charadrius melodus*—what a wonderful name! *Charadrius* being the Latin for "gully," referring to its simple, concave nest, and *melodus*, of course, for "melody." A scrape and a song—it seems to get at the essence of the bird.

The presence of these plovers represents another spare continuity on this beach. When Thoreau walked this same beach 160 years ago, seeing the same birds, he, too, appreciated their ethereal song and affectionately described them as "a pinch of down on two legs." Surely it is an admirable extravagance to set off several acres of beach for the sake of a bird no larger than a sparrow. And yet, in spite of the plovers' freedom to enter and exit these wire exclosures, I cannot help but see them as cages, albeit cages to keep something out rather than in. I cannot help but feel that all of these well-intentioned protective measures—signs, roped-off areas, wire exclosures, and Seashore patrols—are indications that we probably shall never again experience plovers on the beach as Thoreau did, that is, with the birds nesting freely, openly, unfenced, invisible, unmarked—and vulnerable—on our foredunes and beaches. I know that this may very well be the price we pay for the continued survival of the piping plover and other wildlife on Cape Cod, but once again I feel that old conflict between, on the one hand, appreciation of the genuine achievements of conservation measures like this in halting the slide of a species toward extinction and, on the other, a recognition of what a sad substitute it is for the original untrammeled wilderness that we have lost.

Would I wish the bird gone rather than preserved and protected in such an obstructed manner? Of course not. But there *is* something in me that does not want to be signaled by a metal pillbox a quarter mile off that there is a plover nest on the beach. It is the piping plover's *invisibility*, the very quality that makes its survival so precarious on our heavily trafficked beaches, that is also part of its essence, part of the true experience of a piping plover. Though I acknowledge the value of these wire cages, I also acknowledge what I have lost, which is the quality of unpredictability, the mere *chance* that such a nest might appear anywhere, anytime, like the phantom apparition of the bird itself out of the sands.

June 1997

WOMAN IN THE DUNES

The story of Peg Watson and Charlie Schmid will not, it seems, be easily laid to rest. It haunts the Provincelands and sur-

faces, in slightly different forms, at unexpected times and in unexpected places. One evening last week I gave a reading to an Elder
Hostel* group at the Outer Reach Motel, which overlooks the Provincelands from Route 6 in North Truro. Before the reading I had
been talking to one of the group, a woman in her sixties with short
gray hair and a very hoarse voice (she said she had been inhaling
sheetrock dust for six weeks). Her name is Caryl Zachery, and she
told me that she had lived year-round in Zara's shack in the dunes
in 1977. She had come back to the Cape after an absence of more
than two decades to "reacquaint" herself with the area. She said
she wanted to write a book about the last generation of year-round
shack dwellers.

"They're all gone now," she said, "except for me. Hazel [Haw-
thorne] is still alive, I guess, but she's on a sheet at the Manor and
can't speak."

She said she had met a young artist who was so pleased and excited
because he had leased Seascape, now one of the artist-in-residence
shacks, for February. He felt very daring and adventurous

"Hah!" said Caryl. "'*Seascape*'! Real shack names are never 'quaint.'
They're either plain and designatory—Peg's, Boris's, Zara's, Frenchy's,
Charlie's, the Wellses'—or extravagant and mythic: Euphoria, Tha-
lassa. But never 'quaint.' 'Seascape'—hah!"

Zara's shack burned down in 1990, and when Caryl walked out
there yesterday afternoon she didn't know it had been rebuilt. She
thought it was a mirage.

I read to the group an essay I had written about Peg and Charlie,
in which Peg, having left Charlie's shack in her jeep, apparently got
stuck in the sand. It ended: "Peg, using her walker, tried to get to
the nearest shack, Zara's, for help. There were two women staying at
Zara's, and one of them had a dream that night in which she seemed
to hear someone crying for help. The next day they found Peg's body

---

*   The name of this organization has since been changed to "Road Scholars," which
is much more reflective of the adventurous and curious nature of its participants.

in one of the wild cranberry bogs, a place still marked with a cairn of stones."*

When I finished the reading, I noticed that Caryl seemed visibly shaken. I asked her if she had known Peg.

"Know her? I was one of those women. I found her body." And then she told the following story:

"I was staying at Zara's with another woman, Jean Robertson. We didn't know Peg was in the dunes. I did know her, and I knew Charlie, and yes, they were lovers. The reason she came back out was that she 'wanted to walk in the dunes one more time.' That's what she said, but we thought she was in Boston, or maybe in town, but not in the dunes.

"About 3 a.m. I woke up. I had had a dream. I had heard Peg crying out, 'I need you!' I woke up Jean and told her the dream. She said, 'It was only a dream—she's not out there.' But I couldn't go back to sleep, and about 5 a.m., shortly before dawn, I got up and took our jeep and drove out on the roads. I didn't see anything, and then, just when I was going to give up, I saw this—glint—caught in the headlights. It was her metal walker. Then I found the jeep hung up near some snow fencing. I followed the jeep road up toward the Saddle on Big Dune, where the sand road went through then, and there, just before the crest, I found her. She was lying in a rut, her hands folded across her chest, her eyes open, looking east.

" 'Well Peg,' I said, 'I guess you got to walk the dunes after all.' I brushed the sand off her face, closed her eyes, and drove back to Zara's. I woke Jean and said, 'Peg needs us.' We drove into town and got the paramedics, and they got her body off before the dune traffic started.

"We had a wake for her a few days later, Frenchy, Charlie, Jean, and me. You know how it is on the dunes. You get shit-drunk and laughing. Nobody had known how old Peg was, but somebody said she was seventy-four.

---

* See "Ghost Music on the Dunes," p. 292.

" 'Seventy-five!' Charlie corrected. 'Jesus Christ, I went to bed with that woman when she was sixty-eight—and she was *good!*' "

September 1999

UBER

Two friends from Oregon visited last weekend, and on Sunday I took them out to the dunes, following a series of familiar sandmarks that I have traced across this ever-changing and forever-unchanging landscape for more than half a century.

We parked at the Snail Road entrance off Route 6 and walked beneath the leafless canopy of oaks to the remarkable Sand Ramp, a structure more than a hundred feet long that looks like an engineered runway of sand, but was actually created by casual foot traffic and is maintained by wind blowing sand through the cut, a serendipitous dynamic tension of human and natural forces; then up the ramp to the dune field proper, a great wall of slanted sand that is slowly, patiently, inevitably burying the trees in its path; then a ten-minute slog up the wide flanks of undulating dunes to the summit of Big Dune, where an enormous blowout has formed over the past several decades, creating a bowl a hundred feet long and thirty feet deep, across which we trekked like ants across the sand-pit trap of a giant ant lion; then a sudden vista to the north, like coming upon a town one has been away from too long: the long ridge-and-valley landscape of the outer dunes, the ridges sculpted into fantastic stop-action shapes by the wind, the valleys covered with a tattered carpet of dwarf pitch pine and scrub oak, pocked with flooded bogs of wild cranberry, where foxes, deer, black snakes, and box turtles creep, bed, slither, and hide; coming eventually to a grand intersection of several sand roads (over which Art Costa's Dune Tours buggies have been traveling for more than seventy years) overarched and blessed by a single, desiccated, constantly dying but never quite dead scrub oak; and beyond this, scattered east and west for over three and a half miles, the dozen and a half remaining dune shacks perched like limpets on the final ridge of sand; until at last, through a cut in the foredunes, we gained the beach.

From there we walked east a half mile or so to a spot where, through most of the winter, a herd of some three hundred gray seals had hauled out at low tide, but today there were none to be seen. As we stood, speculating on where they might have gone, we saw a couple walking toward us. They were young and tall, perhaps in their late twenties or early thirties. The man ruggedly handsome, with thick, curly black hair, and looked as if he had just stepped out of a GQ photo shoot. He wore a pressed black suit, a silk tie, and black leather boots. The woman was wrapped in a large black shawl. The man had a camera with a huge telephoto lens slung around his neck and was staring at his cell phone as he approached us and asked:

"Is there a road nearby?"

"A road?"

"Yes. My GPS shows a road nearby here."

"Well, there's a sand road just behind the foredunes—beach buggies use it."

"Oh. Well, you see, we've walked the beach from Head of the Meadow—must be three or four miles—and I was hoping to call an Uber to take us back to our car. Any chance of that?"

March 2016

14

....

Long Point

HARBOR VIEW

Sitting on the beach at Long Point, my legs stretched out toward the town that sat in unmistakable outline across the harbor, I have, as it were, Provincetown at my feet. This is surely the best vantage point from which to view it, nestled, in WPA writer Joseph Berger's sly image, "like a piece of silver that has just crossed the palm of Cape Cod."

Provincetown is generally considered the most commercial of any Cape town, even advertising that fact in the name of its main street. But the gaudy human carnival that swamps Commercial Street each summer is essentially a veneer, and at most dominates a small stretch of the town. More than any other town on this peninsula, I think, Provincetown has managed to remain a community, in the traditional sense of that word—an identity unto itself. It is still primarily a collection of distinct neighborhoods, full, even in summer, of their local residents, tending gardens, painting chairs, walking dogs, riding bicycles. It strikes me, in fact, as a kind of poem, not in any sentimental sense, but rather as fitting Robert Frost's hardnosed description of his art as "a unity of bursting opposites." It contains a greater—and more notorious—social diversity than any town over the canal (not the least part of which is its high-level dosage of seasonal tourism and money), yet its diverse parts not only manage somehow to coexist, but to form a recognizable and vital identity.

Much of its visual appeal—that random compactness that is one of the few genuine examples left of the "Rural Seaside Charm" marketed like saltwater taffy by the Cape Cod Chamber of Commerce—depends, of course, on a certain consistency of architecture over time, marred only at its edges by ill-conceived high-rises and condos. But it also depends, as much or more, on the broad blue apron of the harbor that sets it off in front, and on the "palm" in which the silver coin of the town lies: the unspoiled setting of ponds, forest, and dunes of the National Seashore that backs up and surrounds the town in concentric, protecting layers.

The Provincelands has defined and shaped the character of the town as much as anything else. Ironically, its public ownership—or public confiscation, depending on your point of view—has long been and continues to be a bone of contention. The people of Provincetown have always used the "outback" for their own purposes—cutting wood, pasturing cows, drying fish and fishnets, nude bathing, dune-buggy joyrides—though it has been under public ownership—first colonial, then state, and now federal—long before the town was incorporated. Local inhabitants have always bristled at what they consider unfair and unnecessary restrictions. It is a question of suitable use that has been going on now for almost three hundred years, and it is not likely to be resolved soon.

But however enforced its preservation, it is Provincetown's unspoiled surroundings that also make it the last Cape example of the traditional New England village; that is, a tight cluster of houses surrounded by a preponderance of open space. It is the nature of that open space—the freely moving dunes, and the bright blue blade of the inner harbor, turning the eyes of the inhabitants around, curving us back to look at the rest of the Cape spilling down the inner shoreline of the Lower Cape, up the Sandwich Moraine, across the canal, and finally around to the floating hills of Manomet across the bay—that gives Provincetown its special position, its unique environs and perspective. Here we come to the end of things, standing at its tip and staring back to where we have come from, discovering that place anew, a "presence among us," as Archibald MacLeish said of the earth as seen by the first moonwalking astronauts.

A large blue dragger, the *Little Infant,* is moored nearby on my side of the harbor, which is deepest just inside the curve of the spit. The entire crew of seven or eight (including, perhaps, some shore-recruited hands) is standing in a line on its port side, shucking sea scallops and throwing the gurry over the rail to the raucous delight of the gulls swarming below on the surface of the water. A U.S. flag, which is usually not run at all, is at half-mast in the rigging, a tribute to the crew of the scalloper *Cap'n Bill,* which went down with all hands lost a few weeks earlier.

The men stand at the rail in large yellow rubber overalls and shirtsleeves, with the intermittent winter sun beaming down on them and small flocks of eiders scudding by, as they deftly slip their knives into the yielding shells and flip out the large "eyes," or adductor muscles. There is a rhythmic competency and camaraderie to their work, almost as if they are a band performing out there for their own pleasure.

Watching them, I can understand in part what has been called the "irrational adherence" of New England fishermen to their ancient and (in the world's eyes) unprofitable profession and inefficient methods. Despite a lot of big talk, mundane concerns, and a current of righteous grievance, most fishermen exhibit a genuine pride and independence in their trade. They share—indeed, seem to have invented—the best of many other vocations. Who, for instance, can deny they were the first to attend schools? And the rotating work schedule, so touted now as an innovation to relieve monotony in the life of both students and employees, has always been part of the fisherman's life. He lives and moves by the tides still, which are at pleasant odds with our twenty-four-hour schedule and twelve-month year. He is always meeting the day at a new angle.

If fishermen are more at the mercy of the elements than most professions, they still have more freedom in deciding how to circumvent them. Their line of work is in their own hands. Their casual speculation and planning on runs and trips show that fishing still is not, at this level anyway, so patterned and systematized that they don't need to play some of it by ear, or by wave. By comparison, even a carpenter is continually nailing himself to his work, each spike driven and each stud raised setting more irrevocably the predestined form and the necessity for completion. It is impossible to leave a house half done, as one can leave a bank half fished. The fishermen's object is so simple—the taking of a fish—that it is continually being completed, continually left unfinished. A property owner or developer throws out a hook for a builder and nets him with a contract, but a fisherman throws out his own hook and makes no contract, no pact with the other party. Just as the fish is not there primarily to be caught, so one thinks the fisherman is not there only to catch.

He handles far more profound and complex commodities than Wall Street. In the doughnut shops I hear them inquiring, "How's the stock off Peaked Hills this morning—up or down—running strong or slacking off?" "What about that new breakthrough below the Coast Guard Station—any chance of running through?" "What do you care how far out you have to go—what care how far? Head out now— *now!*" Here, a fisherman who hesitates on his bid may be literally lost.

Sometimes, watching these beat-up, rusty old hulks at sea, I think that our local fishing boats are like the endangered species whose habitat we are continuing to destroy. Of course it's easy to say that they are destroying their own habitat, because they are the ones catching the fish, but it's much more complex than that. It's the whole structure that has them do it. At any rate, they keep doing it. There are animals that people have given up on, but who nonetheless continue to breed and migrate and hunt and eat as if everything were just as it has always been, and these fishermen and their boats strike me that way, too. Maybe it's the way these boats move on the ocean. They're never hurried or anxious or panicked. They assume that kind of grace and deliberateness from the ocean while they are out there, however the individuals aboard them may think and act when they return to land. But I think it must affect them, that it's got to give them a certain stability or centeredness, the sense of being where they ought to be, at least when they're out there. They have outlasted this country's explorers, its hunters and pioneers, its cowboys and most of its farmers. If they survive the oil spills, climate change, growing government regulations, and their own increasing pressure on fish populations, they may just outlast the astronauts as well.

The whole of Long Point itself was once well-populated from here to Wood End, a fishing community that once supported more than two hundred fishermen and their families, as well as a school, in the 1840s. Gradually the inshore fishery gave out and the people left, taking many of their homes with them on barges and scows across the harbor, where they formed the water side of what is now Commercial Street.* Berger says that the Long Point settlement was abandoned by the time of the Civil War, but many of the buildings still show up on the government survey map of 1916.

Apparently the large sand mound against which I am resting is itself a fairly venerable artifact. According to Berger, "the odd, humplike formation was once a fort, thrown up in the Civil War but never used"—and thus dubbed "Fort Useless" by the local populace. Now all there is on the dune is a copper-sheathed wooden cross about six feet high, with no inscription to tell what it marks—a kind of anonymous memorial to all past and future wrecks and abandonments that may come its way.

Over the years I have spent a good deal of time tracing these curved land's-ends of Cape Cod: the spits, hooks, and island necklaces of

---

* The Long Point houses floated across the harbor to the town are generally marked by a blue plaque showing a house on an ark.

this larger curved peninsula. This last place, Long Point, Province-town's elephantine trunk, seems to spin out endlessly, spiral upon spiral, its intricate weavery curving ever in upon itself, orienting the walker in a different direction with every step—toward what?

To ourselves, back where we began. If it is love we can feel for a place like this, then it is for something at once fragile and indestructible, sacred and profane. We cherish its daring, the vulnerability of its incarnations, from the grand sweep of its long beaches down to the finely tooled patterns and subtle colors on the backs of tiny moth larvae hidden inside papery nests on the naked tips of bushes growing out on an exposed, windswept plain.

It is a love of the particular that such places instill, a dangerous devotion in a world that increasingly devalues the particularity of local identity and values. I might withhold myself from this place in fear of its destruction but that its mobile contours speak of Earth's indestructible processes, a depth of purpose and resourcefulness that, as the Cape author John Hay once wrote, "includes me in its passionate heart." It possesses a buoyant vitality of numbers, forces, and fittedness that is exhibited in those same worm cases, in the scallop shuckers on the dragger out in the shining harbor, and in all the life around me that day—sand and seabirds, seals and shells, whales and wrack lines, worlds whirled without end.

March 1981

A WALK TO LONG POINT
WITH RALPH MACKENZIE

I took a trip to Provincetown on Saturday with Ralph and his two Brittany spaniels, Hannah and her daughter, Goober. At low tide we walked across the rock dike at the west end of town out to Long

Point and back, about a three-hour walk. It was the first time I had been out there in nearly a decade, not since the aftermath of the Great Blizzard of February 1978. The cut in the barrier beach made by that storm at Wood End is still quite wide—a thousand feet or more, and seemingly unredeemed.

For the trek Ralph had brought along his "walking hoe"—a self-fashioned tool composed of a blade attached to a three-foot handle with two pieces of shiny plumbers' strapping. With it he ranged, scrounged, and retrieved like the dogs for the entire walk. We had not gone a hundred yards along the dike when he found a rusted quahog-rake head and walked back to the van to drop it off. He then proceeded to hoe out from between the great slab of rocks a dory oar ("there's twenty dollars of oar"), various clams, several dead seagulls, as well as using the hoe as an efficient pooper-scooper for all the dog turds deposited on the rocks. Nothing escaped his notice, everything was of interest or worth noting, and he had a comment, usually unsentimentally empathetic, for everything, including a quahog he found wedged between the rocks: "The good news is, you're wedged down where the gulls can't get you. The bad news is, you're wedged down where you're going to starve to death." Ralph is as curious about the world as a dog, and as spontaneously admiring of its wonders: "Imagine being dropped by gulls on the rocks like these and not breaking!"

He wonders about nearly everything, whether relevant to the immediate situation or not. He told me, for instance, that he had been reading *Hawaii* since returning from a recent a trip there and he questioned the accuracy of Michener's use of some words in the book. One of the words was "sardonic."

"I looked it up. Michener was wrong. Don't they have copy editors to catch these things?"

We passed a group of black-painted soda bottles floating in the shallows on the inner side of the rocks. "Decoys," Ralph said. I questioned him, but Ralph, a duck hunter himself in his youth, assured me that that's what they were and admired their simplicity and effectiveness.

Once we got across the dike, Ralph and I struck off along the beach toward Long Point, examining the remnants of old wrecks in the sand. In one place we found the perfect outline of an old schooner at least sixty feet long, traced by its flattened ribs, and lying perpendicular to the beach. Surrounding it was debris thrown up from the previous Wednesday's snowstorm: a large blue-and-white information booth, quite intact, that we surmised had been blown off MacMillan wharf; a handrail painted sky-blue; and a wooden stoop of four steps that had washed ashore upright and stood, abstract and surreal, on the upper beach, waiting to be climbed.

Ralph quickly dropped behind, ranging back and forth from the lower beach up into the dunes, now oblivious to me, while the dogs themselves ran off separately and ranged loosely together on their own investigations. I became the stable, moving vector around which both the dogs and Ralph continually revolved. (Apparently this is the general nature of most walks with Ralph. Later that evening, after we had returned to his house, I said to his partner, Georgene, "You spend a lot of time with yourself on your walks with Ralph, don't you?" She laughed and said, "Pretty much.")

We shared the beach with a flock of snow buntings, fifty or more birds, the first I've seen this year. They are most common on the Cape in November, and this one of the best places to see them. More than most birds, they are usually visible only when in flight. On the ground they blend perfectly into the small dark stones that seem to be their preferred habitat. In the air, however, they are brilliantly pied with wing patterns of bright black and white, like a flock of miniature willets. They have a habit of moving, while on the ground, with little fluttering leaps, two or three feet off the ground, almost as if playing leapfrog, which easily distinguishes them from small shorebirds. Whereas the latter run about very independently on the ground, buntings *shuffle* along together rather compactly (except for these occasional belated leaps), like pedestrians crossing a crowded city street.

By the time I reached the lighthouse at Long Point it was 2:00 p.m. and Ralph had been long out of sight. I sat at the base of the lighthouse, which, like the one at Wood End, is a squat, white, slightly tapering rectangular column with a black cap. There is an intriguing legend stenciled on its black iron door: "LONG POINT LIGHTHOUSE WOULD NOT HAVE LASTED LONG WITHOUT THE ASSIS-TANCE OF THE USCGC [United States Coast Guard Cutter] BIT-TERSWEET. OCTOBER 1981." Both Long Point and Wood End lights have foghorns that sound at uncoordinated intervals, the one at Long Point slightly more than a half-tone higher. It has recently been converted to solar power, with photovoltaic panels mounted just below the light itself. This caused Ralph to comment later: "I guess it's good that, well, you know . . . but it does distract from the aesthetics of it."

After another half hour Ralph finally appeared, an odd vision in silhouette against the declining sun. His walking hoe was slung over his shoulder, from which there depended, like a hobo's bindle, a large plastic sack bulging with his various finds. In his other hand he carried something that looked like a dish with short legs. With his long angular frame, sculptured Scottish head, and bristly mustache, he looked like a fantastic figure out of an old novel—Diggory Venn, perhaps.

One of the dogs appeared behind him, loping through the beach grass on the foredune ridge and carrying a large dead seagull in its mouth. "That's Hannah," said Ralph. "She likes to bury gulls." Perhaps, but she must be a fussy gravedigger, for she carried the same bird carcass back and forth for more than half an hour.

"You missed the good things," Ralph announced, spilling his treasure out of the plastic sack in front of me, commenting on, narrating, storying each object. Like a dog, he finds a thing and mentally worries it, enjoying the probing of its essence, taking as much pleasure in the things he throws away as the things he keeps.

The dish with legs was a small dead Ridley's turtle. Its shell was olive-green and its genital region a striking light pinkish color. "Poor thing," said Ralph. "Should I take it to Mass. Audubon? No, I guess not." There were also two large badly corroded copper pennies, probably from the late 1700s; a thin copper button, also, according to Ralph, likely eighteenth century. ("Boy, that's a worn button—boy, that was a worn shirt!"); and several lead slugs: white, heavy, and coiled like miniature Ammonite fossils. The slugs, he said, were old, "from the 1860s, I'd guess, which would be about right. They're probably from one of the old Hell Town houses that were out here in the early 1800s. After they were abandoned, they probably used them for target practice"

Finally in his catch of "good things" was a large, clean fish head, over a foot long. "It's better than the one I've got at home, so I thought I'd take it back and replace it."

He sat down, noting a brass plaque above the door commemorating the first Long Point lighthouse keeper, "John Thomas Dunham—1877 to 1889." "Gee," he commented, "they started young but didn't last long, did they?"

Ralph's family has deep roots in Provincetown. He told me that his father used to ride his bicycle across the dike (which raises the question not so much *how* as *why?*) and that his paternal great-grandfather, John MacKenzie, had been a lighthouse keeper at Race Point in the early twentieth century. "He was a soldier of fortune, forever leaving his family to go off fortune hunting. He'd come back long enough to get his wife pregnant and then leave again. Once he walked across the country to go prospecting for gold; when he didn't find any he walked back."

I found this feat not only remarkable but much more interesting and impressive than contemporary self-styled "featists" who do similar things solely in order to chronicle them in *National Geographic* or to get them logged in the *Guinness Book of World Records*. Truly memorable physical feats are almost always accomplished for practical reasons.

Ralph had barely started lunch when he got up and climbed the knoll that was beside the lighthouse. On top of the knoll was a large wooden cross set into a concrete piling. A gull perched sentinel-like on top of the cross. When Ralph approached within a few yards, it flew off, replaced even as it left by another one, as if it were a changing of the guard. A tattered and knotted flag waved from the top of the cross, and attached to it was a small plaque painted with white letters on a blue surface: "CHARLES S. DARBY / 'GALLANT SOLDIER' / KILLED IN ACTION/OCT. 17, 1944."

"Why the quotation marks?" Ralph asked.

As he came down off the knoll he scrounged a plastic bottle off the beach with his hoe and fashioned it into a water dish for the dogs. He also found a large rubber float and a complete bluefish skeleton, both of which he momentarily considered, but decided to let them lie.

After lunch Ralph said he was going to walk out to the end of Long Point with the dogs. I told him I would meander back toward the dike on the Outer Beach side to see what "good things" I could find on my own.

On the outside shore the beach was smooth and curved and dropped off steeply into the offshore race. Though it was not yet three, several colorful trawlers, including the black *Shirley and Roland,* which I remember seeing during my first winter here twenty-five years ago, came steaming up the shore, trailing scarves of white gulls.

The Long Point section of the Provincetown hook must be one of the most stable of the Cape's barrier spits. Its contours, length and outline are very little changed since the 1941 plain-table surveys were done—and this despite its delicacy of shape, very exposed position, and the existence of several deep and wide tidal valleys that cut in from the harbor side and are regularly scoured by storm washovers.

I walked down several of these sand valleys and in the upper reaches of one came upon two objects that demonstrated the extent of the tidal flow here. One was a massive block of oak timbers some thirty feet long and three to four feet in girth, spiked together and securely lodged against the bank of the cut. What its original identity had been I could not guess, but it seemed now to be functioning as a garden box for seaside goldenrod and other beach plants. Even farther toward the head of the valley was a barge or floating dock about ten by three by thirty feet painted sky-blue and filled with Styrofoam floats, with a prow shape on one end and several large cleats around the edge.

I walked "east" into the late-afternoon sun (the beach at this point having curved around 270 degrees), following for a while the old power-line crosses, many of whose bare copper wires now looped low and touched the sand. The beach-plum bushes were still heavily infested with web worms, whose tough papery cocoons were wrapped like a wet Kleenex around the new growth, and when torn apart revealed the wintering larvae, three-eighths inch long, writhing sluggishly in the unaccustomed frigid air and hard light.

I reached the dike and sat on one of the large granite boulders reading a paperback copy of *The Garden of Eden* until Ralph and the dogs finally arrived and we set off back across the dike. All the way back on the beach I had been hearing the reports of guns, which grew more frequent and louder as I approached the dike. About halfway across we encountered two groups of duck hunters. The first were two young men in their late teens or early twenties, one blond and blue-eyed, the other shorter and dark-skinned. They sat quietly hunkered down on the rocks and replied pleasantly when I asked what they were after. "Sea ducks," they said. They seemed to know what they were doing and did not resent our presence or questions. As we talked, a single eider passed overhead between us and the second group of hunters, about two hundred feet on. One of the second group fired at it just as it passed over the rocks. Their shot missed the duck but passed close over us. "Jesus, are they trying to kill us?" the fair-haired man said.

We walked on and came to the second, larger group, two boys in their midteens and an older, chubby man with a beard, two smaller boys, and a wheat-colored dog. They were all laughing and joking noisily, pointing their guns around like toys. Another eider flew over, this time from the harbor side, and one of the teenage boys fired at it as it passed over the marsh. At first I thought he had missed, but then the bird tailed down, still flapping, coming in on a low, curved descent and hitting the water hard with a smack. It stayed upright for a few minutes, and then keeled over, lying still on its side. The boys were very excited and laughed even more. For a while they just stood about staring out at the duck and appearing confused in their excitement. Finally the man with the beard took the dog down to the base of the stones and began urging it to go in: "Go get it, Nessie! Get the bird!" The dog looked up at the man and out at the water, began wagging its tail and getting very excited and eager to please. The others all began urging it to go in as well, and the dog got even more excited, barking and looking back and forth from the man to the boys. "I want my bird," the boy who shot it began shouting, but the dog did not appear to see it. Finally, however, overwhelmed by the urge to please, it jumped in, swam out a hundred feet or so, and then circled back to the dike. The boy said, "Oh well, I sure am a good shot anyway. You see how small it was? I got him anyway." The sun had just set.

As we left them, Ralph said he was sure the bird was dead. "Those guys shouldn't be allowed out here. What a shame—a bunch of retards with guns. I guess it doesn't matter to the duck, but it makes me sick."

November 1987

DEAD WHALE, DREAM WHALE

On that bright, shining April day I, like hundreds of others, made the pilgrimage on foot across the Provincetown Harbor stone dike to see the young humpback whale that had been discovered on the inner beach of Long Point early that morning. It was a fine day for such a trek, warm and sunny, near sixty degrees.

Word of a whale stranding spreads fast. The rotary where the dike begins was already packed with cars when I arrived, though the stranding had not yet been reported in the media. Several dozen people were out on the stone causeway, and about the same number were spread along the stretch of beach from the far side of the dike to the form of the whale, about a quarter mile to the east. From the rotary the whale looked like a large black eyebrow, or a giant leech, gently draped on the tidal flats.

The tide was half out as I strode across the broken, flat top of that massive mile-long mound of granite blocks. The head of water on the marsh side, pushed by the tongue of the tide, was flowing strongly through the cracks in the stonework like seawater straining through baleen in a whale's mouth.

The whale, a young humpback that measured twenty-six-and-a-half feet long, lay on its belly on a slight mound of sand flat. Staff from the Center for Coastal Studies had looped a thick nylon hawser around the narrow tail-end of its spine, securing it to the flats with a large anchor. It was intact and freshly dead, with no serious visible wounds. Its skin was scarred and peeling, blistering in the sun; blood stained the sides of its jaw and the feathered, scalloped edges of its flukes; and its five-inch-long, almond-shaped eyes were red. But its great winglike flippers were clean and composed. In fact it had an air of peaceful repose about it, as if it had stretched out for a midday nap from which it had forgotten to awake—an effect heightened by the besotted faux-smile formed by its uptwisted mouth line.

The whale was softly armored in its hard, rubbery exterior and stiff baleen. Only the rounded edges of its enormous, soft, black tongue, protruding around the perimeter of the baleen like a half-filled water-bed, suggested its organic, fleshy nature.

People gathered around the whale in small groups, generally respectful of the corpse. There was the usual picture taking, several highly conjectural explanations (all by men to women and children) of its presence here, and a lot of touching, caressing, and petting, as if tactile exploration would bring us closer to its death.

How many dead and stranded whales have I seen in my years here? Hundreds, I suppose. And what more do I know about the mystery they represent than I did when I came? Though every individual death deserves recognition, and one of this dimension commands it, apparently it was not significant in the larger context of marine mortality. The necropsy, performed the next day, would show that the whale was a young male, likely a calf from the previous year, whose death was chalked up to a lack of sufficient food at a critical time in its development. Certainly it was of less import than the dead right whale that had washed up in Wellfleet in March, apparently a victim of a ship collision, one of a half dozen right-whale deaths this past winter in a global population that now numbers less than three hundred. Compared with that, this dead humpback was of dubious import. It seemed primarily a spectacle, a school-vacation-week attraction, and I decided I would not try to make more out of it than it asked. I started back, and turned my attention to finding mussels in the low-tide caverns of the breakwater rocks to steam for supper.

But the whale apparently had its own agenda. Following me across the flats, it dived deep into my subconscious. That night I had a dream, mysterious in its presentation and emotional texture. When I wrote it out the following morning, its meaning seemed at once transparent and enigmatic. This was the dream:

> I was swimming out in Provincetown Harbor to retrieve some shellfish for some trivial purpose. Others had been out before me, and I was told there were not very many left. The harbor seemed more like an enclosed basin, with high, age-stained concrete walls, such as one might find in the inner harbors of old East Coast cities. The harbor floor was concrete, too, and painted white, like a municipal swimming pool. On top of the walls were some small wooden houses, deserted, as in the off-season, though the water was comfortably warm and clear.
>
> I was there with a woman I know, who seemed to be acting as a kind of proprietor, or caretaker. In one corner of the basin she showed me the shellfish, clear in the water and easily reached. There was a circular group of them four or five yards across, quahogs, scallops, and oysters in a heap, like a display in some fish-market pool, all white and gathered together. *This is all there is left*, she said, with a tone of cheerful accusation. At first I was struck by the loss, by the painful finiteness of the remnants. But they were so easily gotten that I dived down and brought up a handful.
>
> When I surfaced I saw above me the huge, black, glistening,

faceless form of a great whale. It had arrived soundlessly and seemed to be poised on the top of the wall, teetering above us and dripping sheets of water. The woman seemed to know that it would not hurt us, but we retreated a few steps nonetheless. Suddenly the enormous form seemed to regain momentum and continued along the wall and through the middle of a green-and-white wooden house, making a large breach in the center of it and plunging back into the water. I thought of the conjectures—sudden, like the wind, and all wrong—that would pass through the owners' minds when they returned and saw it next summer.

The whale continued around and around the rim of the basin, scaling the walls again and devastating more of the houses—not with the intent to destroy, it seemed, but as a wolf might mark with its urine the limits of its territory. The woman and I stood and watched, spellbound, still holding on to our clams. The whale seemed to become two whales, then three, then four, their huge bulks passing close to us like stage sets on wheels, and at last vaulting over the wall and heading out to sea. At the sight a strong tremor of sheer gladness moved through me, followed almost immediately by an equally intense longing to follow them—a deep sense of bereavement at having been left behind. . . .

April 1997

L'Envoi:
The Rain of Time

The other day I was reading yet another article about yet another threat to the future of Cape Cod: water pollution, disappearing wildlife, clogged highways, rising sea levels—I forget what else. Whenever I find myself thinking too much about "the fate of the Cape" and feel a case of cosmic jitters coming on, I know it's time to get to the Outer Beach, preferably during a northeast storm. There I can watch the foundations of this land being eaten out from under me. There I can recover what the local historian Henry Kittredge called the Cape Codder's "true perspective," where the ocean, the final arbiter of the Cape's future, speaks without ambiguity or riddles.

Whenever I do this, I'm usually joined by dozens of fellow storm watchers. As they watch the land disappearing beneath their feet, the expression on their faces is not anxiety or dread, but fascination, enjoyment, even exhilaration. During the Great Blizzard of February 1978 I was one of hundreds of people gathered at Coast Guard Beach to watch huge swells pound in the walls of the National Seashore's bathhouse and break up the six-hundred-car parking lot that once occupied the now-empty dunes. We cheered at each wave.

Every year some fifty-five acres, or 880,000 cubic yards of precious Cape Cod earth, slide into the sea, and what do we do about it? Where is our communal outrage? After the break in Chatham's North Beach occurred in 1987, a dozen houses on the mainland fell into the sea and owners sued town officials for not letting them build seawalls.

When I served on the Brewster Conservation Commission in the 1970s and 1980s, I noticed an interesting phenomenon. Most shorefront owners who sought to build their houses near the beach or to erect protective seawalls would usually accept our Orders of Conditions if they seemed to guarantee the owners at least fifty years of use before the ocean claimed their houses. In other words, people's concerns about the longevity of their dwellings, and of the land beneath them, seemed to go no further than their anticipated individual lifetimes. This was the case no matter what the value of the property was. We're not so attached to permanence as we sometimes think.

Even without the potential increase in sea level from global warming, geologists estimate that all of Cape Cod will be gone in six thousand years or so, give or take a millennium. (Granted, this is considerably more than Nantucket's estimated remaining time of eight hundred years, which is a shorter term than that of the British monarchy. Better make those ferry reservations now, folks!)

But think of it: Six thousand years before the Cape is utterly gone! Sixty centuries—the *wheel* has been around longer than that. And who's protesting? Who's taking the ocean to court to "save the Cape"? We make such a mighty fuss, as if it matters, even to us. We are spindrift, and we know it.

If this sandy peninsula, thrust so presumptuously out into the ocean, has taught me anything, it's been how to live with change and loss, how to face whatever winds blow. Each day the sea takes a little here, adds a little there. Each day the Cape is saved and lost, lost and saved. The ultimate outcome isn't in doubt. On any shore the waves whisper or shout it to us an average of 14,400 times a day. Whose fault is it if we don't listen?

Cape Cod is a cherished face, deteriorating in the rain of time. Like drops of water on a hot stove, we roll around madly on its skin, trying to escape the inevitable. In the meantime, within its shrinking boundaries, everything else is up to us.

ACKNOWLEDGMENTS

The author would like to thank these publishers for their kind permission to republish the following essays:

"Night in a Dune Shack" and "After the Storm" from *Common Ground: A Naturalist's Cape Cod*, by Robert Finch. Copyright © 1981 by Robert Finch. Reprinted by permission of W. W. Norton.

"The Sands of Monomoy" and "North Beach Journal" from *Outlands: Journeys to the Outer Edges of Cape Cod*, by Robert Finch. Copyright © 1986 by Robert Finch. Reprinted by permission of David R. Godine, Publisher.

"Barren Ground," "Dancing with Lights," "Long Nook," "Off Hours," and "Ghost Music on the Dunes" from *Death of a Hornet and Other Cape Cod Essays*, by Robert Finch. Copyright © 2000 by Robert Finch. Reprinted by permission of Counterpoint.

In addition, I would like to acknowledge my debt to the many previous books written about the Outer Beach, but especially these four: *Cape Cod* (1865) by Henry David Thoreau, *The Outermost House* (1928) by Henry Beston, *The House on Nauset Marsh* (1955) by Dr. Wyman Richardson, and *The Great Beach* (1963) by John Hay. They were my constant companions.

Finally, I am grateful to the many friends and family members, implied and overt, who accompanied me on the beach, but especially to Ralph MacKenzie, who makes everything more interesting.